The COMPLETE GUIDE
to INDOOR GARDENING

The COMPLETE GUIDE to INDOOR GARDENING

Jenny Raworth and Val Bradley

Special photography by

Michael Newton and Howard Rice

Green Frog Publishing

The New Indoor Gardener

First published in Canada in 1998 by Green Frog publishing

(an imprint of Guy Saint-Jean Éditeur), 674 Place-Publique, Suite 200B,

Laval (Québec), Canada H7X 1G1. Tel. (514) 689-6402.

A Berry Book, conceived, edited and designed for Collins & Brown Limited.

First published in Great Britain in 1998 by Collins & Brown Limited,

London House, Great Eastern Wharf, Parkgate Road, London SW11 4NQ.

Copyright © Collins & Brown Limited, 1998

Text copyright © Val Bradley and Jenny Raworth, 1998

Illustrations copyright © Collins & Brown,1998

ISBN 2-89455-048-0

DISTRIBUTION IN CANADA

Prologue Inc.

1650, boul. Lionel-Bertrand

Boisbriand (Québec)

Canada J7H 1N7

Tel. (514) 434-0306

Printed and bound in Italy.

A CIP catalogue entry for this book is available from the

National Library of Canada.

CONTENTS

Allamanda cathartica

Sinningia speciosa

Fittonia verschaffeltii

Caladium bicolor

Lilium 'Casa Blanca'

Introduction

Variegated ivy (Hedera *'Mona Lisa')*

Maidenhair fern (Adiantum pedatum)

Flaming sword (*Vriesea splendens*)

Scutellaria costaricana

Arrowhead plant (Syngonium podophyllum)

M OST OF THE plants we grow indoors are simply outdoor plants from warmer countries. They have their origins in rain forests and deserts, mountainous regions, and wide, open plains. They have the same likes and dislikes in terms of light and water as the plants we have in our own gardens, the main diffcrence is that they usually have a higher requirement for warmth and humidity.

The effect of trying to grow a plant in unsuitable conditions is the same indoors as out − it will become stressed as it tries to cope, vulnerable to attack by pests and diseases, and will ultimately give up the struggle and die. Unfortunately, as far as indoor plants are concerned, this happens so often that they have come to be regarded as short-term and expendable.

Indoor plantings tend to develop on a much more casual basis than outdoor ones, with most plants being bought because they catch the attention. We have all succumbed to the "impulse buy" at the garden center or nursery, when a glorious display can tempt the most resolute, especially at those special times of year, such as Christmas or Mother's Day. For a few weeks, the plant looks lovely, then it fades and is thrown away — but is this really all there is to it? How much longer would the plant flower if its growing needs were really attended to? Could it survive to flower again next year? Could that one plant produce others to fill out the display or to share with friends?

All the tender, loving care in the world will not help a plant which has been poorly treated before you buy it. It is much better to buy from a nursery or garden center where attention has been given to the plants' well-being. Some centers grow their own plants, so there is no stress from transportation, drying out in a storage area, or sudden changes in temperature. Even centers without growing facilities can generally be relied upon to keep the conditions as good as possible until the plants are sold.

At the opposite extreme, a plant sold from a garage driveway may have been subjected to cold wind and exhaust

Dieffenbachia *sp.*

Flaming katy
(Kalanchoe blossfeldiana)

Schefflera *sp.*

Cape primrose
(Streptocarpus *cvs*)

Paper flower
(Bougainvillea glabra)

Cyclamen persicum

Callisia repens

fumes, which will already have put the plant under stress from which it may never recover.

Take the time to find out where your plant prefers to live. Most houses have a variety of conditions available, from a warm, humid kitchen to a cool bedroom. Whether it is bright or dark, warm or cold, there is almost always a plant to fit the situation. The key is finding out which one. In this book , we have tackled each area in turn, giving a list of suggestions for plants in each case. Whether you want a lush foliage plant or a pretty flowering one, something to climb or something to trail gracefully from a hanging basket, there is a plant for all but the most inhospitable of situations.

Having chosen your plant, the next step is to keep it alive and thriving, and the key to success is to take time to get to know the plants in your care. The Indoor Plant Directory is an alphabetical list of popular indoor plants, with family and well-known groups first, followed by an A-Z of plants in botanical Latin (genus or species) name order. Full cultivation information is given for each entry, including growing conditions and advice on propagation.

In the Care and Maintenance section of the book, the different aspects of the growing process are explained. There is no mystery to successful growing, it is a matter of patience and attentiveness to the plant's requirements. The need for light, water, and fertilizing are obvious, but what is humidity, and what is its relevance to the way a plant grows?

Finally, there is a section for that moment when you realize that, despite your best efforts, something has gone wrong. By using this section earlier, rather than later, a diagnosis should be possible which will make sure that the correct treatment can be followed, and the problem overcome. Most of the difficulties faced by plants are only fatal if they are allowed to develop.

The Complete Guide to Indoor Gardening aims to help the beginner start up and the more experienced to progress by offering inspiration and explanations. Understanding why something happens (or needs to happen) makes it easier to ensure that it *does* happen.

Tradescantia
zebrina
'Quadricolor'

Peperomia

Polka dot plant
(Hypoestes phyllostachya)

Azaleas
(Rhodendron simsii)

Christmas cactus
(Schlumbergera)

Rubber plant
(Ficus elastica)

9

Containers

MOST HOUSEPLANTS are grown at the nursery in plastic pots. While these are both practical and convenient for growing and watering, they do not look attractive in the home. Fortunately, there are a great many decorative flowerpots and containers available to disguise, or replace, your plastic pot.

Plastic pots have drainage holes in the bottom that allow excess water to drain away, and are therefore unsuitable for use indoors where water seeping from the pot can damage polished surfaces. The first consideration must be a saucer or drip tray under the pot to collect excess water. Remember that your plant must not be allowed to sit in a saucer of water because this is when water-logging occurs, which can rot the roots and lead, eventually, to plant death. Although saucers are a practical method of collecting excess water, they are hardly decorative. Indeed, there is nothing worse than a sad-looking plant sitting on a

Wicker baskets

BELOW LEFT *The natural quality of wicker combines well with many houseplants. Baskets lined with plastic are widely available from garden centers and specialty stores, but if you have an old basket at home that you particularly like, it is easy to transform it into a suitable plant holder. Simply cut a piece of thick plastic from a garbage bag – black plastic is best because it does not show through the wicker – trim it to the correct size and put it inside the basket so that the plastic ends just below the rim. You can now either place the plastic plant pot inside the basket, or take the plants out of their pots and plant them directly in the basket, adding extra potting soil if necessary and finishing with a layer of fresh soil.*

Metal buckets, baskets, and bowls

BELOW RIGHT *Metal containers range from metal buckets, cast-iron cooking pots, baking pans, enamel pitchers, and wire baskets to the humble tin can that can be covered with moss or painted a suitable color. An old-fashioned metal washtub makes an ideal container because it has a flat bottom that can accommodate lots of plants side by side to create a magnificent grouped display (see page 63). A tall florists' bucket, on the other hand, is useful for displaying a single bushy or trailing plant, whose leaves can cascade over the sides. If you don't like the reflective quality of brand new tin, you could try painting it with turquoise acrylic paint to imitate the attractive patina of verdigris.*

windowsill with a chipped saucer underneath — this does not make the most attractive display.

One way to get around the pot and saucer problem is to place the plastic pot in a pot holder or cachepot. These come in all shapes and sizes and can be made of pottery, china, wicker, tin, or metal. Before you rush out and buy new containers, take a look around the home and see if there are any suitable receptacles that you could adapt for houseplants. Household items, such as enamel buckets, copper bowls, wastepaper cans, and log baskets, all make excellent and unusual containers, as do coffee mugs, casserole dishes, or a pretty vegetable dish that has lost its lid. A set of matching ceramic pitchers with necks wide enough to accommodate a plastic pot makes a great way to display similar plants (such as the primulas shown on page 43). The color of the container must complement the plants and not compete with them. A highly decorated pot in bright colors, for example, would completely overwhelm a delicate flowering plant. While a white container may seem like a safe option, this will contrast sharply with the foliage and draw attention away from the plant.

The container must be the right size for the plastic flowerpot, which should sit easily inside with the rim hidden. If the plastic surround is still visible, either repot your plant into a smaller container or cover the surface of the potting soil, including the rim of the container, with fresh moss, which will also conserve moisture and provide humidity for the plant.

It is possible to create a really stylish container by painting an old basket or aluminum container to match the flowering plant you have chosen. The easiest method to transform containers is to use spray paints, which come in just about any color of the rainbow. A good tip to remember when spraying anything is to put the object inside a large cardboard box to protect the surrounding area. Spray outdoors and wear a mask to protect your face and lungs. Try planting a group of grape hyacinths (*Muscari* sp.) in a blue-painted aluminum bucket, or arrange a row of dwarf daffodils (such as *Narcissus* 'Tête-à-tête') on a kitchen windowsill in individual clay pots that have been painted yellow. If you can't find a container that will accommodate your plastic flowerpot, you can always grow the

Miniature containers

TOP SHELF *Miniature plants that are popular in garden centers need attractive containers to set them off to their best advantage. Many household containers, such as china egg cups and small cups or mugs, make charming plant holders – especially if the decoration matches the color of the plant – but it is also possible to find more unusual containers at flea markets or secondhand stores.*

Glass vases and bottles

MIDDLE SHELF *Removing the plant from its plastic pot and planting it in a glass container is an unusual but very attractive way to display a plant. However, due to the transparent nature of most glass vases, it is important to disguise the root ball of the plant by lining the pot first with either fresh moss (see page 30), gravel (see page 31), or clear glass marbles sold especially for the purpose. If you are planting spring bulbs in this way, first remove as much soil as possible from around the root ball, then hold the bulb upright in the container while you add the moist gravel. The bulb will be hidden completely by the stones and the flowers will look as if they are growing directly out of the stones. An attractive method of displaying hyacinths is to place them in special glass pots filled with water. The neck of the pot supports the bulb and the roots draw up water from below (see page 51).*

Ceramic pots and dishes

BOTTOM SHELF *China and ceramic cachepots are the most popular type of container, and there is a vast selection on display at garden centers. Bear in mind that a highly decorated china container will overwhelm most pot plants, so it is best to go for neutral blues, creams, or greens that harmonize with the display rather than contrast with it too sharply. Bold stripes and colours may enhance the strong lines of an architectural plant, but they will certainly distract the attention from delicate leaves or flowers.*

plant directly in its decorative container. However, you must make sure that this container is completely waterproof — if it is cracked or porous, you will need to line it first with heavy-duty plastic; a garbage bag is ideal. If there are no drainage holes in the base of the container, or if it is lined with plastic, make sure you don't overwater the plants because the soil mix will quickly become sodden and sour, causing the plant's roots to rot. To encourage drainage, cover the base of the pot with pieces of crockery shards (from a broken clay pot) before you add the potting soil.

Repotting your plant into a clay pot and then painting the pot a single color, or stenciling it to match your interior, makes an attractive way to display your houseplants. The Victorian-style, straight-sided clay pots, known as "long Toms," make charming and simple plant containers. If you don't like the bright reddish-brown of new clay, you can age or distress it. To speed up the aging process, you can paint the outside with cultured yogurt and leave the pot outside in the garden for a couple of weeks. This technique will soon get rid of that newly bought look.

Clay pots

BELOW LEFT *Clay is a very sympathetic material for plant pots and there are many different sizes and styles – from straight-sided pots known as "long Toms" to those with fluted edges or relief patterns. Basic clay pots are probably the cheapest kind of container you can buy to display your houseplants. However, most of them have drainage holes in the base, which means that you must place them on a saucer to collect excess water. In practical terms, plants displayed in clay pots will dry out rapidly, because moisture is lost through the sides of the container as well as through the soil mix. To cut down on moisture loss, soak new clay pots in water for at least an hour before use.*

Wooden tubs, trays, and window boxes

BELOW RIGHT *Wood is a versatile material that suits both modern and rustic settings. Containers range from large, ornate tubs that look attractive placed on either side of a doorway, to wooden garden baskets, window boxes, and even empty seed trays that can be filled with low-level plants for an informal display.*

The main drawback of wooden containers is that they are porous, which means you should either treat them with a horticulturally safe wood preservative before using them, or line them with a strong plastic liner to collect excess water. Alternatively, you can simply place the plastic plant pot inside the container and use a drip tray underneath.

PLANTS FOR THE PLACE

THE POSITIONING of indoor plants is critical to their survival, and this section of the book is devoted to choosing the right plant for the place, offering a situation-by-situation analysis of the home and listing the plants best suited to those positions.

From plants that will thrive on a sunny windowsill in direct sunlight, such as summer-flowering geraniums to those that prefer indirect sunlight, such as gerberas, and those that enjoy the cool light of an unheated spare bedroom or east- or north-facing kitchen, like azaleas, just about every plant and situation is covered. There is a special feature on plants for conservatories and sunrooms, plus advice on a wide range of topics, such as how color schemes and curtaining can affect a plant's health.

ABOVE *The delicate yellow heads of* Narcissus *'Tête-à-Tête' form an attractive display in a wrought iron basket.*

LEFT *Spectacular golden trumpet* (Allamanda cathartica), *from South America, is best suited to a warm conservatory.*

Positioning Plants

M OST OF US buy plants on impulse without really considering where we are going to put them. However, choosing the right plant for the right situation is a key element in successful indoor gardening.

In general, indoor plants are frequently positioned where they can be seen and admired by everyone, such as in the living room or hallway, but these areas do not necessarily provide the best growing conditions. The living room, for example, is usually the warmest, driest room in the house, and therefore not an ideal environment for many of the spring-flowering plants that require cool, humid, growing conditions. The kitchen windowsill, on the other hand, is often cooler and offers good humidity, making it a better place for cyclamen, azaleas, and primulas. In addition to the temperature of the room, you must consider how much light is available in the room.

Many people leave their plants in a permanent position all year round and wonder why they do not flourish. In general, flowering plants require more light than foliage plants, but remember that light intensity varies throughout the year. For example,

DOWNSTAIRS

When choosing a plant for a particular position in the home, make sure that it will receive adequate light, warmth, and humidity.

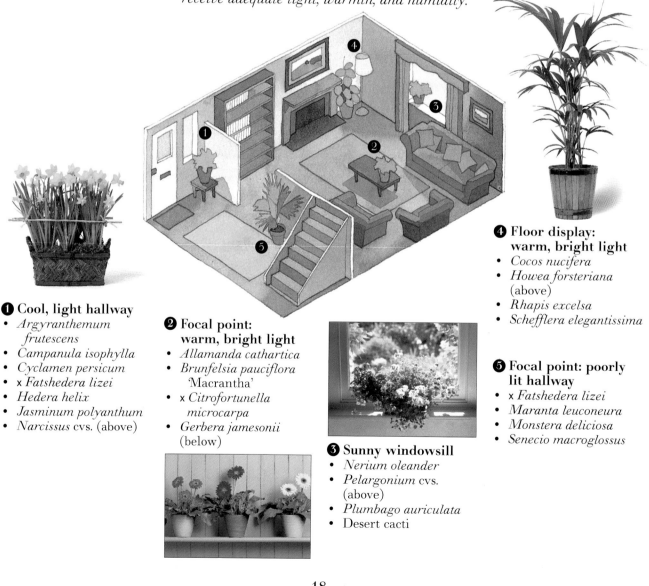

❶ **Cool, light hallway**
- *Argyranthemum frutescens*
- *Campanula isophylla*
- *Cyclamen persicum*
- x *Fatshedera lizei*
- *Hedera helix*
- *Jasminum polyanthum*
- *Narcissus* cvs. (above)

❷ **Focal point: warm, bright light**
- *Allamanda cathartica*
- *Brunfelsia pauciflora* 'Macrantha'
- x *Citrofortunella microcarpa*
- *Gerbera jamesonii* (below)

❸ **Sunny windowsill**
- *Nerium oleander*
- *Pelargonium* cvs. (above)
- *Plumbago auriculata*
- Desert cacti

❹ **Floor display: warm, bright light**
- *Cocos nucifera*
- *Howea forsteriana* (above)
- *Rhapis excelsa*
- *Schefflera elegantissima*

❺ **Focal point: poorly lit hallway**
- x *Fatshedera lizei*
- *Maranta leuconeura*
- *Monstera deliciosa*
- *Senecio macroglossus*

a plant that thrives in the back of a north-facing room in summer, when the sun is strong and the days are long, may need to be placed much closer to the window in winter when the days are short.

The color of the walls and the amount of curtaining provided can both affect the light intensity. Pale-colored walls reflect light, making a room appear much brighter, while dark walls absorb light. Some rooms may not receive any direct sunlight at all, but still have windows large enough to provide good natural light for growing certain houseplants.

Indoor plants are grown in the nursery in a controlled environment and very few can tolerate sudden changes in temperature. A windowsill may offer the best light for your plants, but remember temperatures can drop to below freezing in many geographical regions at night, making it a hostile place for tender plants. Conversely, in summer you must take care that your plants aren't pressed up against the glass, which will scorch their leaves.

Most plants at the garden center are labeled with their ideal growing conditions, and there is a directory of plants at the back of this book with advice on temperature, light requirements, and maintenance. Before you make your selection, check that your home offers adequate growing conditions. Humidity, in particular, is crucial to many house-plants and there are several ways of increasing the humidity in your home (see page 77).

UPSTAIRS

It is sometimes easy to neglect plants upstairs. Always make sure that they have enough water and food.

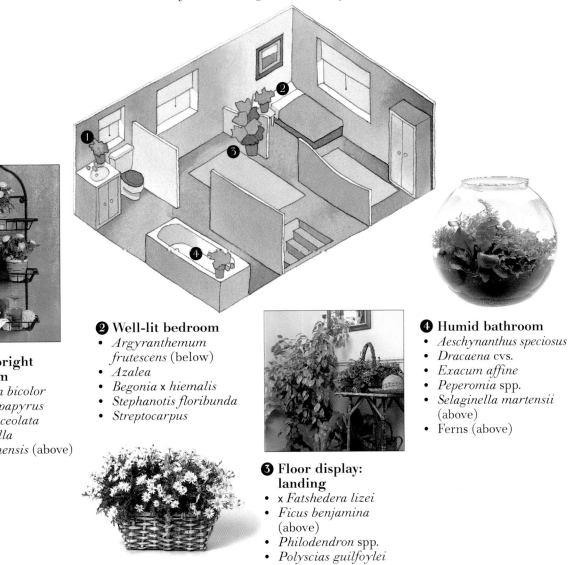

❶ Warm, bright bathroom
- *Caladium bicolor*
- *Cyperus papyrus*
- *Hoya lanceolata* subsp. *bella*
- *Rosa chinensis* (above)

❷ Well-lit bedroom
- *Argyranthemum frutescens* (below)
- *Azalea*
- *Begonia* x *hiemalis*
- *Stephanotis floribunda*
- *Streptocarpus*

❸ Floor display: landing
- x *Fatshedera lizei*
- *Ficus benjamina* (above)
- *Philodendron* spp.
- *Polyscias guilfoylei*

❹ Humid bathroom
- *Aeschynanthus speciosus*
- *Dracaena* cvs.
- *Exacum affine*
- *Peperomia* spp.
- *Selaginella martensii* (above)
- Ferns (above)

Direct Sunlight

This is a really bright position that receives direct sunlight for most of the day – for example, a south-facing windowsill. Shading may be needed in summer months.

A SUNNY ROOM may seem an obvious place to display houseplants, but they have to be chosen carefully if they are going to thrive. A south-facing bay window can give a room the feeling of a desert on a hot summer's day and will be a very hostile place for all but a few sun-lovers, but this very same window could offer an ideal home for many of the winter-flowering houseplants during the dark winter months when light is at a premium.

Desert cacti are a good choice for somewhere that is likely to get hot, and they can provide a vast selection of shapes and textures with their different sculptural forms (see pages 54–5). Other, taller, foliage plants that are suitable for a sunny window in summer include phoenix palms and yuccas, both with tough leathery leaves, but even these need constant turning and attention to keep them happy and growing well.

The summer-flowering geraniums will tolerate a lot of bright sun in the middle of summer and are especially suited to a sunny windowsill. Scented-leaved geraniums, in particular, are a real boon in a sunny situation where the warmth of the sun releases their aromatic scent. Good varieties include *Pelargonium crispum* 'Variegatum' (lemon-scented), *P. tomentosum* (mint-scented), and *P. odoratissimum* (apple-scented).

In winter, jasmines and bougainvilleas are an excellent choice for a sunny windowsill. However, these wonderful plants really don't like dry air and must have humidity to be successful. A moist, but never waterlogged, soil is necessary, and they should be watered with warm, soft water.

Windowsill of geraniums
RIGHT *These scented-leaved geraniums thrive on a sunny windowsill, where the warm sun releases their aromatic perfume.*

TRUE SUN-LOVING PLANTS

Only a few plants like to bask in the sun in the hottest months of summer, and even these must be watched carefully or their leaves will soon become scorched and dry. Many of the bromeliads thrive in hot, sunny conditions.

PLANTS THAT
TOLERATE FULL SUN

The following plants will tolerate a hot, south-facing position in summer:

Bromeliads
Flaming sword (*Vriesea splendens*)
Pineapple plant (*Ananas bracteatus*)
Rainbow star plant (*Cryptanthus fosterianus*)
Urn plant (*Aechmea fasciata*)

Flowering Plants
Geranium (*Pelargonium* cvs.)
Golden trumpet (*Allamanda cathartica*)
Paper flower (*Bougainvillea glabra*)

Urn plant (*Aechmea fasciata*)
LEFT *This striking bromeliad, with its silver-banded, gray-green leaves, produces a long-lasting bright pink flower in the base of the rosette in summer. It is easy to grow, but remember to water into the flower rosette and not over the soil mix (see page 84).*

Pineapple plant (*Ananas bracteatus* var. *tricolor*)
RIGHT *This dramatic looking bromeliad has sharp, serrated leaves.*

HERBS

While herbs really prefer to grow outdoors in the garden, it is always useful to keep a selection handy in the kitchen as a short-term planting. Either make a mixed display like this one, or group several plants of the same type together in one container to give a full planting.

Culinary mixed herbs

RIGHT *Your choice of culinary herbs will depend largely on the sort of food you prepare. This window-box contains a mixture, but if you tend to use a lot of one particular type – for example, parsley – you may be better with a single planting. When the plants start to look leggy and thin, transfer them outdoors to the garden where they will soon rejuvenate.*

Lemon thyme
(Thymus × citriodorus)

Rosemary
(Rosmarinus officinalis)

Bay *(Laurus nobilis)*

Parsley
(Petroselinum crispum)

Tarragon
(Artemisia dracunculus)

Cilantro
(Coriandrum sativum)

Indirect Sunlight

This is a warm position that receives little or no direct sunlight, although the overall level of brightness is still high.

MANY OF THE main living areas in our homes offer good natural light. Rooms situated on the east side of the house are often bathed in sunlight for a few hours in the morning, while those on the west receive soft light during the afternoon. These sorts of conditions are ideal for many houseplants, since very few enjoy basking in hot summer sun all day long. If your home offers good natural light, you have many choices available to you from nurseries, with flowering and foliage plants to choose from throughout the year − from gerberas, busy lizzies, and Cape primroses in summer to chrysanthemums, kalanchoes, begonias, and poinsettias in winter.

One of the most popular rooms in which to display houseplants is the living room, as this is where we spend much of our time. However, since this is probably one of the warmest rooms in the house, you must take precautions to prevent the atmosphere from becoming too dry. Many houseplants enjoy a warm position, but very few thrive in dry conditions and none like to be placed near a direct source of heat. If you have an open fire or central heating, you must find ways of providing humidity for your plants. Regular misting is beneficial to many plants, especially ferns, but it is not suitable for those with hairy leaves, such as African violets, because the water can get trapped in the hairs on the leaves and cause them to rot. A helpful tip is to place the pot on a saucer of moist pebbles, which provide humidity as the water evaporates off the stones and into the surrounding air. Make sure the plant isn't sitting in water, because this encourages bacteria which rot the roots. Another solution

Cheerful gerberas
LEFT *The striking, large, daisylike gerberas are perhaps more familiar as cut flowers from florists', but the flowering pot plant is now widely available in orange, yellow, red, pink, and white throughout the summer.*

Centerpiece of peperomias
RIGHT *A selection of different types of peperomias arranged together in a basket makes a very good centerpiece for a dining-room table. This basket has been lined with plastic, a few pebbles have been added to the base for drainage, and the plants removed from their original pots. The surface of the soil has been covered with fresh moss to conserve moisture. Do not overwater these plants because they are likely to rot.*

is to place your flowerpot inside another larger container and surround the inner pot with damp moss. A useful tip is to place fresh moss over the surface of the potting soil, which not only preserves moisture and provides humidity, but also looks most attractive – especially if you replace the moss regularly with a fresh supply.

Telltale signs that your plant isn't receiving enough humidity are that the leaves begin to shrivel or show signs of scorching, or the buds or flowers fall off prematurely. If your plants have been displayed in a warm, dry atmosphere for several months at a time, they will often benefit from a short vacation in a slightly airier part of the house. Bedrooms and hallways that have good light, but are not as warm as the main living areas of the house, are good places to move your plants to for short periods of time when they are starting to show signs of poor humidity.

One of the advantages of growing houseplants in containers is that they are portable, which means you can move them around according to the season. Different rooms offer different levels of light throughout the year, so if your indoor plants are not receiving enough light in one area of the room, you can move them to a brighter position with little effort. A begonia or African violet, for example, that thrives in the center of the living room in summer when light levels are high, may need to be placed closer to the windowsill in winter, when the sun is weak and the days are short – especially in northern latitudes. Temperatures, too,

WINTER PLANTINGS

There is a wide selection of flowering plants available in winter – from the ever popular poinsettias to more unusual specimens, such as the pentas shown below. A fair amount of winter sunshine will not harm many flowering houseplants.

PLANTS FOR INDIRECT SUN

The following seasonal plants are all suitable for a warm position out of direct sunlight:

Spring
Brazilian jasmine (*Mandevilla sanderi*)
Camellia japonica
Flamingo flower (*Anthurium scherzerianum*)

Summer
Begonia x *hiemalis*
Busy lizzy (*Impatiens* cvs.)
Cape primrose (*Streptocarpus* cvs.)
Gardenia augusta
Gerbera jamesonii
Hibiscus rosa-sinensis
Italian bellflower (*Campanula isophylla*)
Nut orchid (*Achimenes longiflora*)

Winter
Christmas cactus (*Schlumbergera* x *buckleyi*)
Jasmine (*Jasminum polyanthum*)
Ornamental pepper (*Capsicum annuum*)
Poinsettia (*Euphorbia pulcherrima*)

Red and white
LEFT *Flaming katy* (Kalanchoe blossfeldiana) *can be bought in flower at any time of the year, and in a wide range of colors – including red, orange, and yellow. It has fleshy, succulent leaves and a long flowering season.*
BELOW *A new plant to look out for and one that flowers during the winter months, pentas requires a warm bright position. To maintain a compact shape, pinch out the stem tips.*

can fluctuate – especially at night. So if you move a plant onto a sunny windowsill in winter, remember to bring it back into the middle of the room at night when temperatures plummet. The same applies in summer when you must take care that your plants aren't pressed up against the glass, which will scorch their leaves and cause them to turn brown around the edges.

Dramatic, single color displays

RIGHT *The poinsettia* (Euphorbia pulcherrima) *is one plant that everyone associates with Christmas, with its large colored flower heads in brilliant red, pale pink, or butter-cream. The flowers are not really flowers, but are colored leaf bracts with the tiny real flowers at the top of the bracts.*

BELOW *This attractive plant, known as the lipstick vine* (Aeschynanthus pulcher), *produces a mass of bright red lipstick-shaped flowers on long stems with pointed leaves edged in purple. Place it in a bright position with average warmth, and water with tepid water. Provide some humidity by misting the leaves.*

Rotating your plants is an important part of caring for them, because if you leave a plant in a permanent position all year round it will eventually grow towards the main light source and lose its shape. If your plants are grouped in the middle of, perhaps, a dining-room table, make sure you turn them each day so that all sides receive equal shares of light. This is especially important during the winter when light levels are low.

If you like to display your plants together in a large container or cachepot, try to leave them in their own pots so that you can tend to them on an individual basis. Different plants require different levels of food and water, and if you keep them in separate pots you can remove them one at a time, check for dead or yellowing leaves or flowers, and water them individually, before returning them to the main container.

Single planting
LEFT *This Begonia rex, with its large striking leaves, makes an attractive plant for a permanent display. Water well, but allow the top half of the soil to dry out between watering. Mist the leaves frequently and surround the inner container with damp moss to maintain humidity levels.*

Grouped display
BELOW *The Rex begonias, with their attractive and varied foliage, do really well in a warm bright spot away from direct sunlight, which can scorch the leaves and make them turn brown. Several different varieties planted together in a bowl, as here, make a long-lasting, colorful centerpiece. Try to leave the individual plants in their plastic pots, rather than planting them together, so that you can tend them on a personal basis.*

BEGONIA LEAVES
With their magnificent leaves, which have markings in shades of purple, red, pink, and silver, begonias provide as much color as any flowering plant.

Begonia 'Connee Boswell'

Begonia rex

Begonia bowerae

Begonia 'Minuet'

Single foliage display

ABOVE RIGHT *The fresh, grassy stems of these house bamboos* (Fargesia nitida) *are set off by their straight-sided, aluminum containers. A group of two or more plants is particularly eye-catching and works well in a modern room setting.*

Harmonizing colors

RIGHT *A popular flowering plant, which is available from garden centers and nurseries, the Hiemalis begonia comes in a wide range of colors with single or double flowers. For maximum impact, group several plants together in a large container. This basket contains red and pink flowers.*

Cool Light

This is a cool position that receives little or no direct sunlight; for example, a bright window in a north- or east-facing kitchen, hallway, or unheated spare bedroom.

THE POPULAR winter- and spring-flowering azaleas, cyclamen, and hydrangeas that are so often given as presents will quickly drop their flowers and die in the dry air of a warm, centrally-heated living room. These plants prefer a cool position with good light and some humidity.

These conditions can be found in rooms that receive sunlight for only part of the day, either an east-facing window that receives cool morning sun or a really light, large, north-facing window. The color of the walls in a room and the amount of curtaining over a window can both affect the light intensity. Pale colored walls reflect light, making a north-facing room appear much brighter, while dark, somber walls absorb light. Some rooms may not receive any direct sunlight at all, but still have windows large enough to provide good bright light

for growing plants. A windowsill probably receives the most light, but remember that temperatures can drop to below freezing here at night – especially if plants are left behind drawn curtains.

As well as considering the correct light source for your plant, think about the temperature in the

Mini pots
RIGHT *These dainty azaleas would look charming placed on bedside tables.*

Creating impact
BELOW *Grouping several delicate plants together increases their impact because it concentrates their colors at one level.*

room. Temperatures of around 60–65°F (16–18°C) are ideal for most bulbs, azaleas, and cyclamen, but these can be difficult to achieve in most houses. Azaleas really dislike warm conditions and must be kept permanently moist, without being water-logged, if they are to thrive indoors. They also need good humidity, so the secret is to mist your plants daily or place them on a bed of wet gravel. When the flowers have finished, move the plant to a frost-free position – somewhere like a cool conservatory or porch – and when the danger of frost has passed, plant it outdoors in the garden. Plunge the pot into the soil in a shady corner and make sure it doesn't dry out during the summer. You can then lift the pot again in fall, ready to make a lovely display in time for Christmas.

Cyclamen are one of the many flowering houseplants available around Christmas time and popular as gifts. However, these beautiful plants are often short-lived due to a lack of understanding their needs. This is as shame, because well-grown

Basket of azaleas

ABOVE *A basket of azaleas* (Rhododendron simsii) *is a good choice for this cool, east-facing bedroom. When displaying plants in a basket, always line it first with plastic to ensure it is waterproof. If possible, leave the plants in their plastic pots so that you can water and tend them on an individual basis.*

Fluted flowers

RIGHT *The delicate flowers of this* Primula obconica *are set off by a pretty china basket, with its fluted rim and painted flowers around the outside. Although these plants are usually treated as annuals and discarded after flowering, they will flower again if they are kept cool during the summer months.*

cyclamen can last for many weeks and be kept from season to season, getting bigger and bigger each year with a large head of flowers. Cool conditions, a bright room, and careful watering – never directly onto the tuber – are all these plants need if they are going to thrive.

Indoor bulbs need similar conditions and, although their flowers do not last for long inside the house, they are a welcome sight in spring, bringing enormous pleasure. Bulbs like hyacinths, muscari, and daffodils can all be planted outside in the garden when they have finished flowering.

The cymbidium orchids are an easy group of orchids to cultivate, and their exotic, waxy blooms suit many contemporary settings. The moth orchid *(Phalaenopsis)* is particularly striking, and while it may seem an expensive plant to buy, it can flower for several months if kept at an even temperature of around 60°F (16°C) and given good humidity, making it a worthwhile investment.

Handsome clivia
RIGHT *The* Clivia miniata *comes in orange, red, yellow, and cream with bell-shaped flowers. Even when not in flower, the ribbonlike leaves make an attractive feature.*

Orchid behind glass
BELOW *The slipper orchid* (Paphiopedilum *'Grozner Castle')* enjoys good cool light on this east-facing windowsill. Always remove plants from the windowsill at night when temperatures drop.*

Modern display
RIGHT *The amaryllis* (Hippeastrum) *is a very popular indoor bulb, producing a magnificent display of glamorous flowers. It must be grown in a cool position and only brought into a warm room when it comes into flower.*

PLANTS WITH STRONG FLOWER IMPACT

The following plants all have large, striking flower heads:

Pink and red
Amaryllis (*Hippeastrum* cvs.)
Christmas cactus (*Schlumbergera* x buckleyi)
Cyclamen persicum
Oleander *(Nerium oleander)*

White
Gardenia *(Gardenia augusta)*
Gerbera jamesonii
Lilies (e.g. *Lilium* 'Casa Blanca')

Yellow and orange
Clivia miniata
Hibiscus rosa-sinensis
Shrubby verbena *(Lantana camara)*

Blue and mauve
Florist's cineraria (*Pericallis* x *hybrida*)
Hydrangea macrophylla
Passionflower *(Passiflora caerulea)*

Partial Shade

This is a position that receives no direct sunlight, although the overall light quality is not poor. Most plants featured in this chapter will thrive in the back of a room, away from a large window.

FLOWERING HOUSEPLANTS do not thrive in the more shady areas of the home, because they need maximum light to keep flowering and maturing. However, there are many beautiful foliage plants that will thrive permanently in a shady room and will cheer up the darkest corner.

A hallway or landing is often an area that is cool, since it is not heated to the same degree as the rest of the house. This can be a good area to grow leafy foliage plants, because they will not have to put up with the dry, arid atmosphere of the warmer living rooms. The Boston fern *(Nephrolepis exaltata)* is a good subject for a cool, shaded area – although it doesn't like deep shade – and looks very handsome displayed on a large pedestal with its bright green fronds cascading over the sides. If you need a taller plant, a fatshedera or

Architectural display
RIGHT *The fern* (Nephrolepis exaltata *'Bostoniensis')
was favored by the Victorians for its beautiful bushy
habit. This plant is not a deep shade lover, but would do
well near an east-facing window.*

SPECIMEN PLANTS
*These plants have eye-catching foliage and a strong, architectural
form, making them dramatic enough to display on their own
in an attractive container.*

Narrow leaf fig *(Ficus binnendijkii)*
BELOW *The* Ficus binnendijkii *(also known as* Ficus longifolia) *is usually grown as a tall, floor-standing specimen (see page 47), but here it has been grown into a short, compact shape. It is shade-tolerant and would do well standing on a table away from the window.*

Miniature tree fern *(Blechnum gibbum)*
ABOVE *This fern has a crown of stiff fronds and a small trunk that grows as the plant ages. Its arching shape is set off beautifully by the Victorian-style vase.*

philodendron would make a good floor-standing specimen in a shady corner. For a table display, choose a grouped arrangement of leathery-leaved scindapsus and *Ficus pumila*, which will trail over the sides of the container. Another trailing plant, and one that is very easy to grow in partial shade, is the grape ivy *(Cissus rhombifolia)*. This has dark, glossy leaves that are often trained up a pole, although it can be grown as a trailing plant, making it ideal for a hanging basket. If the leaves turn brown at the tips, the air is too dry.

One of the advantages of growing plants in containers is that it gives you the flexibility to move them around. Beware of leaving your plant in a permanent position all year round. Even shade-loving plants enjoy a lighter position at some stage during their growing season to stimulate their growth and regenerate the plant. Rotating your shady plants from low light to stronger light is a good idea, providing it is done gradually and the plants are able to acclimatize slowly. Once the summer is in full swing, give your plants a break by plunging their pots into a shady corner of the garden where they will benefit from being out in the fresh air and an occasional shower of rain. Keep an eye on them as you would in the house to check for pests and diseases, and make sure you bring them back into the house before any signs of frost.

FERNS
Ferns thrive in the humid, shady areas of the home, such as a steamy kitchen or bathroom. The varieties shown below would all grow well in a terrarium or bottle garden.

Hare's foot fern *(Polypodium aureum)*

Bird's nest fern *(Asplenium nidus)*

Cretan brake fern *(Pteris cretica)*

Polystichum tsussimense

Maidenhair fern *(Adiantum raddianum)*

Grouped display
ABOVE *A group of dieffenbachias makes a striking feature in a modern setting. Here, two varieties are grouped in clay pots with* Pellaea rotundifolia *arranged around the front. The variegation on the leaves means these dieffenbachias will not tolerate poor light.*

Single planting
RIGHT *This handsome cristate table fern* (Pteris cretica 'Alexandrae'), *with its long fronds and tipped leaflets, has reached full size, making it dramatic enough to display on its own. These plants prefer a warm environment with good humidity, like a bathroom.*

Conservatories

THE CONSERVATORY offers an opportunity to create an environment for both plants and people. Sunrooms and solariums also make perfect places for growing plants, and even screened-in porches can suit many plants at various times of the year. There is so much more light in conservatories and sunrooms than the average room inside the home and, as long as the conservatory does not get too hot in summer, it will have good humidity and be the ideal place for many plants to thrive. Plants like plumbago, passion flower, jasmine, and abutilon will flourish in the cool and humid conditions of a correctly situated conservatory, and others, such as pot hydrangeas (*Hydrangea macrophylla*) or primulas (*Primula obconica*), that last only a short time inside the house will thrive for many weeks. Conservatories offer the chance to create somewhere quite different from the house or garden for growing plants.

Cascading basket of columnea

ABOVE *Hanging baskets are tremendously successful in a conservatory where they can reach huge sizes. This exotic-looking* Columnea *'Stavanger,' with its red-lipped blooms, needs room for its trailing stems to hang freely.*

Tender rhododendron

ABOVE *A conservatory provides the ideal environment for tender plants that need to be brought inside to protect them from winter frosts. This tender* Rhododendron *'Lady Alice Fitzwilliam' overwinters in the conservatory and produces a fantastic show of heavily scented white flowers in early spring.*

Border display

RIGHT *The bird's nest fern* (Asplenium nidus) *in this north-facing conservatory has grown to full size with fronds of 4 ft. (1.2 m), giving architectural interest in both summer and winter. Variegated ivy provides good ground cover around the base and keeps the roots moist.*

The position of your conservatory is of the utmost importance if you want to fill it with lots of plants, as well as provide extra living space. A conservatory that is situated on a south-facing wall will become its own desert in summer and no plants will be happy there. A south-facing conservatory or sun-room may be comfortable in winter when the sun is weak, but in summer temperatures can soar to 100°F (37°C), making it a hostile place for both people and plants.

Whatever aspect, ceiling ventilation is essential. Side ventilation cannot create the same buoyancy of atmosphere. You must also supply adequate shading with Venetian blinds or shades in summer.

If your conservatory has a solid wall, this is an ideal place to fix trellis or wires for climbing plants. Try and display your plants at different heights to give a natural growing environment — a tiered plant stand is ideal for this purpose, because it enables you to display several plants together. A shelf around the edge of the window makes a wonderful

Mass of Cape primroses
BELOW *The Cape primrose* (Streptocarpus) *is a native of South Africa that will flower over a long season. Because these plants have delicate flower heads, they are best displayed in a group on a low table to increase their impact. Regular deadheading and fertilizing throughout the summer will encourage flowers.*

Basket of begonias
ABOVE *This* Begonia solananthera, *with its attractive waxy leaves on long trailing stems, will flower for many months, if it is kept in the right conditions. Choose a bright position out of direct sunlight and allow the soil to dry out between watering. The trailing stems snap easily, so be extra careful when watering. As begonias are prone to powdery mildew (see pages 116–7), always provide adequate ventilation.*

home for tall or trailing plants, which can either be trained to grow up in front of the window or hang down below the windowsill.

Most conservatories open directly onto the house and one of the joys of having such a room is the wonderful scent it provides when you open the doors in early summer. Scented plants, such as jasmine and trachelospermum, as well as those with aromatic foliage, like scented geraniums and the night-scented *Cestrum nocturnum*, are a valuable addition in this still and warm environment that concentrates their heady scent. Exotic-looking lilies, such as *Lilium regale* or *L.* 'Casa Blanca,' are a must in summer, but be careful not to brush against the pollen-laden stamens, which can stain clothes. Your conservatory can become a magical green cave in summer with pots of many different plants. You could try growing some of the exotic, old-fashioned conservatory plants so favored by the Victorians, such as the poor man's orchid (*Schizanthus*) or salpiglossis (*Salpiglossis sinuata*).

In winter, seasonal flowering plants, such as azaleas, cyclamen, and primulas, will flourish in a cool conservatory. In fact, they are often happier here than inside the house where the dry central heating can scorch their leaves and stunt their growth. If a cyclamen or azalea begins to look unhappy indoors, it will often revive completely if given a short spell in a cool conservatory. The conservatory also provides sanctuary for some of the tender rhododendrons and camellias that like to spend the summer in a shady spot in the garden, but must be brought into a frost-free environment during the winter months.

It is important to grow a selection of green foliage plants in the conservatory, which will provide all-year-round color and interest. Ivies and ferns are relatively trouble-free and can be planted in pots and moved around according to the season. Pots of leafy palms, both floor-standing specimens, such as the kentia or phoenix palm, and smaller varieties grouped on a table, add to the charm of many conservatories. And even "difficult" houseplants, like the maidenhair fern (*Adiantum raddianum*), will flourish in a conservatory where they have adequate humidity and light.

Wall of geraniums
LEFT *A solid wall is the perfect place to attach wires to train climbing plants. Here, variegated ivy (Hedera cvs.) provides all-year-round interest, while ivy-leaved geraniums – including the mauve P. 'La France' – give a splash of color in summer and early fall.*

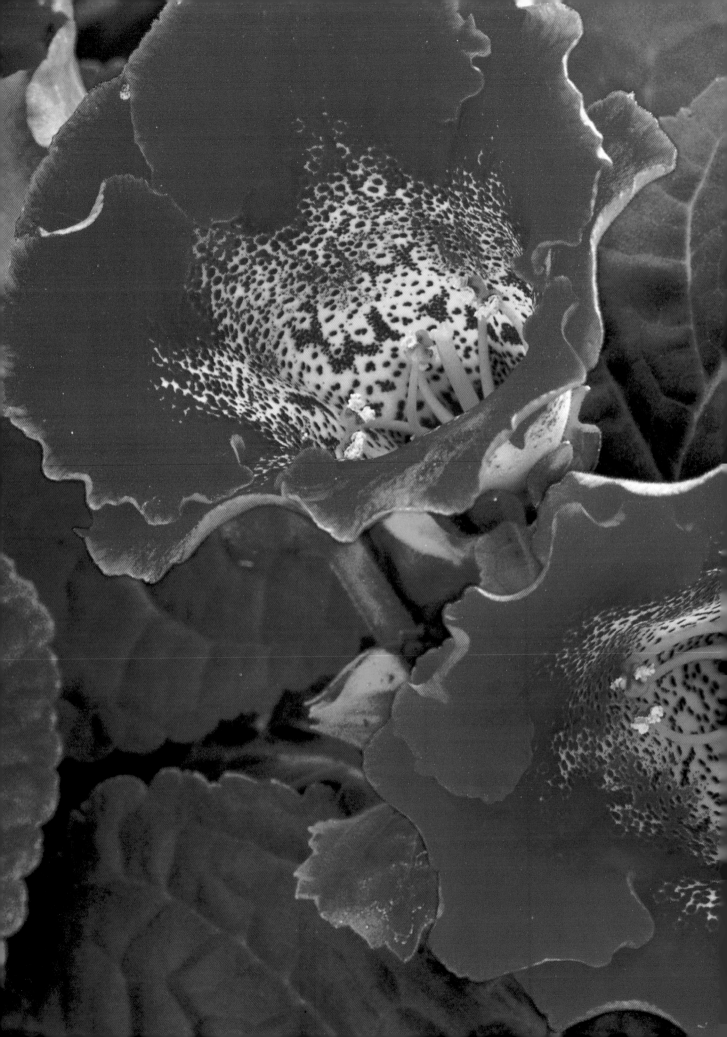

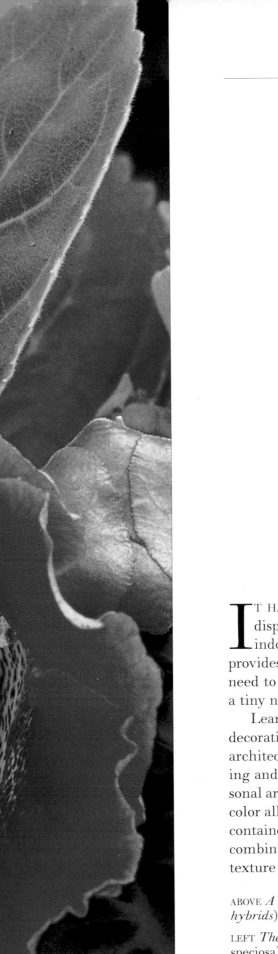

PLANT DISPLAYS

I T HAS NEVER BEEN easier to create stunning plant displays in the home. Whether you are a keen indoor gardener or a complete novice, this section provides all the know-how and inspiration you will need to create arrangements for every situation, from a tiny nook or cranny to a spacious conservatory.

Learn how to group plants successfully, stake them decoratively, and make a focal point of a handsome architectural display. There are ideas for small flowering and foliage displays, succulents and cacti, and seasonal arrangements that will ensure a brilliant show of color all year round. Finally, there are tips on selecting containers, choosing plants to suit the decor of a room, combining colors, and making the most of foliage texture and shape.

ABOVE *A group of busy lizzies* (Impatiens *'New Guinea' hybrids*) *in mixed colors.*

LEFT *The singularly beautiful flowers of gloxinia* (Sinningia speciosa) *have speckled throats and large petals.*

Grouping Plants

PLANTS LIKE TO BE grouped together because they give off water vapor, which makes the surrounding air humid and gives them a happy growing environment. From an aesthetic point of view too, a group of well-thought-out plants will make a stronger statement in a room than several individual pots spaced around randomly.

The decor of your home plays an important role in your choice of houseplants, so make this your starting point. Consider the style of the room and your choice of wallpaper or paint. An ornate wallpaper, for example, would completely overwhelm a delicate flowering plant or feathery fern. A room decorated with large, vertical stripes needs a bushy plant that will contrast with the stripes and stand out against the walls. A fireplace is a popular place to display houseplants in summer, but consider how much light is available here before making your selection. A group of flowering plants may seem the ideal choice to brighten up a dark space, but they will not survive in shady conditions – whereas ferns will thrive in them (see page 32).

Once you have decided on the location for your plants, you are free to make your selection at the garden center. You might decide on contrasting colored flowers to suit a modern living room, or soothing mauves and whites for an airy bedroom. However, don't concentrate on color alone – consider the shape and form of the leaves too.

The next consideration is a container. You can either choose a large single container, such as a bowl or dish, which looks good as a centerpiece on a table, or a series of individual containers to suit a shelf or windowsill. If you choose the latter, pick ones that complement each other in color and shape, as this will help to unify the arrangement.

Creating a balanced display

LEFT *A ceramic sponge-painted bowl makes a perfect container for this bedroom arrangement in soothing shades of blue, silver, lilac, and white. Note how the trailing stems of the scindapsus complement the branches on the toile de Jouy wallpaper behind. When making a group of different plants, check that they all require the same growing conditions – these plants would all enjoy a warm situation, out of direct sunlight.*

Matching pair

RIGHT *Plants with delicate flower heads, such as these* Primula obconica, *look most dramatic when displayed together in a group. Here, they are placed on a kitchen shelf in matching ceramic pitchers for an informal feel. The plastic pots fit neatly inside the rims. Note how the plain green of the containers does not detract from the flowers.*

Decorative Staking

WHEN YOU GROW trailing or climbing plants indoors, it is important that you stake them successfully to create an attractive display. This can be done in several ways, using bamboo canes (see below), moss poles (see page 109), topiary frames (see opposite), or hoops made from garden wire (see page 108).

Tabletop topiary, which involves training plants around a wire support, is fun and easy to do, and you can create lots of interesting shapes. Start by selecting an evergreen plant with dense compact foliage and pliable stems. Ivy is ideal because it is fast-growing and comes in many attractive forms with silver, white, and gold markings. It also grows easily from cuttings, making it an excellent choice for growing over topiary frames where several plants are needed. Simply snip off short lengths with some roots attached and plant them around the edge of a container. Another good foliage plant is the miniature creeping fig (Ficus pumila), which can also be obtained in variegated forms.

Many flowering plants can be encouraged to grow around hoops and frames. The wax flower (Stephanotis floribunda) is easy to train around a hoop and carries the added bonus of beautiful, scented white flowers. Another scented flowering plant that will quickly cover a trellis or pyramid is Jasminum polyanthum, with its pink tubular buds that become white as the flowers open.

Once you have selected your plants, decide what shape you want to train them. There are lots of commercial wire supports readily available from nurseries and garden centers. You can choose from spirals, hoops, columns, and wreaths. If you can't find one the correct size, try making your own from a wire coat hanger.

USING BAMBOO CANES

The most popular staking device is the bamboo cane, which can either be used with plastic ties to support individual stems (see left) or in a framework to prop several stems at once (see below).

'Casa Blanca' lilies
ABOVE *This large pot of lilies must be well-staked to support the large flowers. Place the bamboo canes in the pot as soon as the bulbs show through, because you may damage them by adding canes at a later stage.*

'Jetfire' narcissus
RIGHT *Individual pots of narcissus are crammed together in this basket and bamboo canes are used to support the plants' stems.*

USING A TOPIARY FRAME

Commercial topiary frames can be bought from garden centers, or you can make your own using coat hangers or garden wire. Don't forget to paint the wire first to prevent it rusting.

Wire hoops
ABOVE *Madagascar jasmine* (Stephanotis) *and ivy are ideal for training around a wire hoop because their stems are pliable.*

Ivy pyramid
ABOVE LEFT *Ivy is a fast-growing foliage plant that will grow over a wire frame like this one in about 18 months, depending on the cultivar.*

Ivy ball
LEFT *This topiary frame has been filled with sphagnum moss to form a firm support for the ivy tendrils to cling to. Keep the moss moist at all times and feed the plants regularly.*

CLIMBING PLANTS
The following plants are all suitable for growing up a topiary frame:

Flowering plants
Black-eyed susan *(Thunbergia alata)*
Hoya lanceolata
Jasmine *(Jasminum polyanthum)*
Mandevilla sanderi
Wax flower *(Stephanotis floribunda)*

Foliage plants
Cape ivy *(Senecio macroglossus)*
Creeping fig *(Ficus pumila)*
Ivy *(Hedera cvs.)*
Philodendron scandens
Pothos vine *(Scindapsus spp.)*
Rhoicissus spp.

Architectural Displays

A NUMBER OF INDOOR plants are dramatic enough to be given the spotlight and stand alone in a room, making a real focal point. This is particularly true of large plants, such as palms, which make handsome specimens and soon become part of the room's furniture, adding elegance and style and lifting the decor. But not all architectural plants need to be large. A pair of small dracaenas, with their striped leaves of red and yellow, make an eye-catching display placed at either end of a table in an entrance hall, and these plants are ideal if you don't have the space to accommodate a large floor-standing specimen. In many situations, a large specimen plant can present

fewer problems than a group of smaller plants. Although it might take up a great deal of space, there is only one plant to care for, while a group of small flowering plants will all need individual attention. One of the main problems with large indoor plants is that they can become dusty, just like the furniture, and need regular cleaning and sponging to keep the leaves dust-free (see page 118). Plants like the rubber plant *(Ficus elastica)*

Kitchen display
RIGHT *A tall* Ficus binnendijkii *stands in the corner of this north-facing kitchen. Its long spiky stems contrast beautifully with the variegated spider plant on the pine dresser.*

STANDARDS

Standard trees of all shapes and sizes make an eye-catching feature. They are an expensive investment, but will last for many years if they are well cared-for.

**Rainbow plant
(Dracaena marginata)**
LEFT *This elegant plant has been carefully grown into a beautiful upright shape. Tall varieties look good placed on either side of a doorway, while small plants suit a table display.*

**Weeping fig
(Ficus benjamina)**
RIGHT *This popular, low maintenance plant is also available in a variegated form with cream-splashed leaves, making it a wonderful specimen plant for a modern interior. Here, the stems of several plants have been braided together to create an interesting twisted trunk.*

and the fiddle-leaf fig *(Ficus lyrata)* both have large leathery leaves that need regular care to keep them clean and healthy.

Finding an appropriate container to display a really large plant can often prove to be a problem, but it would spoil the elegance of a large plant by placing it in an unattractive plastic pot. Large clay containers, with a plastic dish placed in the base to collect excess water, are available in every size and shape from garden centers and garden architecture stores, or you could make your own container from a painted tin cannister or wastepaper basket.

Grouped foliage display
FAR RIGHT *This fresh-looking grouping of bird's nest ferns and fig plants* (Asplenium nidus, Ficus benjamina, *and* F. pumila) *brightens up the corner of a north-facing hallway. A hall is an ideal place to display plants, since it is not usually heated to the same degree as the rest of the house, but make sure it is not drafty.*

Specimen plant
ABOVE *While most plants benefit from being displayed in a group with similar plants, some, like this polyscias, are dramatic enough to stand on their own.*

Kentia palm *(Howea fosteriana)*
RIGHT *The kentia palm is a graceful and elegant plant, which would look as good displayed with other plants as it would on its own.*

Canary date palm *(Phoenix canariensis)*
RIGHT *Palm trees were favored by the Victorians, who displayed huge examples in their houses and conservatories.*

Small Flowering Displays

THERE IS A SMALL flowering plant to choose from for every season of the year. Aim to grow a few different varieties that flower at different times so that you can keep the display going for as long as possible. Starting in the fall, there are the delightful *Cyclamen persicum* cultivars that come in a variety of soft colors. These small cyclamen are really much more charming than their larger cousins, and they often have attractive silver-green leaves. In spring, there are a large number of bulbs and primulas to choose from, followed by geraniums, miniature roses, and marguerites in summer.

Small flowering plants usually look best if they are displayed together, rather than randomly spacing them around the room. When growing several plants together in one pot, make sure you buy enough plants to fill it entirely — you may need three or four to create a really full display. A favorite place to show off houseplants is on the kitchen windowsill, where a row of three or four identical pots or ceramic pitchers can make a real feature filled with small flowering plants, such as cyclamen, in harmonizing colors.

Flowering plants make popular gifts and many will flower for long periods of time. Choose from African violets *(Saintpaulia)*, which are available all year round in many colors, and kalanchoes, with their abundant star-like flowers that flower non-stop throughout the year. Cineraria *(Pericallis hybrida)* is a pretty plant to give as a gift, with its mass of daisylike flowers covering the bright green, heart-shaped leaves. However, these plants should carry a warning, as they won't survive in an overheated room and will also soon wilt and die if left on a hot windowsill.

Lisianthus *(Eustoma grandiflorum)*
RIGHT *Lisianthus are most often seen in florists' as cut flowers, but dwarf houseplants in blue, purple, and white are popular during the summer months. These plants are best treated as shortterm investments and discarded after flowering has finished.*

Gloxinias *(Sinningia speciosa* hybrids)
LEFT *These exotic-looking plants are actually quite easy to look after. They come in a wide range of vibrant colors, their handsome flowers and leaves needing no additional adornment.*

BULBS

Bulbs are very easy to grow indoors and usually flower several weeks earlier than they would outside. Buy bulbs as soon as you see them at the garden center, when they are at their freshest, and plant them immediately.

Hyacinths
ABOVE *These hyacinths are grown in special hyacinth glasses without the need for soil. Simply place the bulb in the top of the glass and fill it with water until it just touches the base of the bulb. Put in a dark place and bring into the light when shoots appear. The bulb can be planted in the garden after flowering.*

Grape hyacinths *(Muscari azureum)*
ABOVE *Being small, grape hyacinths are best grouped together in a large container, as here, or planted as part of a bigger group of mixed bulbs. They have the same cultivation requirements as hyacinths, and can be planted in the garden when they have finished flowering.*

Tulips *(Tulipa 'Red Riding Hood')*
LEFT *This variety of tulips has been specially treated for indoor culture. Here, six individual pots have been grouped into a large metal filigree tray, lined first with plastic, then filled with moss. Do not overwater the bulbs, but keep the surrounding moss damp, which will provide welcome humidity.*

Small Foliage Displays

LEAVES, AS MUCH as flowers, contribute to the attractiveness of houseplants, and you can create some excellent displays using a selection of small-leaved plants just as easily as the more dramatic, architectural-leaved varieties (shown on pages 46–9).

When growing plants with small, fine leaves, you may have to group them together if the plants are naturally small, or still in their infancy, but once they reach full size, they look imposing in their own right. If you browse around garden centers, you will be surprised by how much color and variegation there is in any group of foliage plants that are grown for their leaves alone.

As well as plants with variegated foliage, such as the spider plant *(Chlorophytum comosum)* or the *Ficus pumila* 'Sonny' shown opposite, there are a wealth of plants with red, pink, brown, and purple leaf markings. An eye-catching foliage plant that would do well as a permanent planting is the *Begonia bowerae*, which has beautiful rust-colored leaves with green markings and a bushy habit. One of the most popular colorful foliage plants is the polka dot plant *(Hypoestes phyllostachya)*, with its brightly spotted leaves of pale pink. This is a plant that can grow quite big, but as it generally becomes straggly with age, it is best used as a young plant to add interest to a small foliage display. A good ground-cover plant for a bottle garden is club moss *(Selaginella martensii)*, with its fresh green, creeping stems that form a dense mat of foliage.

Another group of small foliage plants that need mentioning are the miniature ferns seen frequently in nurseries. These are baby versions of the bigger, full-grown plants, but when bought as small foliage plants they, too, can look attractive displayed in a group. The maidenhair fern *(Adiantum raddianum)* often shrivels and dies in an overheated home, and is especially suited to the warm humidity of a bottle garden.

CREATING HUMIDITY

Many small or miniature foliage plants — ferns and mosses in particular — require high levels of humidity to prevent their leaves from shriveling and going brown. Finding ways to create humidity is one of the secrets of success with your houseplants.

Club moss
(Selaginella martensii)

Maidenhair fern
(Adiantum raddianum)

Bird's nest fern *(Asplenium nidus)*

Glass garden
LEFT *Glass bottle gardens and terraria offer high levels of humidity and are ideal for growing many small ferns and "baby" plants. Under normal conditions, water vapor given off by plants evaporates in the air, but in a bottle garden it condenses on the sides of the container and trickles back into the soil. This bottle garden is created from an old fish tank, which has been filled with an assortment of miniature ferns and plants.*

Braided fig

LEFT *A Victorian-style "long Tom" container is perfect for this charming, dwarflike tree, with its head of delicate leaves. Creating topiaried shapes with houseplants is easy to do (see page 45). A pair of these trees placed on an occasional or dining table would make an attractive and long-lasting feature in the home.*

Trailing display

BELOW *The creeping fig (Ficus pumila 'Sonny') is a versatile plant that looks as attractive grown up a pole as it does creeping along the surface of the soil. Here, it is displayed in a tall florists' bucket, which allows the foliage plenty of room to tumble over the sides. Small foliage plants such as this are often used as fillers in large arrangements, but when given their own space, they become star performers on their own.*

Single fern

LEFT *When a plant is really well grown, and has formed a good rounded habit, it can make a single architectural feature. This maidenhair fern* (Adiantum raddianum), *with its graceful bright green foliage, is a rather temperamental subject, but is happiest in a warm position with plenty of humidity. Keep the foliage well-misted and place in a bathroom or kitchen, where it will enjoy the humid atmosphere.*

Cacti and Succulents

ACTI AND SUCCULENTS are two fascinating groups of plants. The difference between the two is that cacti have modified side shoots, called areoles, carrying spines or hairs, while succulents have fleshy stems or leaves that store water. Some cacti are smooth and round, while others are knobbly, but they have all adapted themselves to give off as little water vapor as possible in their natural habitat. Most garden centers stock a good selection of cacti and succulents (see pages 125–127 and 136–137 for the best plants available), and these are ideal plants for children, because they are easy to maintain and tolerate a little neglect. Their main growing requirement is lots of warm sunlight, so find a warm, bright position for your plants. Although cacti are drought-tolerant, they do need watering during the summer.

Modern cactus garden
BELOW *Silver-painted pots of different heights, grouped on a pewter tray and surrounded by smooth pebbles, make a striking and stylish way to display a mixed group of cacti and succulents.*

When choosing a pot for your cactus, try to keep it fairly small because this will stimulate the plant and encourage it to flower. Tiny miniature clay pots are sold especially for the purpose, which should be filled with a purchased cactus soil mix or one with plenty of grit added. Cover the surface of the soil with ornamental gravel and add a couple of smooth stones around the outside to give your cactus garden the impression of a desert.

Succulent hanging basket
RIGHT *The trailing stems of this donkey's tail plant* (Sedum morganianum) *can reach up to 2 ft. (60 cm) long. Allow plenty of room around the plant, since the leaves will drop off if brushed against.*

DESERT CACTI

Desert cacti are not to be confused with forest cacti, which have completely different growing requirements.

Cereus peruvianus

Opuntia microdasys

Spiny desert cacti
ABOVE *A pair of silver-painted toothbrush mugs sets off the sculptural nature of these desert cacti, which would look spectacular in a modern setting. Desert cacti require hot, sunny conditions and should be watered less in winter when they need a rest period.*

SUCCULENTS

Succulents are easy to propagate from stem or leaf cuttings. These varieties would do well on a sunny windowsill.

Echeveria secunda var. glauca
RIGHT *This blue, rosette-forming echeveria flourishes in a large clam shell in a soil mix with plenty of grit added.*

Kalanchoe 'Primavera'
BELOW *The hollow inside of a ceramic ornamental swan makes a comfortable home for this silver-leaved succulent, which produces masses of purple-pink flowers in early summer.*

Miniature Displays

DISPLAYS OF miniature plants have a charm all of their own and they make an attractive gift when displayed together in a small container. Some of the most popular miniature plants on sale at nurseries and garden centers are ferns and small foliage plants, and many of these are ideal for growing in a humid terrarium or glass bottle garden (see page 52).

Miniature versions of their full-size relatives, like mini roses, mini kalanchoes, mini African violets, and mini chrysanthemums, are all perfect plants to display in a row on a kitchen shelf. You can either choose the same plant for each container (see right) or grow a different plant in each pot (see below). If you display your miniature plants in individual containers, make sure that you check them every couple of days to ensure they have enough water, because the potting soil will dry out rapidly. Most people have a wide variety of suitable plant holders in their own homes – many of them unusual. Delicate flowering miniature roses (*Rosa chinensis* 'Minima') look pretty in small coffee mugs, while large egg cups are ideal for displaying individual dwarf cacti (see far right).

Cacti are particularly popular with children, and they are often the first houseplants children notice. There is always a very big selection of cacti in all shapes and sizes at garden centers, and with a little imagination, it is possible to create a contemporary and stylish grouping. Try putting various sizes of cacti in small clay pots of slightly different sizes and painting the pots in bright colors, either different shades or the same color (see far right). A group of four or five miniature cacti, arranged on a metal dish, can look really striking in a contemporary setting and require little maintenance (for more information on growing cacti and succulents, see pages 54–5).

Same pots, different plants

BELOW *A row of three or four different miniature plants can look very attractive on a kitchen shelf. Mixed ferns and a creeping fig are ideal in this situation, where they are grown out of direct sunlight, but where humidity levels are high.*

Different pots, different plants

ABOVE *Repotting miniature cacti into hand-painted china cups of different heights and sizes is a novel way of displaying these sculptural plants. Making a collection of miniature cacti and succulents is an inexpensive hobby, and since the plants are easy to look after, ideal for beginners.*

Same pots, same plants

LEFT *These miniature roses (Rosa chinensis 'Minima') are potted into small yellow and green striped china pots that exactly match their yellow flowers and green foliage. Because the pots are small and will dry out quickly, make sure you water the plants on a regular basis. Remove dead or dying flower heads to maintain a healthy display.*

Low-level display

LEFT *A low foliage arrangement like this one would be ideal for the center of a table. Here, two types of club moss (Selaginella martensii) are planted in rows on a kitchen tray, creating a patchwork effect. These plants should be placed in a semishaded position, away from any bright sunlight. They need misting regularly to maintain humidity levels.*

Spring-flowering Displays

AS SOON AS CHRISTMAS is over, and all the decorations have been cleared away, how nice it is to see the early spring bulbs and spring flowering houseplants in the garden centers. While many bulbs are traditionally considered as outdoor features, some can be grown successfully indoors.

Bulbs, such as dwarf narcissi, crocus, and hyacinths, appear in the stores in bud well before any of the spring bulbs in gardens show through. These bulbs have been forced, but once you have enjoyed them inside the house you can plant them outside in the garden to flower again the following year. After they have finished flowering, remove any dead flowers. When the fear of frost has passed, transfer them to the garden, keeping their leaves intact, where you must feed them with a high potash fertilizer every two weeks to encourage them to flower well into the following year.

Primula obconica, with its delicate petals, makes a lovely spring plant for the kitchen windowsill. When the flowers eventually die, you can encourage extra flowering by placing the plant in a cool conservatory or on a frost-free porch where, after a short rest away from the central heating, a second flush of flowers will soon appear.

The hydrangea *(Hydrangea macrophylla)* is a popular spring plant, which makes a nice change from some of the smaller flowering specimens. Although you tend to buy these plants in spring, they will flower well into the summer months if given the correct treatment. Hydrangeas need a great deal of moisture, preferring rainwater to hard tap water, and they are best placed in a flat-bottomed container so they can absorb water freely. Surround the plants with damp moss to encourage humidity and keep them in a cool, bright situation. After they have finished flowering, prune back the stems and repot them into a larger container. These plants benefit from a short stay in the garden during the summer months. Simply bury the pot in a shady part of the garden, watering and feeding periodically with a high potash feed. In fall, bring the plant indoors to a cool, frost-free room and reduce watering to encourage the plant to rest. In early spring, gradually increase watering to bring the plant back into flower once again.

Line of three
LEFT *Three pots of yellow primroses have been placed in this twiggy pot holder to make a pretty feature. Keep the plants well-watered by removing their pots from the holder and submerging them in water. These plants will not last long inside, but will recover if put outside for a short time, away from central heating and dry air.*

PLANTS FOR SPRING

The following plants all flower in spring:

Amaryllis (*Hippeastrum* hybrids)
Azalea (*Rhododendron simsii*)
Begonia x *hiemalis*
Blue-flowered torch (*Tillandsia lindenii*)
Clivia miniata
Crocus cvs.
Flamingo flower (*Anthurium scherzerianum*)
Hyacinth (*Hyacinthus orientalis*)
Hydrangea macrophylla
Lotus berthelotii

Narcissus cvs.
Paper flower (*Bougainvillea glabra*)
Parodia chrysacanthion
Primula obconica
Red crown cactus (*Rebutia minuscula*)
Shrimp plant (*Justicia brandegeeana*)
Shrubby verbena (*Lantana camara*)
African hemp (*Sparrmannia africana*)
Tulips (*Tulipa* cvs.)
Urn plant (*Aechmea fasciata*)

Scented basket

ABOVE *Forced Dutch hyacinths provide a welcome splash of color and wonderful fragrance early in the year. If the flower heads are heavy, insert a few twigs to give extra support. Here, the necks of the bulbs are hidden by fresh moss.*

Indoor window box

BELOW *The delicate yellow heads of* Narcissus *'Tête-à-tête' look very attractive displayed in this wire basket, which has been made waterproof by lining it with plastic and fresh moss. When flowering has finished, the bulbs can be planted outside.*

Summer-flowering Displays

MOST GARDEN plants are at their best at this time of year, and there are many varieties that you can bring indoors to decorate your home, including roses, busy lizzies, lilies, marguerites, and fuchsias.

Be careful of displaying your plants on a south-facing windowsill in summer. Although plants may be happy there in winter when the sun is at its weakest, most varieties will scorch and dry out during the hot noon summer sun.

Geraniums are one of the few plants that will tolerate a warm, sunny position in summer, but even these need constant care and attention to keep them healthy. Display regal and zonal geraniums on the windowsills of a conservatory or plant them into hanging baskets. If you don't have a conservatory or sunroom, you can make an eye-catching display by standing several different types together on an occasional table or sunny windowsill. Look out for the old-fashioned varieties with their exotic-colored flowers.

The Cape primrose (*Streptocarpus*) is another exotic-looking plant that is increasing in popularity. A relative of the African violet, it comes in similar colors and should be displayed in the same way, massed together in a shallow bowl on a low table. This plant has a long flowering season, and providing you feed it regularly throughout the summer, will flower well into the fall. Always water this plant from below and never directly onto the leaves, which will rot if they become wet.

Basket of roses *(Rosa* 'Grand Palace')
ABOVE *Miniature roses should be regarded as short-term houseplants, because they do not flourish in the dry atmosphere of the average centrally heated or air-conditioned room. Treat them as outdoor plants, bringing them indoors when they come into flower and returning them to the garden immediately after.*

Busy lizzies (*Impatiens* hybrids) are a really good choice if you want a plant that will go on flowering throughout the summer. They are available in red, orange, purple, and white, and can look striking if you group several contrasting or complementary colors together in a matching container.

Summer daisy basket
LEFT *These marguerites* (Argyranthemum frutescens), *planted together in a gray and white basket, will tolerate a sunny position, but need to be kept moist if they are to continue flowering over a long period. Keep deadheading regularly to encourage more flowers to form.*

Informal grouping

ABOVE *A variety of exotic-looking, old-fashioned geraniums – including 'White Bonanza,' 'Vicky Claire,' and 'Dark Venus' – make an informal display in this rustic-looking garden basket. When displaying plants in a large group such as this, keep them in their own pots so that you can tend to and water them on an individual basis. Here, we have balanced the ones at the back on upturned flowerpots, using handfuls of fresh moss to keep the pots upright. These plants really hate being overwatered, so make sure you allow the soil to dry out between watering. Fertilize throughout the summer and deadhead regularly, as this will encourage a long show of flowers.*

FLOWERING PLANTS FOR SUMMER
The following plants all flower in summer:

Basket plant *(Aeschynanthus speciosus)*
Begonia bowerae
Bleeding heart *(Clerodendrum thomsoniae)*
Brazilian jasmine *(Mandevilla sanderi)*
Busy lizzy *(Impatiens* cvs.)
Cape leadwort *(Plumbago auriculata)*
Freesia cvs.
Gerbera jamesonii

Golden trumpet *(Allamanda cathartica)*
Italian bellflower *(Campanula isophylla)*
Lily *(Lilium* spp.)
Miniature wax plant *(Hoya lanceolata* subsp. *bella)*
Orchid *(Cymbidium* hybrids)
Pelargonium cvs.
Persian violet *(Exacum affine)*
Zebra plant *(Aphelandra squarrosa* 'Louisae')

Winter-flowering Displays

AS THE DAYS BECOME shorter and the plants in the garden start to die off, many of us turn to the garden center or nursery to look for ways to brighten up our homes. Fresh flowers from the florist are often expensive at this time of the year, so it makes sense to invest in some well chosen flowering houseplants that will give you pleasure as you watch them grow and flower throughout the winter months.

This is the season when mass-produced "gift" plants come into their own – begonias, cyclamen, kalanchoes, and Christmas cacti. These plants will all bring a welcome splash of color into your home, but remember that they are cultivated in the nursery in a controlled environment and like to be kept at a constant temperature. Azaleas, in particular, hate being exposed to sudden drafts of cold air – even the short journey home from the garden center or nursery can shock these plants and make them shed their flowers – so make sure you have them packed up carefully in plastic before you leave the building.

Massing plants together

BELOW *You can increase the impact of a display by massing several individual plants together in one pot. Here, eight shocking pink Christmas cactus plants* (Schlumbergera sp.) *are grouped in a large clay pot to give the impression of a single plant.*

Leaf texture and shape

ABOVE *The delicate white flowers of this* Begonia *'Bettina Rothschild' are pale by comparison with its huge, dark, hairy leaves.*

Most houseplants will benefit from being massed together in one container, rather than being positioned all around the house randomly, so try to buy as many plants as you can afford to create a really impressive display. This is particularly true in a large room, where a single display of four or five Christmas cacti or Hiemalis begonias, grouped together in a large clay bowl or rustic-looking basket, can appear quite spectacular.

FLOWERING AND BERRYING PLANTS FOR WINTER

The following plants all flower in winter:

African violet (*Saintpaulia* cvs.)
Azalea (*Rhododendron simsii*)
Begonia x *hiemalis*
Calamondin orange (x *Citrofortunella microcarpa*)
Christmas cactus (*Schlumbergera* x *buckleyi*)
Chrysanthemum (*Argyranthemum* spp.)
Cyclamen persicum
Egyptian star cluster (*Pentas lanceolata*)
Flamingo flower (*Anthurium scherzerianum*)
Jasmine (*Jasminum polyanthum*)
Monkey plant (*Ruellia makoyana*)
Ornamental pepper (*Capsicum annuum*)
Poinsettia (*Euphorbia pulcherrima*)

One of the drawbacks of "gift" plants, such as cyclamen and begonias, is that they rarely go on flowering for more than a month. These are generally regarded as short-term houseplants that should be discarded after flowering. One plant that has a slightly longer flowering season is the pot chrysanthemum, which comes in almost every color except blue.

If you don't like the idea of throwing your plants away after they have finished flowering and you do not have a conservatory, sunroom, or spare room where you can give them a rest before bringing them into flower again next year, then the best alternative is to invest in a flowering houseplant with attractive foliage, such as a zebra plant

Large mixed arrangement

ABOVE *This preserving pan makes an excellent home for an exotic display of winter-flowering plants in shades of red, orange, and pink, including flamingo flower* (Anthurium scherzerianum), Calamondin orange (x Citrofortunella microcarpa), Begonia bowerae, *azalea* (Rhododendron simsii), *and* Cyclamen persicum. *When grouping several different houseplants together in this way, it is important to check that they all have the same cultivation requirements.*

(Aphelandra) or Rex begonia, which will provide interest throughout the year. The peace lily *(Spathiphyllum wallisii)* is another good houseplant for winter, with elegant pure white flowers held above glossy, long, pointed leaves, which look attractive even when the plant is not in flower.

63

Grouped Flowering Displays

OST FLOWERING plants look best when they are massed together in a group, either with identical plants or with an assortment of different varieties that all require the same growing conditions. There are several aesthetic points to consider when grouping flowering plants together: the color of the flowers; the shape and form of the flowers; the size of the container; and the room setting.

Color is one of the most significant features of flowering plants, and this is particularly important indoors where you want to create splashes of brilliant color in lifeless living rooms. Your choice of color will usually be influenced by personal taste and this means the style or decor of your room. In general, cool, subtle color harmonies – blues, pinks, mauves, and whites – are easier to live with than

Cool white arrangement

BELOW *This closely planted basket contains a white azalea and a white African violet, with a pteris fern at the back to provide height and some trailing ivy around the front to soften the container. The advantage of a grouped display is that when the flowering plants are over, you can replace them with something different.*

vibrant, clashing colors – reds, yellows, and oranges – which tend to dominate or overpower. Even so, the latter are particularly useful in winter when light levels are low and a rigorous treatment is needed to lift an otherwise dull room.

When planning a grouped arrangement, try to choose plants that complement each other in form as well as in color, rather than picking several plants that compete for attention and spoil the potential harmony. In general, smaller plants benefit from being massed together in a group, while those with large flower heads are best displayed as single specimens. Lilies, gerberas, sunflowers, and orchids all have dramatic-looking flowers which can frequently overwhelm and detract from the quieter charms of small flowers. These plants are best displayed on their own in single pots or grouped with similar varieties. Some will need discreet staking to keep them growing in a good shape, but even this must be done with care, or it will detract from the beauty of the flowers.

The size and shape of the container is another important factor when combining flowering plants. Not only must it match the scale of the plants, but it must also harmonize with the flowers. Some people think that white containers are a safe choice for displaying indoor plants, but unless your scheme incorporates a lot of white flowers, they can often look very stark when set against healthy looking plants. A safer choice is green or terracotta, which

COOL COLORS

*Flowers with a hint of blue or white in their make-up appear much cooler
than those with yellow or red. A toning display of white, pink, or
blue flowers can have a very calming effect.*

Cape primrose
(*Streptocarpus* 'Kim')

African violet
(*Saintpaulia* cv.)

Pelargonium
'White Bonanza'

Marguerite
(*Argyranthemum
frutescens*)

African violet
(*Saintpaulia* cv.)

Pelargonium
'Imperial
Butterfly'

Mauve and silver
ABOVE *The silver-leaved foliage of* Kalanchoe
'Primavera' *combines particularly well with
cool colored flowers, especially blues, mauves,
and whites.*

Purple and blue
LEFT *This harmonizing arrangement of cool blue campanulas and
mauve African violets is soothing on
the eye, making it a successful
scheme for a bedside table.*

65

tends to look good with most color schemes and never dominates. If you have a group of attractive containers that are all roughly the same size, try painting them in different colors and displaying them in a row along a shelf or work surface.

When creating an arrangement that relies on flower power alone, it is important that you keep your plants in tip-top condition. Keep in mind that most flowering plants are grown in nurseries in a controlled environment and that very few thrive in the arid atmosphere of centrally heated or air-conditioned homes. If the leaves show signs of scorch marks or the buds or flowers fall off prematurely, this is a sure sign that your plants are not receiving enough humidity (to increase humidity, follow the advice on page 77). Most flowering plants need feeding throughout their flowering season to keep them going for as long as possible and constant deadheading will also encourage an additional show of flowers. The same applies to leaves. It is pointless to concentrate your attention on growing spectacular flowering plants if the leaves are yellowing through neglect. Nothing will induce them to turn green again, so remove any that have become discolored immediately.

While many flowering plants are considered as short-term investments and thrown away after flowering, some can be encouraged to flower again the following year if they are given a rest period when watering is reduced. If you don't like the idea of throwing away your plants and have a cool spare room where you can care for them during the winter, follow the advice on overwintering in the Care and Maintenance section (see page 93).

HOT COLORS

*The flowers below all have yellow or red in their make-up, and combine
well with other yellow, red, or orange flowers
to create a contrasting display.*

Pelargonium
'Paton's Unique'

Gerbera cv.

Cape primrose
(*Streptocarpus*
'Susan')

Busy lizzy
(*Impatiens*
walleriana)

Pelargonium
'Royal Ascot'

Busy lizzy
(*Impatiens* New
Guinea Hybrid)

Pelargonium
'Pulsar Scarlet'

Alternative display
ABOVE *A line of dwarf sunflowers would look
very striking in place of the gerberas shown
on the left. Sunflowers have the same
cultivation requirements as gerberas (see page
162), and they grow quickly from seed.*

Contrasting arrangement
LEFT *Three cheerful looking gerberas
provide a splash of color on a wooden shelf.
The painted clay pots give the scheme
a fresh, contemporary feel.*

Grouped Foliage Displays

MOST PEOPLE are seduced by a plant's flowers, rather than by its foliage, and this is particularly true of houseplants. Many flowering plants are bought on impulse, seasonal plants that are choosen as short-term investments to brighten up the home. Foliage plants, while not always the first choice, have a much longer lifespan, and these plants are indispensable in partially shaded rooms, where flowering plants rarely survive due to poor light. Many of the large foliage plants are covered in the section on Architectural Displays on pages 46–49. In this chapter, we concentrate on

some of the smaller specimens that often look best when they are massed together in a group.

Plants like growing together because they give off water vapor, which makes the surrounding air humid and gives the plants a happier growing environment. From an aesthetic point of view, too, a group of well-thought-out plants will make a strong

Combining leaf color, shape, and form

RIGHT *A wrought iron chair in this north-facing conservatory makes a comfortable home for a group of foliage plants. See how the variegated spikes of the ivy contrast with the feathery fronds of the adiantum.*

SMALL GROUPED DISPLAYS

Small foliage plants are available from the garden center throughout the year and really benefit from being grouped together. For best results, concentrate on choosing plants with different leaf shapes, colors, and forms.

Combining leaf color and form

BELOW *When creating an all-foliage display, it is important to pick leaves that contrast in color as well as in form. Here, the stiff, upright foliage of the dracaena contrasts with the soft, trailing leaves of the hypoestes.*

Polystichum tsussimense

Hare's foot fern (*Polypodium aureum*)

Maidenhair fern (*Adiantum raddianum*)

Pteris ensiformis 'Evergemiensis'

Cretan brake fern (*Pteris cretica*)

Dracaena fragrans Compacta group

Polka dot plant (*Hypoestes phyllostachya*)

Bird's nest fern (*Asplenium nidus*)

Hare's foot fern (*Polypodium aureum*)

Combining leaf texture and shape

ABOVE *This fern grouping relies on a combination of variously textured leaves in various shapes and sizes for impact. The bird's nest fern, with its large glossy leaves, contrasts well with the feathery spires of the maidenhair fern. Ferns need a lot of humidity, so mist your plants daily and keep the soil on the moist, but not wet, side.*

statement in a room and look much more imposing than a single plant sitting on its own. One of the most important considerations when grouping different plants together is to make sure you choose ones that originate from the same habitat – not only will forest ferns look odd set against desert cacti, but they need different growing conditions.

When you visit the garden center, you will soon discover that foliage plants are far more colorful and varied than you previously imagined. The reason for this is that when they are exhibited with flowering plants, the brilliant color of the flowers detracts from their leaves, making them appear less spectacular. Only when you single out foliage plants on their own do you start to appreciate their immense variety – not only of color and size, but of leaf shape and form. Colors range from the meadow green of maidenhair fern (*Adiantum raddianum*) and golden-green of *Scindapsus* 'Neon' to the deep red of Rex begonias. When grouping different foliage plants, try to choose a variety of

Combining trailing plants
BELOW *A pair of wooden receptacles make unusual containers for these trailing plants. Here, we have selected* Scindapsus pictus, Scindapsus *'Neon,' and variegated ivy* (Hedera *cv.*).

colors and forms for a really spectacular display. Large plants, such as the weeping fig *(Ficus benjamina)*, will often benefit from being grouped with small variegated plants, such as the creeping fig *(Ficus pumila* 'Sonny'), which is fringed with white. Not only do variegated plants break up the monotony of the evergreen leaves, but the trailing habit of many varieties looks pretty spilling over the top of the container and is useful for concealing the bare soil surface. If possible, try to keep the smaller plants in their original pots, so that you can tend them on an individual basis. If they require extra height, support them on upturned flowerpots.

Hanging basket
RIGHT *A hanging basket for the conservatory or porch contains a mixture of different foliage plants, whose leaves (below) contrast well together to give an interesting planting of shape and texture. The hanging stems of the saxifraga can reach up to 2 ft. (60 cm), so this basket needs lots of growing space.*

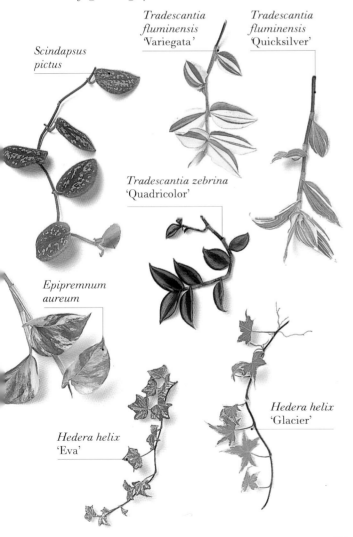

Scindapsus pictus

Tradescantia fluminensis 'Variegata'

Tradescantia fluminensis 'Quicksilver'

Tradescantia zebrina 'Quadricolor'

Epipremnum aureum

Hedera helix 'Eva'

Hedera helix 'Glacier'

TRAILING PLANTS
The following plants have a trailing or creeping habit, making them suitable for displaying in a hanging basket:

Variegated leaves
Cape ivy *(Senecio macroglossus)*
Creeping fig *(Ficus pumila* 'Sonny')
Golden pothos *(Epipremnum aureum)*
Ivy *(Hedera* cvs.)
Pick-a-back plant *(Tolmiea menziesii)*
Spider plant *(Chlorophytum comosum)*
Tree philodendron *(P. bipinnatifidum* 'Variegatum')
Wandering Jew *(Tradescantia fluminensis* 'Albovittata')

Pink or purple leaves
Mosaic plant *(Fittonia albivensis)*
Mother of thousands *(Saxifraga stolonifera)*
Wandering Jew *(Tradescantia zebrina* 'Quadricolor')

Green leaves
Creeping fig *(Ficus pumila* 'Minima')
Ivy *(Hedera* cvs.)
Kangaroo vine *(Cissus antarctica)*
Miniature wax plant *(Hoya lanceolata* subsp. *bella)*
Sweetheart plant *(Philodendron scandens)*

CARE AND MAINTENANCE

THE COMPLETE GUIDE to keeping your indoor plants in the very best of health, this section of the book deals with every aspect of their care and maintenance.

It discusses how plants grow, what they require in terms of humidity, light, food, and water, and how they are affected by various factors in the home, such as heating. It gives advice on growing mediums, potting, repotting, and propagation methods, plus how to choose healthy plants and buy and set up the equipment to care for them, such as mini-tools and stakes. Among other topics covered include hydroculture, forcing plants into flower, pruning, staking, supporting and training plants, and planting and caring for containers and hanging baskets.

ABOVE *Regular, but not excessive, watering is essential to the health and well-being of indoor plants.*

LEFT *Mosaic plant* (Fittonia verschaffeltii) *is best planted in a bottle or terrarium as it needs high humidity to grow well.*

The Plant's Needs

ANY PLANT – whether large or small, for the short term, or a permanent addition to the home – is an investment, and a little research before buying will save wasting money. A plant for indoors is usually destined for a certain position – such as a windowsill, shelf, or table. The wide range of plants available in the nursery or garden center ensures that there is something to suit almost every situation (see Plants for the Place, pages 16–39). All plants differ in their demand for light, warmth, humidity, and space, so it is worth assessing how much of each is available before you make your choice. Conditions vary throughout the year, so make sure you assess them continually. Remember that indoors, the plant has no natural resources to call on, so you must provide everything for it or it will die. Give a plant the right conditions and treatment, however, and it will flourish.

HOW THE PLANT GROWS

In order to thrive, every part of the plant has to be kept actively growing and in good condition. This can be achieved by creating as ideal an environment for the plant as possible.

Leaves

During daylight hours, carbon dioxide in the air is absorbed via stomata on the undersides of the leaves. Green pigment (chlorophyll) in the leaf cells absorbs light, causing water in the cells to separate into hydrogen and oxygen. Oxygen is released through the stomata at night while hydrogen combines with carbon dioxide to form sugars and starches that feed the plant.

Stems

Transportation of carbohydrates down from the leaves and nutrients up from the roots to the rest of the plant is achieved through a series of cells in the

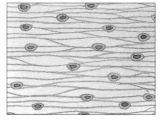

Stomata
The underside of the leaf is covered with tiny pores (stomata), through which gases and moisture are exchanged, enabling photosynthesis and respiration to take place.

stem of the plant. The flow is continuous, unless there is a shortage of water, when an interruption will cause the plant to wilt. Indoor plants in warm conditions tend to dry out quickly, so regular watering is essential.

Roots

Water and nutrients in the soil or potting mix are absorbed by thin feeder roots. They are then transported to the rest of the plant along thicker, more fleshy roots. These larger roots also serve to anchor the plant in the soil mix and hold it steady. If the roots dry out, they are unable to function, and any restriction in their growth will limit the growth of the rest of the plant.

The growing medium

A good-quality growing medium, which is kept moist and well-supplied with nutrients, will provide all the stability and nourishment a growing plant requires. It should be checked on a regular basis to make sure that the roots still have enough space in which to grow, and that no soil-dwelling pests have taken up residence (see Pests and Diseases, pages 116–7).

Photosynthesis
During photosynthesis, the green parts of the plant convert carbon dioxide into carbohydrates, which feed the plant.

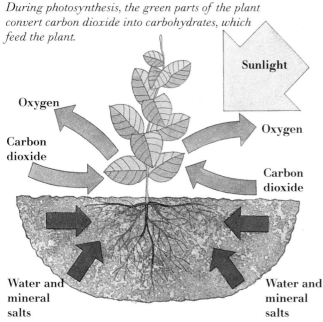

Sunlight

Oxygen

Oxygen

Carbon dioxide

Carbon dioxide

Water and mineral salts

Water and mineral salts

LIGHT

A healthy plant depends on an adequate supply of light to allow the process of photosynthesis to take place. Photosynthesis provides the carbohydrates essential to a plant's existence. Without it, the plant's growth and flowering will begin to slow down.

Light intensity
The amount of light received varies according to the plant's position. The plant at the window is in direct sunlight, the other two receive indirect sunlight.

Light is essential to the plant in order for the process of photosynthesis to take place, when chlorophyll within the leaves reacts with light to produce sugars and starches that nourish the plant. Inadequate levels of light mean that the process slows down, and the plant begins to suffer slow growth and a lack of flowers. Prolonged exposure to poor light will result in a pale-colored plant that becomes elongated in its search for light, and is left weak and floppy in the process.

Many indoor plants – especially those with large leaves – are prone to a build-up of dust in the home, and this can interfere with photosynthesis. Plants with smooth leaves should be wiped regularly with a damp cloth or sponge (see page 118), while those with hairy leaves should be brushed gently with a soft paintbrush.

Variegated leaves have no chlorophyll in the white, cream, or yellow parts of the leaf, so the area available for photosynthesis is restricted, and the need for light is correspondingly higher. If there is inadequate light, the plant will adapt by increasing the pigment in the paler part of the leaf, resulting eventually in a total loss of variegation.

Sources of light

As well as the intensity of the available light, the duration of the light is also important. Nearer the equator, light levels are consistent all year round, whereas farther away there is a marked difference between levels in summer and winter. Flowering plants, in particular, demand long periods of light to initiate the formation of the flower buds. All flowering plants fall into one of two categories: long-day plants, which flower when the light lasts for 12 hours or more over a given period, or short-day plants, which flower when the light lasts for less than 12 hours a day over a given period. It makes no difference to the plant whether the light is natural or artificial (supplementary), which is how growers are able to produce flowers on plants such as poinsettias and azaleas outside their natural flowering season. They manipulate the plants' day using a combination of black plastic sheets to simulate the darkness of night and electric lighting to simulate daylight.

Plant tolerance

In a situation where the light received by a plant is from one side only, the plant's natural instinct is to grow toward the light source, making the plant losided. This is called phototropism and is best avoided by either moving the plant to a position with a more even supply of light, or by turning it around by a quarter every day (so that over a four- day period, the whole plant has received equal shares of direct light).

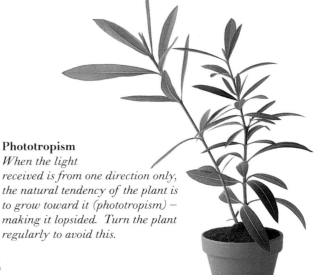

Phototropism
When the light received is from one direction only, the natural tendency of the plant is to grow toward it (phototropism) – making it lopsided. Turn the plant regularly to avoid this.

TEMPERATURE

Indoor plants originate from all over the world – from both tropical and temperate regions – and this is reflected in the temperatures they require to grow well. Try to match plant and position as closely as possible.

Every plant has an ideal temperature range in which it prefers to grow, and a wider one that it can tolerate. When grown in its ideal range – if all other circumstances, such as moisture, are also adequate – the plant will thrive, maturing to produce lush foliage and rich flowers. In the range it can tolerate, growth will be slower, foliage harder and darker, and flowers smaller or nonexistent. Outside these ranges, the survival of the plant cannot be guaranteed.

Most plants can survive short-term seasonal changes, such as in winter when central heating is turned on. However, they are less tolerant of sudden fluctuations of temperature, such as a draft from a door or window. Since many indoor plants hail from countries as warm as Brazil and Africa, it is understandable that they do not like the cold, and prefer a warm, humid environment. Check the growing requirements on the label *before* you buy.

TEMPERATURE CHECKLIST

- during the growing season, most indoor plants need to be kept at temperatures of 59–70°F (15–21°C)
- plants from temperate regions need a cooler site, at 50–59°F (10–15°C)
- young plants and seedlings grow best at 64–70°F (18–21°C), away from direct sun
- never site plants directly over sources of heat, such as fireplaces, or near air-conditioners
- keep sensitive plants away from drafts
- most plants need a winter rest period in cooler conditions
- in winter, remove plants from the windowsill at night, since temperatures behind drawn curtains are generally colder than those inside the room
- an unshaded windowsill facing the sun during summer will be too hot for most leafy plants, and even some succulents

GROWING IN BOTTLE GARDENS

Bottle gardens provide high levels of humidity, making them especially useful for displaying moisture-loving mosses and ferns.

The advantage of growing plants inside a bottle garden or terrarium is that the humidity levels are high, providing the ideal environment for specimens that need moist conditions. All the water given off by the plants during transpiration is condensed on the sides of the glass and runs back into the soil, keeping both the growing medium and the air constantly moist.

3 Gently remove the plants from their pots and position according to how the garden will be viewed, adding more soil around each. Water to settle, adding more soil to bring the level up if it sinks.

1 Cover the base with a layer of gravel, which encourages drainage away from the rooting zone.

2 Sprinkle the surface with a handful of charcoal to keep the soil fresh. Add a layer of potting soil.

HUMIDITY

Humidity and watering are often linked because both involve moisture, but quantifying the humidity requirements of a plant is much more difficult than gauging its watering needs.

The term humidity refers to the amount of water being held as vapor in the air. This can be measured as a percentage, with 0 percent being totally dry air, and 100 percent so saturated that the vapor can be seen (as fog or steam). The amount of water vapor held in the atmosphere varies according to the temperature, since warm air holds more vapor than cold.

All indoor plants, even succulents and cacti, need a humidity level of between 40 and 60 percent to sustain them during transpiration, when water is lost through the stomata in the leaves as they open to allow the intake of gases for photosynthesis (see p.74). The warmer the air, the drier it tends to be, and the more water is lost through the leaves. Thin, papery leaves – in particular, fern fronds – are more susceptible to drying out than thick, leathery leaves, although both can suffer in very dry conditions. If the water is not replaced quickly by the roots, the result will be brown tips and edges to the leaves, where the cells have died. Damaged leaves will not recover and should be removed to prevent infection.

How to improve humidity

Improving humidity means increasing the amount of water vapor held in the air. This can be done in various ways. The easiest method is to use a fine-spray mister around the plant at least once a day, and more often if the temperature is high. This creates a localized increase in humidity, as the spray evaporates off the surfaces of the leaves, stems, and soil, and into the surrounding air. This effect can be enhanced by grouping several plants together, since the evaporation is trapped under several layers of foliage, causing a moist microclimate to form around the plants.

Small, portable electric humidifiers are convenient, and can be used to increase the moisture level of the air indoors, or in the conservatory (if simply soaking the floor or the soil is not an option, or the plants are all in containers). However, these can be expensive, and are therefore not an option for just one or two plants. In the home, humidity tends to be highest in steamy rooms, such as the kitchen and bathroom. As long as the overall temperature is high enough, plants that need humidity often do best in these locations.

Tray of pebbles
Placing a plant on a tray containing pebbles and water allows evaporation up around the sides of the pot and past the foliage. It is important to make sure that the base of the pot itself is above the water level, otherwise the roots will rot.

Moss lining
The clay pot containing this azalea (which prefers cool, moist root conditions) has been set inside a larger container, lined with moist sphagnum moss. The moisture from the moss evaporates, increasing humidity levels around the plant.

Misting a plant
Use tepid water to mist plants that like high humidity at least once a day, and more often in warmer conditions, since the effect is immediate rather than long-lasting.

HUMIDITY PROBLEMS

Low humidity:
- flower buds fail to develop or fall off
- flowers wither soon after opening
- brown edges or tips appear on leaves
- plant begins to wilt

High humidity:
- gray mold is visible on leaves and/or flowers
- patches of rot appear on plants such as desert cacti, which prefer low humidity
- soft, sappy growth

WHERE TO SITE THE PLANT

Plants are generally remarkably tolerant, often surviving periods spent in less-than-ideal conditions without suffering too much damage. However, to get the very best from your plants, try to site them according to their needs.

Plants would not naturally choose to live indoors, where the air is dry, the growing area is severely restricted, and supplies of water are limited. Given these constrictions, it is amazing that plants manage to survive indoors at all, yet they do, and this is a testimony both to the resilience of the plants and to the ability of the collector to provide as good a habitat for them as possible.

What to avoid

The worst places in the house, in plant terms, are in areas of direct heat, deep shade, or strong air currents. Not many plants will tolerate any length of time on a windowsill facing the sun during summer, when the intensity of the heat can bring the water within the leaf cells to boiling point and cause them to die.

While such plants as desert cacti have adaptations that allow them to cope with heat, most others begin to exhibit signs of scorching, such as brown patches on the upper parts of the leaves. Even the heat from a radiator, television set, or refrigerator will damage a plant if it comes into direct contact with it – the upper part of the plant may enjoy the warm environment, but the roots will suffer as the soil dries out far more quickly than it would do otherwise.

In deeply shaded areas of the home, light levels are not great enough to allow photosynthesis to take place, denying the plant the carbohydrates it needs to live; and in drafty positions, poor humidity causes the leaves of more delicate species to wilt and turn brown.

Seasonal change

In winter, plants will need to be repositioned within the house. Those needing a period of dormancy should be moved into a cooler room, such as a spare bedroom, so they can rest before the next growing season. Others, such as those on windowsills, should be brought into the main room overnight to escape the cold. Light intensity will also affect where you position your plants (see pages 16–39). For example, a plant that thrives in the middle of the room in summer, when light levels are high, usually needs to be closer to the window in winter.

WHERE TO POSITION PLANTS AND WHY

Try to make use of the different ways in which plants can be displayed: in floor-standing containers; on pedestals; on furniture; or hanging from the ceiling or wall.

Entrance hall (shady, some drafts)
- tolerant foliage plants
- flowering plants that need less light and will tolerate drafts
- plants that have dark green leaves
- plants with waxy leaves

Stairs/landing (cool, indirect light)
- larger foliage plants
- cyclamen, azaleas, and other flowering plants that prefer cool conditions
- trailing foliage plants

Living room (warm, bright light)
- most indoor plants, foliage and flowering
- seasonal pot plants
- cacti and succulents
- bottle gardens

Dining room (warm, indirect light)
- most indoor plants, foliage and flowering
- seasonal pot plants
- small plants in grouped arrangements
- bottle gardens or terraria

Kitchen (fluctuating temperatures, drafts, steam)
- herbs
- plants with thin, papery leaves, such as *Ficus pumila*
- tolerant plants, such as geraniums

Bathroom (fluctuating temperatures, steam)
- plants that need high humidity, such as ferns
- dramatic foliage plants
- trailing foliage plants
- tolerant houseplants, such as chlorophytum

Main bedroom (warm, bright light)
- flowering indoor plants, including grouped arrangements of seasonal plants chosen to match the decor of the room
- foliage plants

Spare bedroom (cool, indirect light)
- foliage plants
- overwintering plants
- seeds and cuttings
- flowering plants that are between seasons

CHOOSING A HEALTHY PLANT

Indoor plants are sold in a wide variety of outlets, from supermarkets to nurseries, and they will have received very different levels of care. Outlined below are the main points to look for when selecting a new plant.

The better condition the plant is in when it is purchased, the better its chances of survival. A plant that is sold at the nursery where it was raised should be in the best possible condition, because it will be younger and healthier than those which have had to undergo the stress of being transported. Plants sold along the roadside or from a garage driveway are exposed to drying winds, high or low temperatures (according to the time of year), and pollution. In a supermarket, unless there is a separate area dedicated to plants, the watering might be erratic and the lighting poor. In the garden center, they should be well cared for in terms of watering, although the longer they remain unsold, the more they will begin to suffer as their reserves of slow-release fertilizer run out (see pages 82-3).

How to select a healthy plant

Look for a plant with strong, healthy-looking leaves of a good, vibrant color, with no blotches or nibbled edges. The stems should be firm, rather than floppy or limp, and the growth should be compact, not long and weak – the latter indicates a period spent in poor light. Choose a plant which has most of its flowers still in bud to give the longest flowering season, and check the leaves and stems for any pests, such as scale insects or whitefly (see page 116). Disease will show itself as gray, furry mold around the base of the plant, or as pale blotches on the surfaces of the leaves. Check the condition of the potting soil, too – if it is smelly or white-encrusted, the plant has probably been overwatered at some stage and the roots may be damaged. If the soil is dry and hard, or if it has shrunk away from the sides of the container, the plant has been underwatered.

Size is a matter of preference: a small plant will cost less, and although it will soon need repotting, it will adapt quickly to its new surroundings and mature rapidly. A larger specimen will have instant impact, although it will cost more and may take longer to adjust to the conditions in its new home.

Some plants that are bought in flower, such as primroses and spring bulbs, have the attraction that once they have finished flowering, they can be planted outside to be enjoyed for years to come.

PROBLEMS TO LOOK OUT FOR

- weak, pale, spindly growth
- a plant that has already finished flowering
- leaves with blotches, wiggly lines, holes, or nibbled edges
- insects anywhere on the plant
- curled or twisted new shoots
- oval brown lumps on the stems or leaves
- gray mold anywhere on the plant
- soggy, rotting patches on the stems
- shrunken, withered roots
- smelly or white-encrusted soil
- dry, hard soil that has shrunk from the sides of the pot
- pests amid the roots
- wilting leaves, limp stems

Plant with healthy roots
Ease the plant out of its pot to check that the roots are light-colored, firm, and free of insect larvae. If they protrude through the base of the pot, the plant is pot-bound and needs to be repotted as soon as possible (see pages 88–92).

Buying and Setting Up

FROM THE MOMENT you purchase your first plant, the business of acquiring equipment begins – whether it remains fairly basic or progresses to the level required by the dedicated collector. Most garden centers sell a bewildering array of tools and equipment, most of which falls into the "nice to have," rather than "need to have" category, although there are certain items that are important. The essentials include: a clean, sharp pair of pruners for pruning and propagation; a mister for increasing humidity; a watering can with a long spout to reach through the foliage of the plant directly to the soil; a dibble for when the plant is young, and a gardener's trowel for later on; a measuring jug for mixing fertilizer or chemical treatments; and labels to identify each plant. Tools do not have to be bought, they can be improvized from the home. Cutlery is always useful, and can be attached to short canes with string or insulating tape for dealing with plants in a tall bottle garden. The main rule is to keep all your equipment clean to prevent cross-infection.

BASIC EQUIPMENT

This is a range of equipment used in the care and maintenance of indoor plants, at various stages in their lives. The better the quality, the longer the tools will last.

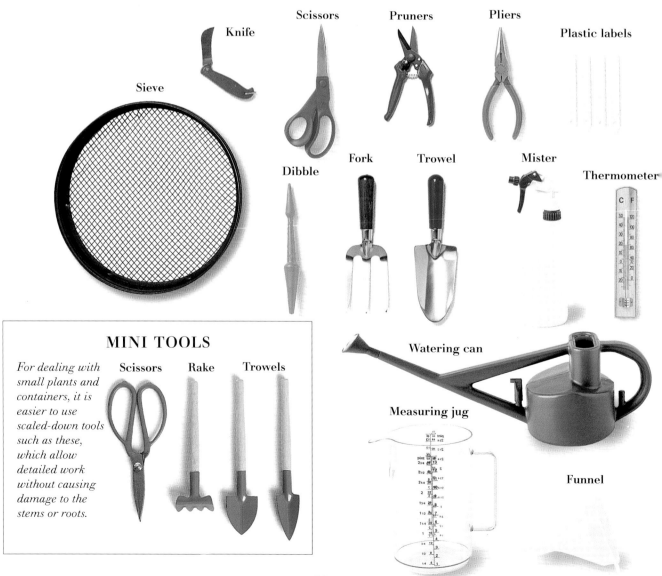

Knife
Sieve
Scissors
Pruners
Pliers
Plastic labels
Dibble
Fork
Trowel
Mister
Thermometer
Watering can
Measuring jug
Funnel

MINI TOOLS

For dealing with small plants and containers, it is easier to use scaled-down tools such as these, which allow detailed work without causing damage to the stems or roots.

Scissors
Rake
Trowels

PROPAGATION EQUIPMENT

Growing plants from seeds or cuttings needs only a little extra equipment and is very satisfying.

Many plants can be grown from seed or cuttings using this equipment, although some will respond better if they are given a little extra warmth in the early stages in a propagation case with heating cables laid in. The propagator and plastic bag both serve to keep the humidity high around the plants, reducing stress and speeding up rooting.

Sowing seed in cell-packs rather than trays takes up more room, but eliminates the need for transplanting. This means that there is no check in growth, producing a larger plant more quickly, and is particularly suitable for larger, easy-to-handle seeds. When seedlings need to be transplanted, the widger can be used to ease them out of the soil by levering beneath the roots to cause as little damage as possible. They can then be planted in the new soil mix using a dibble to make the hole and then firmed in.

STAKING EQUIPMENT

Canes, ties, wire, raffia and string are all used to encourage a plant to grow in a specific direction.

Staking plants is often part of their training, to encourage them to grow straight. However, it can be used on indoor plants to alter their natural growth habit – if, for example, you want to train a trailing or climbing plant to grow as a pillar or ball (see pages 44–5).

When the plant is young and growing quickly, its stake will need replacing regularly to keep it growing correctly. Bamboo canes are cheap and convenient at this stage, and can be used together with string, wire, metal rings, twine, or ties (covered in either paper or plastic) to hold the stems in place. As the plant grows, the support can be changed to a more ornamental one. Keep a close watch on the ties, particularly metal ones that have no flexibility – if they become too tight, they will bite into the stem and constrict it. Each time the stake is replaced, the ties should be changed.

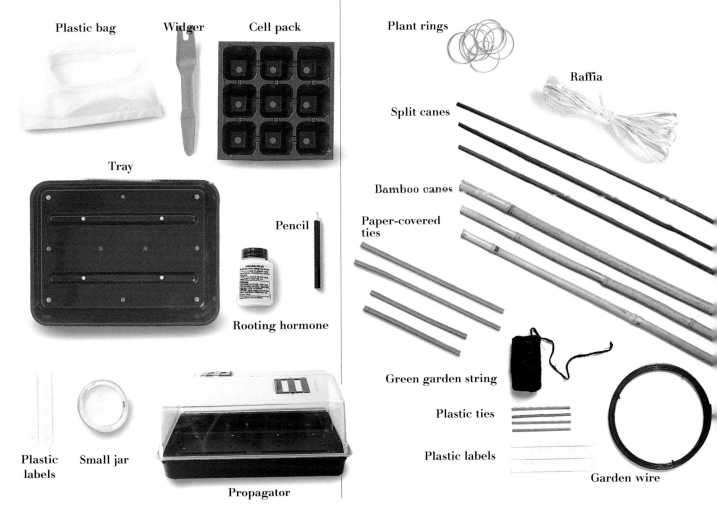

Plastic bag   Widger   Cell pack

Tray

Pencil

Rooting hormone

Plastic labels   Small jar

Propagator

Plant rings

Raffia

Split canes

Bamboo canes

Paper-covered ties

Green garden string

Plastic ties

Plastic labels

Garden wire

Fertilizing Plants

IN THE WILD, plants draw the nutrients and minerals they need from the soil by extending their roots. In containers, however, the room for root expansion and the amount of growing medium is drastically reduced, making it vital to replace nutrients on a regular basis.

Types of fertilizer

The two main types of fertilizer available for plants are classed as organic and inorganic. Organic fertilizers are made from a plant or animal base, and tend to be absorbed slowly by the plant, which means they are longer-lasting. Inorganic fertilizers are mineral-based and tend to be faster-acting, which means that they are used up more quickly.

All plants require three main chemical elements for healthy growth: nitrogen (N) for shoots and leaves; phosphorus (P) for roots; and potassium (K) for fruit and flowers. The amount of each of these in relation to the others in a soil mix or fertilizer is shown on the pack as the N:P:K ratio. A balanced general fertilizer should contain equal quantities of each. Different plants require different levels of these elements, as well as needing a number of trace elements, including iron, copper, zinc, magnesium, and manganese. For example, foliage plants have a lower requirement for potassium than a plant being grown for flowers, but a higher need for nitrogen. Flowering plants need a balance of all three main elements, changing to an emphasis on potassium as the buds develop.

Plant fertilizers contain the three main nutrients, plus a full range of trace elements. They are available in a variety of forms, as either quick-

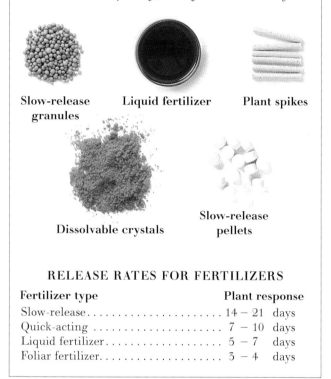

FORMS OF FERTILIZER

Always follow the manufacturer's instructions, since some types are very concentrated. Liquid fertilizers are absorbed quickly, solid fertilizers slowly.

Slow-release granules

Liquid fertilizer

Plant spikes

Dissolvable crystals

Slow-release pellets

RELEASE RATES FOR FERTILIZERS

Fertilizer type	Plant response
Slow-release	14 – 21 days
Quick-acting	7 – 10 days
Liquid fertilizer	5 – 7 days
Foliar fertilizer	3 – 4 days

release or slow-release, depending on how quickly they dissolve in water. Liquid fertilizers (including soluble powder, granules, and crystals) have an immediate effect because they are readily absorbed, and the plant should respond within a week. Foliar fertilizers are useful for plants that do not take nutrients easily through the roots, such as bromeliads, since they are absorbed directly by the leaves, acting as a rapid "pick-me-up." Pellets, spikes, and pills are placed in the soil in a solid form. These dissolve slowly, taking longer to become available to the plant. High-potash (potassium) fertilizers are often referred to as "tomato fertilizers," because they are used widely to promote the production of flowers and fruit on tomatoes. These are ideal for indoor plants that need a boost to produce a good display of flowers.

When to feed

Fresh soil contains nutrients, but these will not last forever. How long they last depends on the type of

MIXING LIQUID FERTILIZERS

Measure the fertilizer into a clean watering can, dilute with water (as directed on the pack), and stir to mix together. Liquid fertilizers offer a very quick and effective means of delivery, since the nutrients are supplied along with the water and are distributed evenly.

plant, its growth rate, and whether the soil is loam-based or loamless. Loam itself contains nutrients, and holds additional ones better than peat, which tends to release them as water passes through. Start fertilizing plants after 6–8 weeks in a loamless soil, and after 10–12 weeks in a loam-based one, and then feed regularly during the active growing and flowering season. Plants bought from the garden center will not have been fed for two weeks before leaving the nursery (to guard against root damage, caused by a build-up of fertilizer resulting from erratic watering), so you must fertilize these plants immediately.

Most plants have a rest period during the winter months, when they do not need fertilizing, the exception being plants that flower at Christmas and need feeding then, rather than in spring or summer.

How to fertilize

Liquid formulations come as a concentrate or as dry granules or powder, to be diluted with, or dissolved in, water. These are applied with a watering can, or in the case of a liquid foliar feed, with a mister. Dry formulations are added to the soil when the plant is potted, or as a top-dressing on the surface of an older plant. Pins and spikes are pushed into the soil using the end of a pencil – but do not to place them too close to the roots, since localized burning can occur as a result of the high concentration of fertilizer. The drawback of pins and spikes is that they cannot be "switched off" as the plant goes into its winter rest period, which may result in weak, elongated growth. Slow-release granules break down over three to six months, so can be adjusted to the needs of individual plants.

Foliar fertilizers
These are absorbed through the leaves, making them ideal for bromeliads. They are also useful as a quick "pick-me-up" for ailing houseplants.

Fertilizer pills
These small, pill-shaped balls of fertilizer are designed to dissolve and release nutrients over a period of time. They are inserted into the potting soil at regular intervals, as recommended on the pack.

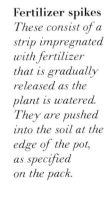

Fertilizer spikes
These consist of a strip impregnated with fertilizer that is gradually released as the plant is watered. They are pushed into the soil at the edge of the pot, as specified on the pack.

EFFECTS OF FERTILIZER

Effects of underfeeding:
- the plant has slow, sickly looking growth
- there is little resistance to disease or pest attack
- the flowers are poorly colored and small, or absent altogether
- the leaves are small, dull, and pale-colored, or are shed prematurely

Effects of overfeeding:
- the leaves show signs of wilting and/or malformations
- there are brown spots and/or scorched edges on the leaves
- a white encrustation develops on the surface of the soil mix
- the growth is long and drawn in winter, and stunted in summer

Watering Plants

PLANTS CAN TOLERATE deficiencies in light and feeding for a while, but if you deprive them of water they will die. How long this takes depends both on the plant and on the growing conditions. For example, a succulent that stores moisture within its tissue will last much longer than a young seedling, which has no reserves on which to draw. And a plant that is kept in a humid environment, such as a steamy bathroom, will survive much longer between waterings than one that is kept in an arid, centrally heated living room.

The water taken up by the plant is used to transport chemicals around within the cells, moving nutrients up from the roots, and sugars and starches down from the leaves. It keeps the plant turgid (firm to the touch and able to support its own weight), the cells full and rigid, and allows the chemical reactions that keep the plant alive, such as photosynthesis. Without adequate water, chemical reactions stop and the cells start to deflate, resulting in a flaccid (pale and floppy) plant. Nutrients and sugars no longer pass through the plant, causing the structure to collapse as moisture is lost through transpiration and not replaced.

Each plant can tolerate wilting to a certain point and still make a full recovery, although some permanent cell-death may show as brown ends to the leaves. This permanent wilting point varies from plant to plant, as does the amount of water needed on a daily basis. The only sure way to maintain adequate levels of water is to get to know your plant's individual needs (see page 86).

Watering from above
Fill the pot to the brim and let the water soak through, adding more for larger containers to make sure that the soil is wet.

Watering from below
Water droplets spilled on hairy leaves cause scorch, so water from below.

Water indicator
This changes color as the soil dries out, indicating when more water is needed.

WATERING HINTS

Such plants as rosette-forming bromeliads need watering into their central cup, rather than the pot, because they absorb moisture through their leaves as well as their roots. Plants with hairy leaves should be watered from below, because water spilled on the surface of the leaves can become trapped by the hairs, resulting in scorch marks where it is magnified by the light. Acid-loving plants, such as azaleas, benefit from being watered with rainwater (which is generally soft), especially in areas where tap water is "hard." For most plants, a little water done frequently is far better than periodic drowning followed by drought.

Rosette plant being watered
Make sure that the rosette of the bromeliad always contains a reservoir of water to be absorbed through its leaves.

CONTINGENCY WATERING

*Plants do not need to suffer while you are away from home. There are various
ways of ensuring that they are well-watered in your absence.*

During a short vacation, plants can survive without special treatment, as long as they are thoroughly watered beforehand and moved to a cool position. For a longer period, however, it will be necessary to make contingency plans.

There are a number of ways in which plants can still be watered, even during a vacation period, when no one is available to care for them. Wicks and capillary matting both work by allowing plants to absorb as much water as they need from a reservoir. However, these methods will not work if the matting dries out and the capillary column is broken. Each presoaked wick is placed into a pot by pushing it through the base or by removing the plant from the pot, placing the wick at the side and replacing the plant – the more growing medium the wick is in contact with, the better. Presoaked capillary matting can cope with a greater number of plants. This is placed partially into a plugged sink containing 4–6 in. (10–15 cm) water, and partially on the draining-board. The pots are then placed directly onto the matting, which will remain moist as long as there is water in the sink. Note that this system relies on contact between the soil mix and the matting, and that it will not work if the pots have a layer of crockery shards in the bottom (see page 87). A less controlled method of keeping plants moist is by grouping them together on a tray of moist pebbles. The roots stay moist as long as the water level in the tray does not drop too far. However, it is important that the level is not too high initially, or the roots may rot.

Humidifying plastic bag
*Transpired water condenses
on the sides of the bag, to be
taken up by the roots (do not
use for longer than one week).*

Wick watering kit
*Water is taken into the pot by
a wick, which extends into a
plastic bag filled with water.*

Making your own wick watering kit
*Cut a strip of capillary matting long enough to reach from
the pot to a reservoir filled with water. (In hot weather, cover
the wick with a small piece of plastic to prevent it drying out
through evaporation.)*

Capillary matting
*Lay the matting
in the sink and up
onto the worktop.
(If necessary,
protect your
surface first with
plastic.) Place pots
on the matting to
ensure good
contact with the
soil.*

Water-retaining crystals
*These tiny crystals absorb
many times their own weight
of water, hold it, and release
it back to the plants on
demand. Each time you
water the soil, they
absorb more water,
maintaining the moisture
levels and compensating for
erratic watering.*

WATERING QUANTITIES

Achieving the correct watering levels is often a matter of trial and error, because every plant is different, and each will change throughout its life, and at different times of the year.

There are various indicators to help the beginner decide when to apply more water (see page 84), but these are no substitutes for practice and observation. By the time the plant wilts, it may be too late to save it, so check it regularly. Lift up the pot (the lighter it is, the drier the potting soil), feel the soil to test dryness. For clay pots, look at the outside — the wetter the soil, the darker the pot.

How much water to apply

Different plants need different levels of watering in order to thrive. In the Indoor Plant Directory (see pages 120–185) the terms "thoroughly moist," "moist," "slightly dry," or "just moist enough to prevent the soil drying out" are used to indicate how much water each plant needs. To keep the plant *thoroughly moist*, apply enough water to keep the soil completely moist all the time, though never actually wet. Do not allow even the surface to dry out. Check every day. To keep it *moist*, apply water to moisten the soil completely, but allow the top $1/_2$–1 in. (1–2 cm) to dry out before rewatering. Check every 2–3 days. To keep it *slightly dry*, moisten the soil completely, but allow the top half of the soil to dry out before rewatering.

> ## QUICK-REFERENCE WATERING GUIDE
>
> **Water your plant more frequently if it:**
> - is growing quickly (for example, when it is young, or if it has just come out of the rest period)
> - is coming up to, or is in, flower
> - has filled its current container, and is in need of repotting
> - is in a hot or dry atmosphere
>
> **Water your plant less frequently if it:**
> - is resting – usually, although not always, during the winter months
> - stores moisture within its leaves and/or stems
> - has a waxy covering on its leaves, which reduces moisture loss
> - is grown in cool or humid conditions
> - has recently been repotted

Check once a week. The plant might only need to be kept *moist enough to prevent the soil drying out* during the rest period. Check once a week and give only enough water to keep the potting soil barely moist. Once growth starts again in spring, increase the amount immediately.

WATERING PROBLEMS

Experience is the key to successful watering but in the meantime, recognizing and dealing with problems quickly will help ensure a good recovery.

Underwatering symptoms include: wilted, limp leaves; flowers that fade and fall quickly; a slow rate of growth; falling lower leaves; and leaves showing brown edges. If a plant has been underwatered, fill the saucer with water repeatedly, until no more is being absorbed, and then pour away the excess. Never allow your plants to stand in water for long periods of time, since you will deprive the roots of air and, eventually, kill them.

Overwatering symptoms include: soft or rotten patches on leaves; flowers turning moldy; old and young leaves being shed together; leaves curling, wilting, and turning yellow; leaves with brown tips; and the plant having a moldy smell.

Reviving a wilted plant
Plunge the pot in a bucket of water (containing a drop of dishwashing detergent to speed up penetration of the soil, particularly if it is peat-based). Keep it submerged until bubbles stop rising, then leave to drain.

Draining an overwatered plant
Overwatering does not compensate for underwatering, and causes additional problems. Slant the pot at an angle against the rim of a saucer until the excess water stops running out.

The Growing Medium

PLANTS HAVE certain requirements of the medium in which they are growing, whether it is indoors or out. They need a firm anchorage for their roots, the correct pH level, and a readily accessible supply of air, water, and nutrients in an environment free from pests and diseases. In the case of a medium for indoor use, this means that the potting soil has to be sterile, pH neutral (unless it is for acid-loving plants), firm enough to support the plant, but lightweight enough to hold air and able to supply the roots with water and nutrients, without letting the plant become waterlogged.

There are two main choices of soil mix: loam-based (which contains soil) and loamless (based on peat or a peat-substitute). Loam-based soils hold nutrients and moisture better than loamless ones, and are more stable, but they are heavier, and more suitable for older plants that are likely to be in their pots for some time, or floor-standing specimens that need the extra weight to prevent them being knocked over. Loamless soils are light, clean, and easy to handle, but are inclined to dry out (and difficult to re-wet), and nutrients wash through them fairly quickly.

Soil additions

In order to tailor the soil mix to the plant, there are various substances that can be added to the basic ingredients, including perlite, vermiculite, sand, and grit, all of which serve to allow more air into the soil and speed up drainage.

Other ingredients can be used with the soil mix to cater for certain plants. Crockery shards (stones or pieces of broken clay pot) can be laid in the bottom of the empty container before planting to help speed up drainage if the plant will not tolerate wet soil for any length of time. Charcoal is often used in bottle gardens and terraria to absorb waste and keep the soil fresh. Sphagnum moss is another useful addition, which can be incorporated into the soil mix or placed over the surface of the soil to retain moisture.

TYPES OF GROWING MEDIUM

Without the right medium, a plant will struggle to grow well. The consistency, pH, and content of the soil all play a part in the plant's overall health. See the top line, below, for growing mediums, the middle line for drainage additions, and the bottom line for hydroculture mediums.

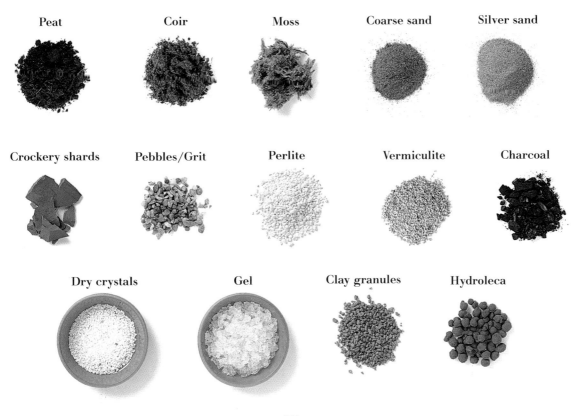

Peat Coir Moss Coarse sand Silver sand

Crockery shards Pebbles/Grit Perlite Vermiculite Charcoal

Dry crystals Gel Clay granules Hydroleca

Planting and Potting

I N THE WILD, a plant's roots can grow unrestrict- ed into new soil in their search for food and water. In a container, however, the limited room for expansion means that instead of stretch- ing out freely, the roots are forced to circle around inside the pot. Unless more space is provided, in terms of a larger pot, this results in a "pot- bound" plant, with slow growth and a poor show of flowers. Most plants need to be moved into a new, slightly larger pot with fresh potting soil once a year, normally in spring as the new growth for the season starts.

PLANTING UP AND POTTING ON

"Planting" indicates that a dry bulb or corm is being put into a new soil mix. "Potting on" refers to the moving of a plant from a smaller pot into a larger one.

Houseplants are usually bought in containers and so the terms "planting" and "planting-up" only apply to young plants grown from seed (see page 101) and bulbs, corms, and tubers (see opposite). Young, actively growing plants should be moved into larger pots on a regular basis to make sure that they have enough room to grow, without suffering a check as a result of their roots becoming cramped. This process is known as "potting on." How often this is done will depend on the plant itself, with quick-growing specimens in ideal con- ditions requiring potting on more often than slow- er growing ones.

The newly bought plant

When a plant is first purchased, the chances are that it is already becoming pot-bound (see page 91), because most plants – especially foliage ones – are sold in the smallest practicable pot in order to make the plant look larger and, therefore, better value. The easiest way to tell if this is the case is to examine the base of the pot for protruding roots – the more there are, the more pot-bound the plant

is likely to be. If there are lots of protruding roots, it should be potted on into a larger pot immediate- ly to keep it actively growing. Teasing out a few of the main roots when planting will help the plant establish in its new pot and start to grow. Carefully trimming off a few of the main roots at this stage will slow down the growth of the plant if it is like- ly to grow too quickly for its surroundings.

How to pot on

Check that the new container has drainage holes in the base to prevent waterlogging, and that it is at least 2 in. (5 cm) larger in diameter than the old one. If the plant dislikes excess moisture around the roots, first cover the base of the pot with pieces of broken crockery, then add a layer of potting soil. Remove the plant from its existing pot and place it inside to gauge the level, adding more potting soil underneath if necessary, then fill up around the sides, firming it gently with your fingertips. Fill the pot to 1 in. (2.5 cm) below the brim, then water it to settle the soil. If the soil level sinks back, add more potting soil.

1 *Place the old pot inside the new one so there is at least a 2 in. (5 cm) gap all around. Layer crock- ery and soil inside the new pot.*

2 *The old soil should sit below the final level of the new one. Remove the plant from the old pot and place in the new container.*

3 *Fill around the sides of the root ball with fresh soil. Water to set- tle it, adding extra potting soil to bring the level back up if it sinks.*

PLANTING BULBS, CORMS, AND TUBERS

There is something wonderful about the way an uninspiring dry lump can burst into a mass of lush greenery and fragrant flowers just by planting it.

Bulbs, corms, and tubers vary in size from delicate freesias to large hyacinths, and as a general rule, should be covered in three times their depth of soil when planted. However, as there are exceptions, always refer to instructions on the pack. Most bulbs prefer free-draining soil, so incorporate a layer of pebbles in the base of the pot, and include a good proportion of grit or coarse sand.

Bulbs, corms, tubers
Each is a food-filled plant waiting to grow.

Planting corms
Space them evenly around the pot and cover with soil.

Planting tubers
Shoot buds or old roots show which way up to plant.

Planting bulbs
A bulb should be planted with its tip facing up.

REPOTTING

This term is used when a plant is put back into the same container with fresh potting soil, rather than being moved to a new one.

Every plant benefits from an annual supply of fresh potting soil, but this doesn't mean changing the container – especially if the plant is already in as large a container as you can accommodate. Likewise, as a plant ages and its rate of growth slows down, it may only be necessary to move it into a larger pot in alternate years rather than every year. The way to refresh the soil if the container is not being changed is to replace some or all of the soil. Remove the root ball from the pot and very gently wash some of the old soil away from the roots, without damaging them in any way. Return it to the same container and fill around the roots with a new soil mix, containing a slow-release fertilizer, which will last until the plant needs repotting again.

WHEN TO POT, REPOT, OR POT ON
You will need to repot or pot on your plant if:

- the root ball is congested (roots show through the base of the pot or are visible on the surface of the soil)

- the plant is drying out more quickly than usual on a regular basis (this means that there are too many roots in the pot and too little soil)

- the rate of growth has slowed down so that it is noticeable

- the top growth has become lopsided (this can be corrected by centralizing the plant in a larger pot)

- the plant has become overcrowded in the pot due to offsets (these can be separated and propagated on their own)

- the growing medium is changed (for example, to hydroculture)

- an attack of pests or disease is damaging the roots (make sure that you wash them with water or fungicide before replanting them in fresh soil)

- you repot annually every spring

Pot-to-root ball ratio
The container should be at least 1 in. (2.5 cm) larger all around the root ball to allow room for a year's growth. If there is not enough room, pot on the plant (see opposite).

Geranium

PLANTING A HANGING BASKET

Although often thought of as an outdoor feature, there is no reason why a hanging basket cannot be used indoors.

It is common to see hanging baskets outdoors throughout the year, but much less common to find them indoors. As many plants will grow as well in a basket as in a pot, there is no reason for this, apart from the practicalities of positioning and watering it. In a conservatory, the basket can be hung from the roof or a wall bracket, as long as the increased weight is taken into account. Methods of watering out-of-reach plants have been devised by manufacturers, with the availability of self-watering baskets and water-retaining gels.

Hanging basket after planting-up

Choosing the plants

Exactly the same rules apply to an indoor basket as to an outdoor one, in that it needs height in the center, color in the middle, and something to trail over the sides. The difference here is that your chosen plants must all have similar requirements in terms of temperature, light, and humidity.

Maintaining the basket

The soil mix in the basket can be enhanced by the addition of water-retaining gel, to reduce the frequency of watering, and slow-release fertilizer to make sure that the plants are well-fed.

Maintenance then only becomes a matter of checking the basket on a regular basis to add water, turning the basket if the light is lopsided, and picking off any fading flowers.

It may be desirable to change the flowering plants once they have faded and replace them with fresh ones. Rather than dismantling the whole basket, which causes disturbance to foliage plants, flowering plants can be left in their individual pots and plunged into the soil. They will be able to take up moisture through the holes in the base of the pots, although they will need fertilizing separately. As they fade, the pots can then be lifted out and new ones inserted, causing little or no disturbance to the rest of the display.

1 *Line the basket using sphagnum moss or a fiber liner to keep the soil in place.*

2 *Put in a layer of potting soil and position the tallest plant in the center.*

3 *Add the other plants, filling in with soil around each to hold them firm. Water to settle.*

WATERING HANGING BASKETS

There are various ways to water a hanging basket that is awkward to reach.

Garden hose watering
Reaching high baskets is made easier by taping a bamboo cane to the hose to make it rigid.

Self-watering
A reservoir of water in the base of this basket is refilled using the pipe.

PROBLEMS WITH MATURE PLANTS

All plants have a "root to shoot" ratio; both elements must be balanced in order for one to support the other. Mature plants grow more slowly than young ones, but they will still outgrow their pots.

As plants age and their root systems expand to fill their pots, the soil is literally squeezed out of the base, leaving progressively less to provide water and nutrients. This may even be the case when a plant is first purchased, with the root ball being so congested that roots are protruding through the base of the pot. In this case, removing the pot in the conventional way (see page 88) may damage the roots because they are dragged back through the holes in the base. Instead, it is better sacrifice the pot by cutting it away using strong scissors or pruners, or break it off in the case of clay. Any long roots will soon re-establish once the plant has more room to grow in its new container.

With established plants, the growth rate of the roots is directly related to the rate of the top growth. This is called the "root to shoot" ratio. Trimming back the main roots will control the top when the plant has reached the desired size. This is useful when you do not have the space to accommodate a new, larger pot.

1 The roots of this jasmine have emerged through the holes in the base of the pot. Pulling them back through would cause damage, leaving open wounds that are susceptible to rot and attack by disease.

2 In order to release the roots without damage, the pot is carefully cut away using pruners. (The cut pot can be used, with the base removed, as a wrap-around slug guard outside in the garden.)

TOP-DRESSING A MATURE PLANT

Removing a plant from its pot, however briefly, can cause it stress. Mature plants find this more difficult to cope with than young ones.

As an alternative to repotting a mature plant on a regular basis, which causes disturbance, you can rejuvenate it by top-dressing it instead. Outdoors, this involves applying a fertilizer around the base of a plant, but indoors it means adding new potting soil as well, at least in the upper part of the pot.

The plant can then stay in place for up to two years before it needs repotting completely. The old soil is gently scraped away with a small rake or fork and discarded, to be replaced by the same amount of fresh soil mix, usually one that contains a slow-release fertilizer.

1 Gently scrape away the upper 1 in. (2.5 cm) of soil, using a small rake or fork, and discard.

2 Replace it with fresh soil, containing a slow-release fertilizer. Water to settle it in place.

Crassula ovata *after top-dressing*

REMOVING A PLANT FROM A SMALL POT

*Whenever you remove a plant from its container, the most important consideration is
to avoid damaging the roots, since open wounds are potential
sites for attack by disease.*

To make the operation smoother, the plant should be watered thoroughly at least an hour before you attempt to remove the pot. This will hold the soil mix together and allow the root ball to be slipped from the old pot easily. Place one hand over the surface of the soil, with your fingers spread to straddle the stem, invert the pot, and knock the rim gently against the edge of a table or a wooden block. The pot should lift off the root ball, which is then ready to transfer to a new pot. To help the plant establish quickly in its new pot, tease out some of the roots around the edge of the root ball.

1 *Place a hand on the soil to support it, invert the pot, and knock it gently against a wooden block to loosen the root ball.*

2 *The root ball should slip easily from the pot without damage to the roots, and can now be transferred to its new container.*

Codiaeum variegatum pictum
after potting on

REMOVING A THORNY PLANT FROM A POT

*This is a good way of handling prickly plants, such as cacti, but it would
work equally well for plants with irritant sap.*

Cacti are wonderful plants, easy to care for, with the most spectacular flowers, but they are among the most awkward to handle. Getting spines in the skin can cause discomfort for weeks. The easiest way to avoid this is to grasp the plant with a piece of folded newspaper or cloth while you invert the pot to loosen the root ball. (Watering the plant an hour before removing the pot will enable the plant to slip out more easily.) The newspaper can be left wrapped around the plant as you transfer it to its new container, and then used to hold it in place as the soil is filled in and firmed around the sides. Only when the whole operation is complete can the newspaper be removed and discarded.

Other plants that can cause skin irritations, such as oleander and primula, can be treated in the same way until they become too large, when gloves become the only viable alternative.

1 *Fold a piece of newspaper several times. It should be long enough to pass around the plant and be gripped firmly. Invert the container, knock gently to loosen the root ball, then remove the old pot.*

2 *Using the newspaper as a handle, gently lift the plant and move it to its new pot. Do not remove the paper until after you have filled and firmed the soil around the root ball.*

Care of Containers

CONTAINERS SHOULD last for many years, provided they are well cared for and not damaged in any way. If they have been used before, it is important to clean them thoroughly to prevent the spread of disease (see right).

1 Use a dry, stiff brush to get rid of loose soil and old roots.

Preparing and maintaining containers

New clay pots should be soaked in water for at least an hour before use, so that they do not draw moisture away from the soil. However, as they age, they gain an attractive outer coating of green moss, which blends the pots into the greenery around them. It is not necessary to remove this when the pot is cleaned, but it is important to clean the inside. Metal containers should be lined with plastic to prevent their minerals contaminating the growing medium. Wooden containers can also be lined with plastic to stop the wood rotting. In each case, holes need to be made in the base to allow drainage.

2 Scrub the pot in warm, soapy water to make sure that it is thoroughly clean.

CARE OF HEAVY CONTAINERS

If you have the space, a large container adds impact and interest, but it presents its own set of problems if it needs to be moved.

Although few indoor plants should have a problem with low temperatures during the winter, those in an unheated conservatory or sunroom, or on a porch, may feel the cold. The result of exposure to low temperatures varies according to how cold the plant becomes, and for how long, but at its extreme, cold kills the plant. A small electric space heater is one way of keeping the temperature above freezing if the plants cannot be brought indoors. Alternatively, plastic bubble wrap or burlap can be tied around both the plant and its container as temporary protection during very low temperatures, but it will need to be removed as soon as feasible, or the plant will suffer from lack of light and air. Repositioning a large container presents its own set of problems because once it is planted and watered, it can weigh a great deal. Even a medium-size container can weigh up to 20 lb. (9 kg) when moistened, and this amount of weight can cause injury if not handled properly. The easiest way to move a heavy pot is to maneuver it onto a board and then use metal pipes as rollers underneath (see right). Lighter pots can be moved by dragging them on a piece of burlap.

Heavy containers can be moved using pieces of metal pipe as rollers under a board. Move the board by taking the front roller to the back. Repeat this action.

Hydroculture

THIS INVOLVES growing a plant without potting soil, using an inert substance as the means of support, and supplying all the nutrients in the water. The plant needs watering less frequently (often only every 2–3 months), and there is less risk of overwatering or drying out. The chosen plant must be suited to moist conditions, able to adapt to a new way of life, and tolerant of partial shade, since if the container is clear glass, algae will be a problem if it is placed in direct sun. Many containers are suitable for hydroculture, from the simple hyacinth glass to more complex double pots where the outer pot is the reservoir for an inner one containing the plant and aggregate.

Supporting mediums

Many inert substances can be used as the supporting medium, including Hydroleca, gel, and clay granules (see page 87). Hydroleca is a lightweight, expanded clay aggregate, available as small pellets that are produced with a honeycomb center and a firm casing, which both holds and conducts water. Gel works on the same principle as the water-retaining gels available for outdoor containers and hanging baskets, but here they are used without soil. Dry crystals, which need to be soaked in water and liquid plant food for several hours before use, can be colored for instant effect. Clay granules are available as a whole kit, with a water indicator and fertilizer. The granules soak up moisture and release it back to the plant as needed.

Care of plants

The roots of the plant should never sit in water, because this will cause them to rot. All excess water not absorbed by the medium after watering should be drained off. For best results, use a cutting rooted in water, since it will already have succulent roots. The younger the plant, the higher the chance of successful conversion.

Fertilizing

Each medium has its own fertilizing regime, particularly if it has been purchased as a kit, so be guided by the advice on the pack. In general, fertilizer is applied when the water is refilled. However, if the plant looks pale or yellow between waterings, the nutrient may not be sufficient, and a foliar feed should be applied once a week.

GEL HYDROCULTURE

This technique involves growing plants in water-retaining crystals, rather than in soil.

1 *Measure dry crystals into a waterproof container and start adding the water, according to the instructions on the pack. As the gel begins to swell, add more water.*

2 *Keep applying more water over several hours, leaving the gel to absorb as much as it can. Drain away any excess water. The gel is now ready to use.*

3 *If clear gel is required, it can be used immediately as it is. For colored gel, add food coloring to vary the shade or match the plant.*

4 *Choose a cutting that has been rooted in water, since it will already have succulent roots to cope with the moist regime. (This* Tradescantia fluminensis *should establish quickly.)*

5 *Plant, gel, and container can all be chosen to complement their room setting, creating an unusual and low-maintenance focal point. Here, a variegated tradescantia is planted in mauve gel.*

Forcing

THE TECHNIQUE of bringing plants into flower outside their natural season is known as forcing. It is routinely practiced by growers to produce plants in flower over a longer period, and involves manipulating the plants' days. Flowering is induced by the amount of light in hours (day length) rather than by its intensity, so if you use black plastic to simulate nighttime and electric light to simulate day, the plants can be fooled into triggering the formation of buds.

Bulbs

Bulbs that naturally flower in the spring, such as hyacinths, can be brought into flower during the winter by planting them in the fall and keeping them cool and dark (and the soil moist) for 6–10 weeks. When the shoots are 1–2 in. (2.5–5 cm) high, the bulbs can be brought indoors into a cool, well-lit spot; the leaves will extend and turn darker green, and the flower buds appear. They can then be moved to a warmer, brightly lit place to flower. Choose bulbs specified for indoor use, and keep the soil moist throughout. As the flowers die down, it is important to feed and water the plants in order to replenish the food within the bulb ready for next year. After the fear of frost has passed, they can be planted outdoors to be enjoyed for years to come. Or you can lift them and store them over the summer in a cool, dry, dark place.

Flowering plants

Plants that flower indoors fall into two categories: those which flower annually without help, and those which are discarded after flowering. Of the latter, some, such as poinsettias and azaleas, can be coaxed to flower again. Poinsettias can be brought back into color, but will be taller than before, because commercial growers use growth regulators to produce a compact, bushy plant. After the bracts and leaves fall, cut the stems down to 4 in. (10 cm) stumps. Keep the plant almost dry until early summer, then repot (in the same size pot), and increase watering and feeding, selecting 4–5 strong stems. In fall, cover nightly with black plastic for 14 hours for 8 weeks, then treat normally to produce bracts for winter.

If you have the time, space, and patience to persevere with them, there are many plants that can be brought back into flower a second time. They may not be as spectacular second time around, but this is much more satisfying than discarding them.

PLANTS FOR FORCING

- **Bulbs**

  Narcissus, hyacinth, crocus, iris, tulip, amaryllis, lily, and freesia can all be brought into flower outside their natural season by controlling their growing conditions (see below).

- **Flowering plants**

  Azaleas and poinsettias can be brought back into flower by manipulating day length and temperature. Other flowering plants can be brought forward or held back when they have set buds by moving them to a warmer or cooler position.

1 *Plant prepared hyacinths with their "noses" out of the soil. Place in a cool, dark situation for 6–10 weeks until the shoot reaches 1–2 in. (2.5–5 cm).*

2 *Bring into a cool indoor room until the buds show color, then move to a warm, well-lit position. Moss keeps the soil moist and maintains humidity levels.*

Hyacinth after forcing

Propagation

THERE ARE MANY reasons to consider propagation in one of its forms: if a plant has outgrown its allotted space; if it is looking old and jaded; if someone has asked for a cutting; or simply for the challenge and satisfaction of producing a thriving new plant. The two basic ways to produce a new plant from another are asexually (vegetative propagation) or sexually (seed). Seed is plentiful, but the results are variable, and may differ quite considerably from the parent plant. Vegetative propagation takes up more room and may be slightly slower, but it gives consistently similar results to the parent.

Vegetative propagation

This is by far the most common means of propagation for indoor plants, and it includes propagation by cuttings (stem, leaf, and root), division, layering, offsets, plantlets, and air-layering. Each technique relies on using part of the parent plant to produce the new one, without necessarily detaching it first. The offspring is genetically identical to the parent, and its growth pattern should also be identical.

Cuttings

Taking a cutting means removing part of the parent plant in order to grow a new one. After the piece is severed, its supply of moisture from the parent's roots is cut off, so an adequate level of moisture must be maintained while the cutting produces its own roots to replace the loss. Some plants produce roots so easily that the cutting can simply be placed in a container of water. Others need the stimulus of a rooting hormone in either liquid or powder form to produce roots. Spring and summer are the best times to take cuttings, because the plant is actively growing and light levels are high. Avoid taking cuttings when the plant is in flower, because flowering shoots will not root successfully, wasting soil, time, and the cutting itself.

CUTTINGS FOR PROPAGATION
Roots, leaves, stems, and shoots can all be used to produce new plants.

Root cuttings
(*Primula*)

Leaf cuttings
(*Streptocarpus*)

Stem cutting
(*Pelargonium*)

LEAF PETIOLE CUTTINGS
This technique involves taking a whole leaf − plus its stalk − from the parent in order to produce a new plant.

Plants such as peperomia and saintpaulia can be propagated by taking a whole leaf and its stalk (petiole). Select an undamaged, fully opened leaf, remove it from the plant, and trim the petiole about 1 in. (2.5 cm) below the leaf. Insert it into moist potting soil at an angle to shed water from the leaf and produce a straighter plantlet. Support a plastic covering with canes so it does not touch the leaf.

Saintpaulia

1 *Using a clean knife, remove the petiole at the base, then trim below the leaf.*

2 *Insert the cut edge at an angle into moist, free-draining soil, and cover with plastic.*

3 *New plants will form at the base of the petiole. Separate and pot into fresh soil mix.*

WHOLE LEAF CUTTINGS

*This technique involves using whole leaves taken from the
parent to produce new plants.*

Whole leaves of succulents, such as crassula, echeveria, and sedum, can be used to form new plants. Take a large, healthy, mature leaf, and leave it to dry for 24 hours before planting. This reduces moisture loss caused by excessive "bleeding." Push the cut end of the leaf into the moist soil. Do not cover the pot with plastic, since succulents are liable to rot. *Begonia rex* can be propagated by taking a whole leaf and making slits through each of the main veins. The leaf is weighed or pegged down to ensure it remains in close contact with the soil (see below) and covered with plastic.

Begonia rex

1 *Remove a healthy, mature leaf with a clean, sharp knife and make small cuts across the veins on the underside.*

2 *Lay the leaf face-up on moist soil and hold down with small stones or hoops of wire. Cover with plastic.*

Vein cuts
New plants should form at each of the small vein cuts. These can later be separated and potted up.

PART-LEAF CUTTINGS

*This technique involves cutting a whole leaf in half or into several horizontal
sections. It is a simple and effective way to produce
a number of new plants.*

The leaves of sansevieria can be cut into horizontal sections about 2 in. (5 cm) deep. Keep them the same way up that they were growing, and insert them into moist soil to one-third of their depth. Two or three plantlets should form from each section.

Streptocarpus leaves can be cut in half lengthways along the midrib (see right) or cut into V-shaped sections horizontally (see opposite). New plantlets should form along the cut surfaces.

Streptocarpus

1 *Use a clean, sharp knife to remove a healthy, mature leaf from the parent plant. Cut along the length of the central vein (midrib).*

2 *Lay the leaf down lengthwise, pressing the cut edge lightly into the moist soil.*

3 *New plants should form along the cut edge. These can be potted up individually.*

STEM CUTTINGS

Young plants can produce roots at every leaf node along their stem, although not all plants retain the ability to do this easily as they mature.

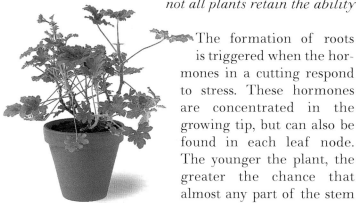

Pelargonium before taking cuttings

The formation of roots is triggered when the hormones in a cutting respond to stress. These hormones are concentrated in the growing tip, but can also be found in each leaf node. The younger the plant, the greater the chance that almost any part of the stem will root if there is a leaf node present.

Stem

Some plants root so well that a growing tip on the cutting is not necessary. From a long shoot it is possible to take the tip cutting, then cut the rest of the stem into similar lengths, making each top cut just above a leaf node, and each bottom cut just below a leaf node.

Tip

Remove the end of a shoot, including the growing tip and at least 3–4 in. (7–10 cm) of the stem. Trim the cut end under a leaf-joint (node), and remove the leaves from the lower third of the cutting. Dip the very end of the cutting in rooting hormone and tap off the surplus. Insert the cutting into a pot of moist soil by pushing it in to ensure that there is a good contact between the stem and the soil.

Heel

Short side-shoots of 3–4 in. (7–10 cm), taken as tip cuttings, can be pulled from the stem complete with a "heel" of bark attached. This strip should be trimmed down to a short point with a sharp knife, to prevent it rotting.

Cane

Plants such as cordyline, dieffenbachia, dracaena, and yucca, which form strong, woody stems, can be propagated by cutting one of their bare stems into several pieces, each 2–3 in. (5–7 cm) long. The pieces are laid horizontally onto the soil or inserted vertically into it. If they are vertical, they must be placed the same way up as they were growing on the parent plant.

1 *Select a healthy, non-flowering shoot and remove the top 3 in. (7 cm), including the growing point, with a sharp knife.*

2 *Trim below a leaf node and remove the leaves from the lower third of the cutting. Insert into fresh soil.*

ALTERNATIVE ROOTING METHODS

While some plants root easily, others need help in the form of rooting preparations designed to enhance the natural hormones that promote root formation.

Rooting hormone, available in powder or liquid form, is designed to mimic the action of the plant's natural hormones and boost the rooting process. Not all plants need it – for example, geraniums tend to rot if it is applied.

The preparation should be kept clean to prevent it from deteriorating, so only pour a small amount into a shallow container, and discard the remainder once the cuttings have been prepared. Never dip the cutting directly into the pot. The powder is quite powerful, and is needed only on the cut surface, so make sure you dip only the very end of the cutting into the powder and tap off any surplus.

Rooting in water

Many plants, especially those with fleshy stems, root easily in water. They can be transferred to a soil mix as soon as the roots appear.

Crassula ovata

LAYERING

This technique is low-risk, since it is the only one that does not involve separating the new plant from its parent until rooting is complete.

The advantage of layering is its lack of risk to either the parent plant or its offspring. The young plant, or the stem to be layered, is bent down and brought into contact with a pot of soil without detaching it from its parent. It is held in position with a U-shaped wire hoop, and remains there until it has formed roots to support itself; the connecting stem can then be severed. If rooting is unsuccessful, the stem is not cut, and the whole process can begin again. Indoor plants, such as hedera and philodendron, which have aerial roots at leaf joints on the stems, can be propagated in this way.

Self-propagating plants

Plants such as chlorophytum and tolmiea produce small replicas of themselves, complete with tiny roots, on long stems or mature leaves as they grow. These are ready to start growing as soon as they come into contact with the growing medium. The plantlets can either be rooted while they are still attached to the parent plant or they can be separated, potted up, and grown on in their own right with a minimum of fuss as they establish. In fact, the only difficulty may be with the sheer quantity of the offspring produced —

although there is no need to remove them from the parent plant, where they can remain indefinitely. If the plantlet already has some roots of its own, it can either be detached from the parent plant immediately and rooted in water (see opposite), or planted immediately in small pots of soil mix. The roots should take only a few days to begin supporting the plant.

Chlorophytum comosum *with plantlets*

Layering a plantlet
Bend the young plantlet down to reach a pot of soil. Hold it in place with a wire hoop until roots form to support it, at which time the connecting stem can be cut.

OFFSETS

Offsets are small plants that develop at the base of mature plants, such as bromeliads, cacti, and succulents.

Aloe variegata *with several offsets*

These small plants either grow from the main stem itself, on secondary stems (stolons) or they arise base-to-base, such as bulblets.

No offset should be severed from the parent plant until it is large enough to survive on its own, and although this is not always easy to judge, it can generally be taken once it resembles the parent plant in shape and characteristics. It may even develop roots of its own before it is severed, which makes success even more likely.

Use a sharp, clean knife to cut the offset from as close to the parent as possible, and place it into a

pot of moist potting soil. Larger offsets may be unsteady, and need supporting with short canes until the roots provide firm anchorage.

1 *Immediately after flowering, remove the plant from the pot and wash the roots gently to expose the young plants.*

2 *Separate those large enough to survive on their own and repot or discard the others. Repot the parent in fresh soil.*

BULBLETS

Such plants as lily and amaryllis can produce miniature bulbs on the stem, offsets from the base, or extra scales that can be separated from the parent.

Many plants that arise from bulbs reproduce themselves as miniature bulbs as well as by seed. The small bulbs reach maturity much more quickly than seed, but lack the variation. Those that arise in the leaf axils on the stem are known as bulbils; those that arise at the base, or are cultivated by breaking the scales from a lily bulb (see below), are called bulblets.

1 *Remove and discard any damaged scales from the outside of the mature bulb. Take healthy ones by breaking cleanly as near to the base as possible. Up to 80 percent of the scales can be taken and the bulb will still flower.*

2 *Place in a plastic bag of moist soil, fold to close, and keep warm and dark for 8–10 weeks.*

3 *Tiny white bulblets will form at the base of each scale.*

4 *Scales can be cut lengthwise to separate bulblets, leaving each a piece of scale as food.*

5 *Pot several bulblets together for the first year. The leaves will initially resemble grass.*

DIVISION

Many clump-forming plants can be increased in number by dividing the existing large clump into smaller ones.

Chamaedorea before division

This technique is suitable for any houseplant that forms a clump as it matures, such as cacti, orchids, ferns, chamaedorea, maranta, saintpaulia, and sansevieria. It is particularly straightforward when the plant has distinct rosettes, such as saintpaulia, separate upright stems, such as chamaedorea, or distinct pseudo-bulbs, such as orchids.

Start by removing the plant from its pot and laying it on a flat surface to examine it. (Watering the plant an hour before removing it from its pot will enable you to remove it more easily.) Select a point where separation looks possible and gently begin to tease the roots apart. It may be necessary to wash the roots first to get a clearer view, but it is important to inflict as little damage as possible to the roots, since this will hinder their recovery.

Plants with a rhizomatous or very dense root system, such as orchids, may need to be severed with a knife, so make sure that it is clean and sharp, and the cut is made in as few movements as possible. For the greatest chance of success, each piece of plant should have both leaves and roots. The new plants can then be planted into separate pots slightly larger than their root system, and watered to settle the potting soil around the roots.

1 *Plants of this size can be divided into many small plants or fewer large ones.*

2 *Each division needs roots and leaves. Plant into separate pots of fresh soil and water to settle.*

SEED PROPAGATION

The production of seed is nature's way of ensuring a continuing mix of genes to give strong, healthy characteristics.

Unlike plants that are grown from cuttings, which are clones of the parent, plants grown from seed can bear characteristics of ancestors going back several generations, rather than just the parents, so the exact appearance of the offspring is very hard to predict.

It is less common to grow indoor plants from seed than outdoor varieties, because so many more are produced than can normally be used, although the surplus can always be given away or exchanged. The attraction is the chance to grow something exotic, such as an avocado or citrus, from a seed which might otherwise be discarded, and this can be a fun way to interest a child in the process of growing. For the keen cook, it is also easy to grow sprouting beans, and herbs like basil and parsley, from seed in a succession of small useable batches to ensure a regular, manageable supply.

For the majority of seeds, germination is triggered as soon as they are sown into soil and begin to absorb moisture through the seed coat. However, some seeds have a particularly hard or moisture-resistant seed coat and need a little help before the process of germination can begin. The key is to carefully break through the outer layer of the seed bcoat without damaging the embryo inside. The easiest way to do this is scraping or "scarifying" the seed with an abrasive, such as sandpaper, or chipping away a tiny sliver of the seed coat with a clean, sharp knife.

SEED SIZES

Seeds come in all shapes and sizes, from huge stones to tiny seeds as fine as dust, and every size in between.

Citrus

Begonia

Avocado

Basil

Solenòstemon

PROVIDING THE RIGHT CONDITIONS

Some seeds germinate readily with little or no help, but others are more fussy and require the correct conditions to grow.

- **Humidity**
A moist environment will prevent the leaves of young seedlings losing water, which cannot be replaced until a good root system has formed. A propagation case is ideal, but a plastic bag sealed around the pot works just as well. When the seeds establish, you may need to support the plastic bag on short canes to prevent it touching the leaves (which can lead to rotting).

- **Temperature**
Most seeds grow well in a temperature of about 65°F (18°C), but some require higher temperatures in order to germinate successfully. A heated propagation case will maintain a constant temperature. These come in various sizes, according to how many seeds (or cuttings) are to be grown. Wean the young plants before they leave the case by gradually lowering the temperature.

- **Light**
Once germination occurs, the seedlings will need to be placed in a brighly lit position, out of direct sun. Too much direct sunlight will scorch the delicate new leaves, while too little sunlight will cause the seedlings to become tall, weak, and spindly. This is also a problem if too many seedlings are left too close together in the seed tray for too long, because they are competing for light.

- **Soil mix**
Seedlings grow best in a light and free-draining soil mix that does not contain much fertilizer. To sterilize pots of potting soil (for example, for spore sowing, see page 102), fill a small pot with seed soil mix and firm gently. Lay a piece of paper towel on the surface and pour boiling water through until it comes out of the drainage holes at the base. Let cool before use.

SOWING FINE SEED

Fine seed should be sown broadcast – sprinkled on the surface – because if buried too deep, it will run out of energy before it reaches the surface.

Seeds have only a limited food supply to last until they form roots and begin to photosynthesize. If they are buried too deep, they run out of food before they reach this stage and die.

The easiest way to handle extremely fine seed is to mix it with silver sand before sowing, so that it can be seen. As with any seed, always be guided by the instructions on the seed packet regarding the depth at which to plant the seed, as well as whether it should be covered.

If there is no packet, the general rule is that the smaller the seed, the less covering it needs; very fine seed may need no covering at all. After sowing, cover the pot with a plastic bag, held securely in place with a rubber band, or place a sheet of glass over the seed tray. Place in a shady spot at a temperature of approximately 60–70°F (15–20°C) until germination occurs.

1 *To sow very fine seed (here,* Begonia x carrierei), *fill a pot or seed tray with seed and cutting soil. Level the surface by scraping off the excess with a straight edge across the rim.*

2 *Use a board to firm the soil very gently and create a level surface.*

3 *Sieve a fine layer of soil over the top to form the seedbed.*

4 *Sprinkle pinches of the seed-and-sand mix evenly onto the soil.*

5 *Water by standing the tray inside a larger one containing water.*

PRICKING OUT

The process of loosening the growing seedlings and transplanting them from their seed tray into individual pots is called "pricking out."

Gently grip the seedling by the leaves and use a dibble to plant it into fresh soil.

Aftercare

Remove the covering when germination starts, and transfer to a bright situation, out of direct sunlight. Turn regularly if the light is lopsided, to prevent the seedlings becoming drawn and bent. As soon as the young plants have two 'true' leaves (which appear after the first "seed" leaves), they can be pricked out into small, individual pots of soil. Handle by the leaves at this stage, not the stem, because bruising the stem now will kill the plant. Settle by watering gently, rather than pressing the soil with fingers or a dibble, because this can damage the roots.

Spores

Select a mature frond with sporangia on the underside and check the ripeness of the spores by touching them gently – a dust-like deposit on the finger indicates that they are ready. Detach the frond with a clean, sharp knife and lay it face-up on a piece of clean, white paper, where any activity is clearly visible. Keep in a warm place for a day or two, so plenty of spores are shed.

Sow the spores onto moist, sterile soil, enclose in a plastic bag, and place in a warm position with plenty of bright light, but not direct sun. Mist twice a week with sterilized water (boiled and allowed to cool) until the soil is covered with green "moss" (this takes approximately 6–12 weeks). Prick out small pieces of "moss" onto sterile soil and mist with lukewarm boiled water.

Finally, seal into plastic bags and keep them in a warm, bright place, misting daily, until tiny ferns develop. These can be transplanted as soon as they are large enough to handle.

SOWING SMALL SEED

This technique is suitable for any seed that is large enough to be handled individually. Citrus seeds are ideal.

Some plants can be raised indoors purely for fun and for the satisfaction gained from the sight of a new shoot emerging from the soil. Citrus seed – from oranges, lemons, and grapefruits – is ideal for children to experiment with, because it is free and would otherwise be thrown away. It will also germinate fairly quickly, producing an attractive plant with fragrant, glossy leaves. Unfortunately, it is unlikely to produce fruit, since the conditions may not be suitable, although citrus plants are certainly worth growing for their foliage alone.

You will need to plant several seeds to ensure that at least one healthy plant grows on.

Citrus bearing fruit

1 The pips from oranges, lemons, and grape-fruits are all easy to grow and quick to germinate in spring and summer. Sow fresh from the fruit or keep in water until you are ready to sow them.

2 Fill a pot with soil and space the seeds evenly on the surface. Press them in carefully to twice their depth.

3 Water with a fine spray to settle the soil, then keep warm and moist. Germination will take about 6–8 weeks.

SOWING LARGE SEED

There are few really large seeds that are grown for indoors. Coconut and avocado are the exceptions.

1 Take an edible fruit and carefully slice it open with a clean, sharp knife. Ease the "pit" out of the middle with a teaspoon or blunt knife, being careful not to cut into it.

2 Push the blunt end of the pit into a pot of soil, leaving the pointed end slightly exposed. Water to settle the soil, then keep warm at 65°F (18°C) until a shoot appears.

The main advantage of large seed is that it is easy to handle, since it does not need mixing with sand or thinning out if too many seedlings germinate. In fact, large seeds can usually be sown into individual pots of soil large enough to support their growth for several weeks, eliminating the need to transplant the seedlings and risk them suffering a check in growth as a result of the shock. Coconut is the largest seed grown for indoors, but as it is impractical to plant in the home, garden centres usually sell seed that has already been germinated. Avocado and date pits are good to experiment with, since they would otherwise be thrown away – there is nothing to lose by sowing them, and possibly a nice plant to gain. Both can be soaked in water first to maintain the moisture levels inside the seed if they cannot be sown immediately.

Be patient with larger seeds after sowing, because they may take some weeks to germinate. Keep the seed warm and the growing medium moist until the first shoot appears.

Pruning Plants

THE MAIN PURPOSE of pruning a plant is to remove dead, damaged, or diseased stems and to prevent rot and fungal attack, as well as any crossing or rubbing stems. Not only does this control vigor, but it can also be used to promote flowering or fruit production. Pruning can be carried out at any time of the year, as the need arises, although the benefit is greatest in spring, when the plant is at its most active and new growth will respond quickly.

Many indoor plants are too small, soft, or sappy to need much in the way of pruning, apart from deadheading as the flowers fade to encourage the formation of more buds and prevent the old ones from rotting. Woody plants need attention to keep the growth healthy and going in the right direction. Plants with a bushy habit need to have their growing points removed from the main shoots regularly to encourage the development of side branches, which should also be tipped to produce a rounded shape. If the plant has variegated foliage, any shoots that revert to plain green must be removed immediately, since the increased chlorophyll in these shoots makes them stronger, and they will take over if left in place.

PRUNING CUTS

The position of the cut is critical – too close to the bud and it will die, too far away and the dying stub of stem is a target for disease.

Alternate buds
LEFT *The cut should slant upward to just above an outward-facing bud, without being too close or touching it.*

Opposite buds
RIGHT *The cut should be made straight across the stem above the buds.*

DEADHEADING

This technique involves removing the flowers as they begin to fade and die. It reduces the risk of fungal attack and conserves the plant's energy.

1 *As flowers fade, they start to look unsightly and waste the plant's energy in the production of seed.*

2 *Using clean, sharp pruners or scissors, remove the flower head, and any seed developing underneath. This encourages additional flowering.*

Dying flowers on a plant not only look unsightly, but they are liable to rot as they fall, making them a prime target for attack by gray mold (botrytis, see Pests and Diseases, pages 116–7). Disease can spread quickly to the rest of the plant if there are any damaged areas where it can enter. The whole of the dying flower head should be removed, including any developing seeds, because unless the seed is going to be collected and used, its production wastes the plant's energy. With many plants, removing the flowers as they fade encourages the production of more buds, since their natural instinct is to produce seed. This has the effect of extending the flowering season and increasing the interest of the plant.

Rose after deadheading

PINCHING, TIPPING, AND BUSHING

Unlike most climbing and trailing plants, which are allowed to grow unchecked, plants with a more rounded habit need to have their growing tips removed regularly to encourage bushy growth.

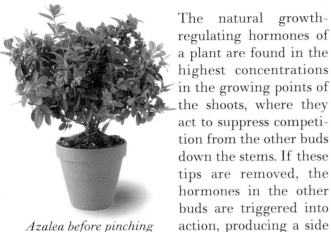

Azalea before pinching

The natural growth-regulating hormones of a plant are found in the highest concentrations in the growing points of the shoots, where they act to suppress competition from the other buds down the stems. If these tips are removed, the hormones in the other buds are triggered into action, producing a side shoot from almost every leaf axil – known as "bushing." In nature, this is intended to provide another leading shoot to assume dominance, but it can also be used on domestic plants to encourage them to form dense, bushy growth. Manipulating growth in this way is known as "pinching" on a younger plant, when it is usually carried out with the finger and thumb, but it can also be used to encourage climbing plants to produce multiple stems. Pruners are often used to trim older plants all over in a process known as "tipping" to keep them growing to the required shape.

Pinching out
Pinching out all of the main growing tips on a young plant, after flowering, helps produce plenty of even growth, rather than a few dominant shoots.

REJUVENATING PLANTS

Cutting a plant right down may sound cruel, but it can sometimes be the best thing for a plant if it is looking straggly or has outgrown its allotted space.

1 *Use clean, sharp pruners to remove the stem in stages, particularly if it has been wound or tied around a frame.*

2 *Cut down to 2–3 buds on each stem or 3 in. (7 cm) if no buds are visible. Water and feed the plant.*

Severe pruning to rejuvenate a plant is a fairly extreme measure, since plants will only respond if they have the ability to regrow from the base. For those which do, it allows them to remain in the home rather than being discarded. It is useful if, as with this bougainvillea, the plant has been purchased in flower but looks straggly as the flowers die off. Cutting the old stems off close to the base will provide strong, new replacement stems – which can be trained as they grow – and although flowering may be sacrificed for a time, the result is a much more attractive plant. Once the new buds have started to grow, trim off any dead stem, as it may rot.

Bougainvillea looking straggly

REMEDIAL PRUNING

Remedial pruning is an operation aimed at maintaining the health of the plant. It is generally carried out on older plants or those which have suffered damage.

Lantana camara
after pruning

Even plants that have been well cared for can fall prey to occasional damage or attack by pests and disease. By taking action as soon as the problem is seen, repercussions can easily be avoided.

Remedial pruning means cutting out the dead and diseased parts of the plant, including any stems that might have been damaged. Woody plants, in particular, often benefit from a remedial trim to thin out over-crowded stems, or to remove any that are crossing each other, since these might rub together and open up a wound in the stems where disease could enter the plant.

A plain green stem on a variegated plant should be removed as soon as it is noticed, to prevent it dominating. This is because there is no chlorophyll in the yellow or white parts of the variegated leaves and their growth is correspondingly slower, making the all-green shoots much more dominant.

Remedial pruning can be carried out at any time of the year, as it is required, but flowers will be lost if it is done as the buds are developing.

1 *Overcrowded and damaged stems lead to ill-health, and leave the plant vulnerable to disease.*

2 *Use pruners to cut damaged stems back to healthy tissue and remove weak, straggly growth.*

3 *Aim for a framework of strong, healthy branches. Airflow through the plant prevents fungal attack.*

CREATING TOPIARY

In a cool conservatory, sunroom, or entrance porch a perfectly-clipped piece of topiary makes a dramatic focal point, in the same way as a statue or ornament.

1 *Small-leaved, slow-growing evergreen plants are ideal for clipping into formal or fun shapes. They can be purchased pre-shaped, or trained from an early age by using a pre-formed wire shape (see page 45). Trim regularly with pruners to keep it within the framework.*

2 *As the plant ages and reaches the desired shape, it will need only a regular trim to keep it within the outline. This can be done by pinching as soon as shoots emerge beyond the outline, or in spring and early fall using hand shears.*

Training Plants

MANY HOUSEPLANTS originate in the wild as rampant climbers, trailers, and scramblers, holding onto their support by means of aerial roots, twining tendrils, or twisting stems. These plants need to be trained against a wall or frame to keep their growth – which is often inclined to be straggly if left to itself – under control. Plants such as hoya, thunbergia, and *Ficus pumila* naturally trail, but they too can be grown against frames to display their flowers or foliage to full advantage. The support should suit the plant – a large plant, such as monstera, needs a sturdy frame, while a delicate plant, such as passiflora needs a more delicate one in order to create a balanced display.

Jasmine after training

Supports and ties

There is a wide variety of frames available, made from wire, bamboo, plastic, and rattan. The plant's stems are tied in place using string, twisties, wire rings, or twine – tightly enough to hold them in place, but not so tight that they constrict or bite into the tissue. Against a wall – in a conservatory, for example – the stems can be held in place using small nails with plastic hoops attached and garden twine as ties.

1 *The vigorous stems of this jasmine will soon outgrow a circular support, which must be dismantled to prevent the stems becoming congested and open to disease, as they wind around and around.*

2 *Unwind each stem carefully in turn, being careful to remove any ties first. Longer stems can be laid horizontally on the table, out of the way.*

3 *Remove the circular hoop and place the new frame inside the pot. Then, carefully weave each stem into the trellis, tying them in place if necessary to provide support.*

PLANTS FOR TRAINING

Young plants can be trained on smaller frames, but large ones need to progress to a more substantial support.

Training on a wall or large frame:
- Bougainvillea
- Cissus
- Hedera
- Jasmine
- Passiflora
- *Plumbago auriculata*
- Thunbergia

Training on a moss pole:
- x *Fatshedera lizei*
- *Ficus pumila*
- Monstera
- Philodendron

Training on a small frame:
- *Ficus pumila*
- Hoya
- Pelargonium

Stakes and Supports

IN THE WILD, climbing plants rely on each other for support. However, indoors – where they are often grown as individual specimens – a support of some description must be provided. Stakes and supports should enhance the appearance of the plant, which often means choosing ones that are as unobtrusive as possible.

Using a frame to support a climbing plant not only allows it to be trained to grow in a certain direction, but it takes the strain off the stems, reduces stress, and allows it to concentrate its energies on growing and flowering. It holds the plant firmly in place, reduces the chance of it falling over, and can be used to increase the air-flow between the stems, thereby lowering the chance of an attack by fungal disease.

Types of support

The type of support used should be chosen to suit both the plant and its situation. Supports are available in a wide variety of materials, including bamboo, plastic, metal, and wood, or as raffia- or moss-filled poles. In an ornamental situation, the support can be of an ornate design, or it can be painted to complement the surroundings. In a temporary or purely functional situation, however, plain bamboo canes may be all that are needed.

Using the support

Whichever means of support you choose, make sure it is firmly anchored in the container so that there is no possibility of the plant pulling it down as it grows. This means that wall supports must be fixed securely to the wall with several heavy-duty screws or nails, and pot-held frames must be pushed down well into the soil. In a pot, the overall height of the support must also be taken into consideration, since a growing plant could make it top-heavy, causing it to fall over.

WHEN TO STAKE
Stems, particularly woody ones, will set into a curled position if not staked in time.

When stems reach the stage where they can no longer support their own weight, and begin to flop over, it is time to stake them.

Push the support down into the soil at the side of the pot to avoid damage to the root ball.

Canes
The straight stems of this tree ivy are tied to green canes to support their weight. This plant would give height to a grouped arrangement.

Bamboo frame
A young bougainvillea is temporarily supported with a homemade bamboo frame, to show off its flowers.

Hoop frame
The delicate foliage of a small-leaved ivy is shown to full advantage on an equally thin wire frame.

Raffia pole
Although it does not hold moisture, the open raffia used here allows a satin pothos to grip on with its aerial roots.

MOSS POLE

Plants that produce aerial roots and enjoy a humid environment will thrive against a moist moss pole. As the plants grow, the pole becomes completely covered in lush, healthy foliage.

Many plants grow in the wild by means of aerial roots, which anchor themselves into moist crevices in the surrounding rocks and trees. Without this moisture, the roots shrivel and die, and the plant's support is lost. Indoors, this environment can be recreated using moist sphagnum moss, either wired around a cane or packed inside a wire tube. The moss must form a continuous column, which can draw moisture up from the soil, because if there is a break in the column, the upper moss will dry out. It will also benefit from being sprayed regularly using a mister, as this will prevent it taking up moisture from the soil, leaving more water for the roots. The stems are held against the pole by wrapping twine around them or using small wire hoops to hold them in place.

Ivy climbing a moss pole

1 *Cut wire for the tube. Keep it in proportion to the plant and pot.*

2 *Wrap it into a tube shape and bend the ends over to hold it closed.*

3 *Use a short cane to push the moist sphagnum moss firmly down inside the tube.*

4 *Put crockery shards and growing medium in the pot, then position the pole inside.*

5 *Hold the stems in place using small hoops of plastic-covered wire, pressed into the moss.*

6 *Space the plants evenly around the pole, fill in with potting soil and mist thoroughly.*

CLIMBING PLANTS

Although many plants can be grown against moss poles, those with aerial roots are most suitable. The plants featured below are ideal choices for moss poles.

Peperomia serpens

Monstera (young plant)

Cissus rhombifolia

Syngonium *sp.*

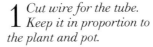

HOUSEPLANT DOCTOR

THIS SECTION OF THE book shows you how to identify problems and deal with them easily so that a plant can recover from an attack by pests or disease, or a physiological condition, with the minimum of damage.

A flow chart allows you to recognize symptoms and make quick diagnoses when a plant is beginning to look unhealthy. A guide to common houseplant pests discusses how they can be brought into the home and how to eliminate them, while a section on diseases provides information on prevention and remedies. Physiological problems, such as drafts and reversion, are also examined in detail. Finally, there is advice on the various controls and chemical preparations available to combat insects and disease.

ABOVE *Keeping leaves dust- and dirt-free helps plants, such as this citrus, to make the most of the available light.*

LEFT *To thrive,* Caladium bicolor *needs a five-month rest period from fall, when the leaves die down, until spring.*

Diagnosing Plant Problems

OURS IS NOT an ideal world, and not everything that comes into contact with our plants is beneficial. Even the best cared-for plant can fall victim to random attack by pests or diseases, or suffer due to a sudden physiological condition. The key to bringing the plant through the problem with the minimum of damage is to identify and deal with it quickly. Keeping plants healthy and well-fed also helps, because a plant under stress, for whatever reason, is vulnerable to attack and lacking in resources to fight it off.

Cleaning is also important, as a build-up of dust and pollution deposits can clog the pores through which the plants breathe, so that they weaken and become more susceptible to infestation.

Not every condition will mean reaching for a chemical, although it may be the only answer to a really persistent problem. Often, inverting a plant into a bowl or bucket of soapy water may be enough to cure a minor attack of greenfly, for example. If chemicals are required, they should be used strictly in accordance with the manufacturer's

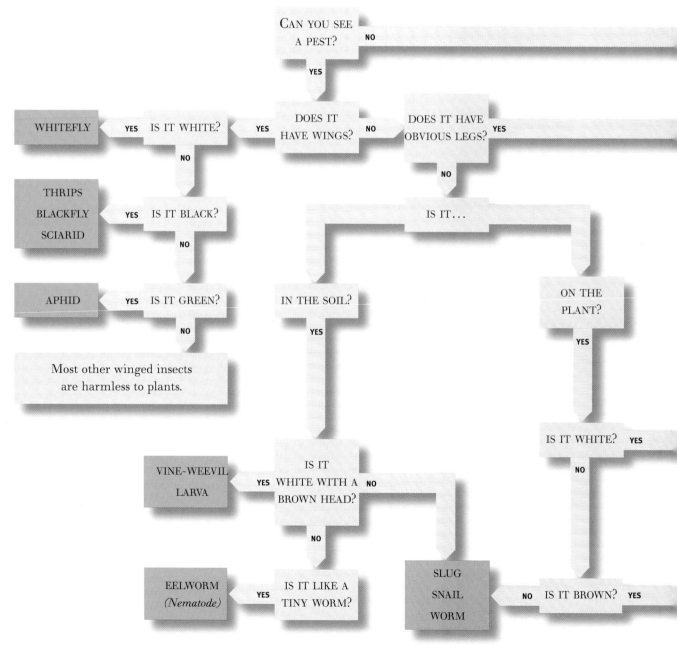

instructions, and sensible precautions must be taken if recommended, such as wearing gloves or a face mask. Children and pets should be kept out of the way while the chemical is being applied.

Whenever a plant begins to look unwell, or just not as healthy as usual, it is worth running through a quick mental checklist to establish a cause. When was it last watered? When was it last fed? Has the humidity level changed recently? Is the pot size right? Is the plant getting enough light? Could it have been chilled or overheated? Is there a visible pest? Is there a sign of disease (such as the fur of a mold, or the slime of a rot)? Correct identification of the problem is crucial to the treatment, but it can be hampered by the fact that identical symptoms may have differing causes. Having identified the problem, the next step is to deal with it effectively. This is easier for some conditions than others, and it may be preferable to put the plant into isolation in a separate room for two or three weeks while it is being treated, before it can become a hazard to its neighbors.

For instance, a fungus such as gray mold will attack any plant that has damaged tissue through which the spores can find a point of entry. If the plant is being treated with a chemical, either as a spray or a drench, it is safer to apply it outdoors on a calm, windless day.

continues on page 114

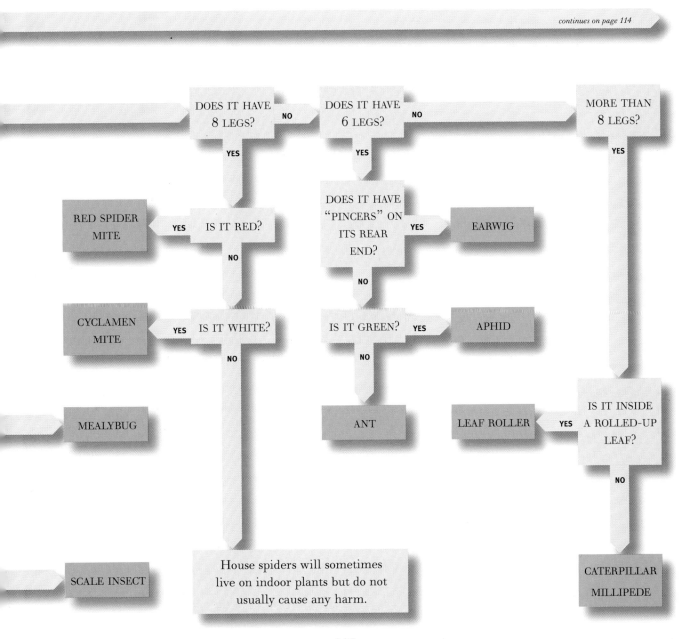

continued from page 113

IS THE PLANT WILTING? — NO

IS THE PLANT LOOKING YELLOWISH? — NO

ARE THE LEAVES NIBBLED AT THE EDGES? — NO

YES → CATERPILLAR

IS THE PLANT WILTING? YES

COULD IT BE DRY? — YES → UNDER-WATERING

NO

IS THE SOIL WET AND SMELLY? — YES → OVER-WATERING

NO

IS THE PLANT A SEEDLING? — YES → DAMPING-OFF

NO

IS THERE ANY DAMAGE TO THE STEM? — YES → SLUGS / STEM ROT / BLACKLEG

NO

IS THERE ANY DAMAGE TO THE ROOTS? — YES → ARE ROOTS MISSING? — YES → VINE-WEEVIL / WIREWORM

NO

ARE THE ROOTS BROWN AND SQUASHY? — YES → OVER-WATERING / ROOT ROT

NO

ARE THE ROOTS DRY AND SHRIVELED? — YES → UNDER-WATERING

NO

Roots can be damaged during repotting, particularly if the plant was pot-bound. Refirm and water well.

IS THE PLANT LOOKING YELLOWISH? YES

IS THE YELLOW COLOR...

SPREAD OVER THE WHOLE PLANT? — YES → NUTRIENT DEFICIENCY

IN A PATTERN ON THE LEAVES? — YES → VIRUS / RED SPIDER MITE / WHITEFLY

EARWIG

ERRATIC WATERING / POOR HUMIDITY

Draughts cause fluctuations in temperature which can cause wilting. Place in a constant temperature to recover.

IS THERE ANY DAMAGE TO THE ROOTS? — NO

HAS THE PLANT BEEN STANDING IN A HOT, DRY, OR SUNNY PLACE? — NO → IS THE PLANT NEAR A DOOR OR OPEN WINDOW? — YES

IS THE PLANT NEAR A DOOR OR OPEN WINDOW? — NO → IS IT WINTER AND THE PLANT IS ON A WINDOWSILL? — YES

YES

Excessive heat and/or sunlight will cause many plants to wilt. Place away from heat or sun to allow recovery.

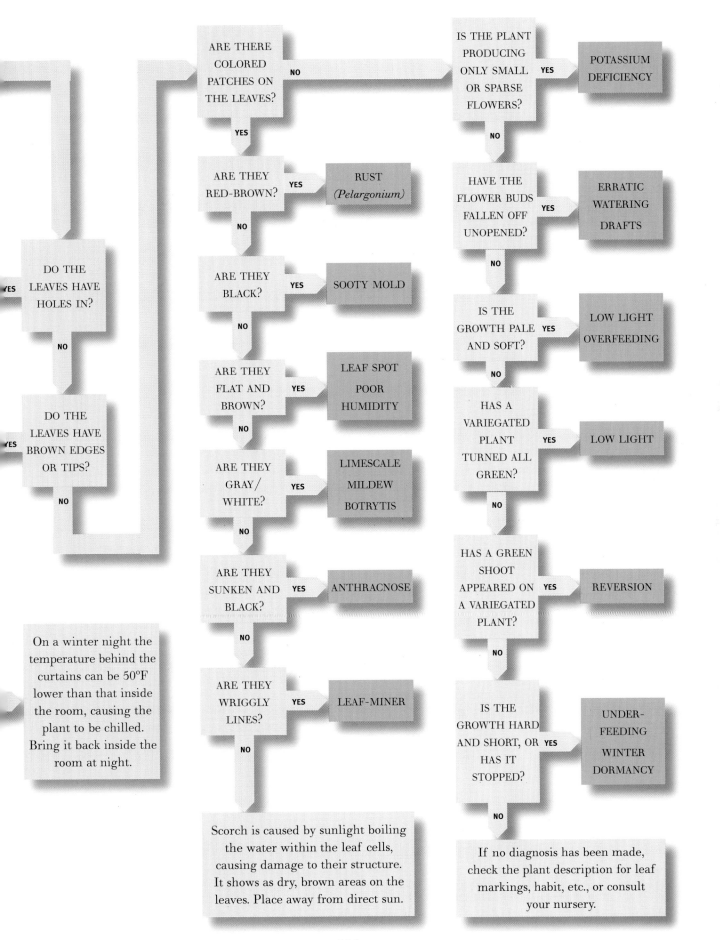

DO THE LEAVES HAVE HOLES IN? — **YES**

DO THE LEAVES HAVE BROWN EDGES OR TIPS? — **YES**

NO

ARE THERE COLORED PATCHES ON THE LEAVES? — **NO** → IS THE PLANT PRODUCING ONLY SMALL OR SPARSE FLOWERS? — **YES** → POTASSIUM DEFICIENCY

YES

ARE THEY RED-BROWN? — **YES** → RUST (*Pelargonium*)

NO

ARE THEY BLACK? — **YES** → SOOTY MOLD

NO

ARE THEY FLAT AND BROWN? — **YES** → LEAF SPOT POOR HUMIDITY

NO

ARE THEY GRAY/WHITE? — **YES** → LIMESCALE MILDEW BOTRYTIS

NO

ARE THEY SUNKEN AND BLACK? — **YES** → ANTHRACNOSE

NO

ARE THEY WRIGGLY LINES? — **YES** → LEAF-MINER

NO

IS THE PLANT PRODUCING ONLY SMALL OR SPARSE FLOWERS? — **NO**

HAVE THE FLOWER BUDS FALLEN OFF UNOPENED? — **YES** → ERRATIC WATERING DRAFTS

NO

IS THE GROWTH PALE AND SOFT? — **YES** → LOW LIGHT OVERFEEDING

NO

HAS A VARIEGATED PLANT TURNED ALL GREEN? — **YES** → LOW LIGHT

NO

HAS A GREEN SHOOT APPEARED ON A VARIEGATED PLANT? — **YES** → REVERSION

NO

IS THE GROWTH HARD AND SHORT, OR HAS IT STOPPED? — **YES** → UNDER-FEEDING WINTER DORMANCY

NO

On a winter night the temperature behind the curtains can be 50°F lower than that inside the room, causing the plant to be chilled. Bring it back inside the room at night.

Scorch is caused by sunlight boiling the water within the leaf cells, causing damage to their structure. It shows as dry, brown areas on the leaves. Place away from direct sun.

If no diagnosis has been made, check the plant description for leaf markings, habit, etc., or consult your nursery.

Pests and Diseases

DISEASES AND physiological problems are much more difficult to identify than pests, where you can usually see a definite culprit. Fungi and bacteria are microscopic organisms, which invade unnoticed; unless the symptoms of attack are seen and dealt with promptly, they can be fatal, not only to the initial host, but also to other nearby plants as the organism spreads.

A virus can be passed on in cuttings from one generation to the next, and while the resulting leaf markings can be attractive (as in several varieties of camellia), they can sometimes cause serious distortion. Physiological problems arise most often when the care instructions for a particular plant have not been followed closely enough. It is important to the health of the plant to try to give it the conditions it needs, regular food, sufficient water, and plenty of room for the roots to expand. If a problem is suspected, the plant in question should be isolated and treated as quickly as possible, before other plants can be affected. Identification of the problem is not always straightforward because it is possible for different causes to produce the same symptoms on the plant. If there is no obvious pest, and the symptoms seem to suggest more than one possible cause, it may be necessary to try more than one course of treatment to help the plant recover.

Sometimes, the most efficient solution is to use a chemical control for the problem, and if this is the case, it is vitally important that the manufacturer's instructions are followed exactly. Apply the chemical outdoors on a calm, windless day, keeping children and pets well out of the way and wearing protection if it is advised.

PESTS

Although some pests can fly in through open windows, and some are picked up if the plant spends time outdoors during the warmer weather in summer, by far the majority are brought into the home on new plants. In order to reduce the risk to a minimum, it is worth buying from a reputable outlet where the plants have been thoroughly cared for.

Ant More of a pest outdoors than in, ants can become a nuisance in the conservatory, tunneling alongside roots (breaking the contact between root and soil so that the root dries out) and "farming" aphids for the sweet honeydew they produce.
Remedy Dust with ant killer and use a systemic insecticide pin.
Aphid Green- and blackfly are most common. Sap-sucking insects, feeding on soft new growth, and leaving behind a sticky residue which attracts both ants and sooty mold. Spray with insecticidal soap, or use a systemic insecticide pin.
Blackfly (See Aphid)
Caterpillar Less common indoors, although sometimes in the conservatory, caterpillars can damage leaves and shoot tips. Size and color varies with variety, but the body is tube-shaped, with a distinct head.
Remedy Pick off individuals, spray with derris, or use a systemic insecticide pin.
Cyclamen mite These minute, whitish-brown sap-suckers (a form of

tarsonemid mite) which resemble dust and cause leaves and stems to become brittle and distorted, and flowers to wither and lose their color. They can be identified under a magnifying glass.
Remedy Destroy affected plant.
Earwig A narrow, brown, six-legged insect with a distinctive pair of pincers at the rear end. Earwigs eat ragged holes in the leaves and flowers of many plants, especially any which have been outdoors during summer.
Remedy Pick off and remove individual pests (wearing gloves).
Eelworm (nematodes) Microscopic, wormlike creatures which damage roots, stems, and leaves by feeding within the plant or attacking the roots. Eelworms enjoy warm and humid conditions.
Remedy Destroy affected plant and sterilize the container.
Leaf-miner Small, caterpillar-like larvae which feed by tunneling between the upper and lower surfaces of leaves, usually in a meandering pattern, before emerging. The larva

or pupa can often be seen if the leaf is held up to the light.
Remedy Remove affected leaves, spray with insecticidal soap, or use a systemic insecticide pin.
Leaf rollers These are larvae of the tortrix moth, and they use sticky webbing to roll up a single leaf or join two together to form a safe haven, from which they emerge to eat nearby leaves and stems. They are $1/2$–$3/4$ in. (1–2 cm) long, thin, green caterpillars.
Remedy Remove affected leaves, or use a systemic insecticide pin.
Mealybug Cacti and succulents are particularly prone to attack. Mealybugs are small, gray-white or pinkish soft-bodied insects, which cluster in leaf axils, on leaf undersides, and among roots, producing a fluffy, white wax to conceal the eggs. They secrete honeydew, which attracts sooty mold.
Remedy Spray with insecticidal soap, or use a systemic insecticide pin. Applying a small amount of paraffin wax on a fine paintbrush (to break

through the wax before spraying) will help make the chemical spray more effective.

Millipede These are outdoor creatures, but may be picked up if the plant spends time outdoors during the summer months. They have long, segmented brown bodies, with two pairs of legs to each segment, and feed on both rotting matter and soft plant tissue.
Remedy Remove the individual millipedes.

Red spider mite The leaf mottling caused by these minute yellow-green, red or pink (according to the time of year) sap-suckers can be confused with a mineral deficiency, but the accompanying spiderlike webbing on the undersides of the leaves is the clue. Attacks can cause leaf distortion and stunted growth. They thrive in warm, dry conditions.
Remedy Isolate plant and spray with insecticidal soap several times to break the life cycle, or use a systemic insecticide pin.

Scale insect Very small, sap-feeding insects with brown or gray, dome-shaped waxy scales (shells). Only young insects move around – once they have found a feeding site, they remain immobile. They attack the stems of indoor plants, excreting honeydew and causing the plant to wilt.

Remedy Wipe off with a cloth or stiff paintbrush dipped in soapy water, spray with insecticidal soap, or use a systemic insecticide pin.

Sciarid fly Minute gray-brown flies which live in and around humus. White larvae feed on decaying matter within the humus, but also on the living roots of seedlings. They are usually more of a nuisance than a real pest, and good hygiene helps with control.
Remedy Sticky traps will catch flying adults. Apply insecticide as a drench to the soil mix.

Slugs and snails Not a problem indoors as a rule, but may attack a plant left outdoors at ground level during the summer. Irregular holes are eaten in the leaves and on the stems, particularly of plants with soft, sappy growth.
Remedy Pick off and remove individual slugs and/or snails. To lay a coarse barrier around the plant, place it on a tray of angular gravel.

Thrips Tiny, sap-sucking insects which cause a silvery mottling on the leaf surface and white spots on flowers. Usually black with two pairs of finely-fringed wings. Young nymphs are creamy-yellow and wingless.
Remedy Remove affected leaves and flowers, then spray with insecticidal soap, or use a systemic insecticide pin.

Vine weevil Larvae and adults are both harmful. Legless larvae are cream-colored with a chestnut-brown head, and eat at the roots of plants, severing them or removing the outer covering, or boring into corms and tubers. Adults are dull black in color, with a long "snout" and bent antennae. They eat notches into the edges of leaves.
Remedy Remove individual adults. Biological control for the larvae (a parasitic nematode) is available. Nurseries often incorporate a chemical into the soil.

Whitefly Small, white, sap-feeding insects. Adults have white wings and feed on the undersides of leaves, flying up if disturbed. Nymphs are like flat, oval scales. Both excrete honeydew, making lower leaves sticky and encouraging sooty mold.
Remedy A biological control (parasitic wasp) is available, spray with insecticidal soap, or use a systemic insecticide pin.

Wireworm Slender, orange-brown beetle larvae with three pairs of short legs near the head. They are outdoor pests, biting through seedlings just below soil level, but may affect plants left outside during the summer.
Remedy Move the plant to another position, check the roots to remove insects, and repot.

DISEASES

Diseases start when a fungal spore, bacterial organism, or virus finds a point of entry into the plant. Maintaining good standards of hygiene, and keeping plants healthy and well-fed, helps to reduce the chances of infection.

Anthracnose Fungi causing sunken, discolored spots on the leaf's surface.
Remedy Spray immediately with a general fungicide.

Blackleg Cuttings turn black at the base, the top becomes discolored and dies. Caused by a fungus, soil- or water-borne, and often carried on dirty tools.
Remedy Discard cuttings. Keep propagation equipment very clean.

Damping-off Seedlings wilt over and die, spreads rapidly to affect whole patches. Caused by various fungi.
Remedy Always use clean seed trays and sterile soil mix.

Gray mold (Botrytis) Covers the affected part of the plant with gray

fluff. It usually enters via a wound and can thrive on living or dead tissue.
Remedy Remove infected areas by cutting back to healthy tissue. Clear away all dead leaves and flowers immediately. Spray with general fungicide.

Mildew All living parts of the plant are susceptible to this white powdery fungus.
Remedy Remove infected areas by cutting back to healthy tissue.

Rot Usually attacks the stem of the plant, making it turn wet and slimy. Often associated with overwatering.
Remedy Parts of the plant may be salvageable for cuttings; otherwise, it should be discarded.

Rust Forms red-brown pustules, normally on leaf surfaces. Spreads rapidly. Affects certain plants such as geraniums.
Remedy Spray with proprietary copper-based chemical.

Sooty mold A black fungus, which grows on the honeydew excreted by many insects. Looks unsightly and interferes with photosynthesis.
Remedy Wash with a soft cloth and soapy water. Identify and treat the pest.

Virus Causes changes in plant cells, resulting in yellowing or mottling of leaves, and distortion of shoots. Often spread by sap-sucking insects.
Remedy There is no cure.

PHYSIOLOGICAL PROBLEMS

The conditions in which the plant is growing will have a direct bearing on its health. Any deficiencies will cause the plant to show symptoms, although on occasion, these may be similar to those caused by disease. Use a process of elimination to identify the cause of the problem.

Drafts Cold air from a door or window lowers the temperature and humidity around the plant. Growth slows and hardens. Tender plants may not survive.

Remedy Move the plant to a position further into the room with a constant temperature.

Erratic watering Plants need water on a constant basis, and giving copious quantities, followed by none at all for days on end will result in poor growth and flowering, and the shedding of flower buds.

Remedy Check the needs of the individual plant and water regularly.

Fluctuating temperatures (See Drafts)

Incorrect humidity The amount of moisture in the air affects how much water is lost by the plant. If the air is drier than the plant likes, the leaves will turn dry or develop brown edges. If the air is too moist, the plant may fall victim to fungal attack.

Remedy Check the cultural conditions for the plant.

Limescale In areas where the tap water is "hard" (contains a lot of calcium), any which drips on the leaves during watering will dry to leave a white, powdery deposit.

Remedy Using rainwater and always watering into the saucer should help.

Low light Low levels of light will cause growth to become elongated, pale, and soft. The plant is unable to support its own weight. Variegated plants will become all-green as the plant compensates for the lack of chlorophyll in the yellow/white part of the leaf.

Remedy Move the plant to a position with more light.

Nutrient deficiency Depending on which mineral(s) is missing, the growth can be stunted, yellowed, purple, mottled, or distorted, with an absence of flowers or fruit, or a susceptibility to disease.

Remedy Apply a balanced fertilizer.

Overfeeding Particularly with nitrogen, this gives a tall, soft, floppy plant, with plenty of leaves but no flowers.

Remedy Give water, but do not feed for several weeks, then adopt a regular feeding regimen, according to the pack.

Reversion Variegated plants occasionally produce a plain green shoot, which will assume dominance over the others if it is left in place due to its extra vigor (it contains more chlorophyll).

Remedy Cut out any all-green shoots as close to their base as possible.

Scorch Hot sun on leaves causes overheating and cell damage. If droplets of water are left on the leaves, the effect is magnified.

Remedy Plants with sappy leaves need keeping out of direct sunlight. Those with hairy leaves (which trap water) need watering from below.

Too much water The more water in the soil mix, the less room there is for air. Without air, the roots will die and rot.

Remedy Slant the pot at an angle to allow the excess water to drain away.

Too little water Without enough water, the roots will shrivel up and die. The plant needs water to transport nutrients and if this cannot take place, the plant will die. If the plant has become too dry, it will never be able to recover.

Remedy Submerge the root ball in water until bubbles stop rising to the surface.

Underfeeding Growth is slow and hard, and there are few flowers. The stems may have a purple tint.

Remedy Begin a regular feeding regimen, according to the pack.

Winter dormancy Many plants need a period of dormancy between growing seasons, and this often coincides with winter, when light levels and temperatures are at their lowest. Growth slows right down or stops.

Remedy Leave the plant alone until it shows signs of growth again, then begin to apply fertilizer and water. Within three weeks, it will be back in full growth.

KEEPING PLANTS CLEAN

The plant lives by using photosynthesis to produce sugars and starches. If the leaves are clogged with dust, less sunlight gets through, slowing the process down and affecting growth. Smooth leaves should be wiped with a very soft cloth or a sponge dipped in soapy water to get rid of the build-up, while hairy leaves should be brushed with a soft brush. Small plants can be carefully inverted into a bucket of water for a few minutes and then left to drain. Leaving old flowers on the plant can encourage mold, so they should be removed as they fade, as should brown leaves.

Any leaves that fall should be removed from the surface of the soil before they start to decay. Trim any stems which have died back after pruning to avoid leaving disease-prone stubs.

Cleaning a Leaf
Dust that builds up on leaf surfaces should be removed regularly using a soft cloth, sponge, or leaf wipe.

CONTROLS

Once the cause of the plant's difficulties has been identified, the next job is to take action to control and eradicate it. There are a number of means of control available, both homemade and commercially prepared.

Insects and diseases can be controlled using chemicals, and physiological problems will need changes to the environment, but with a virus, control is impossible, and it can be spread from plant to plant by such sap-sucking insects as aphids. The only answer is to get rid of the plant and start again.

Pesticides

Chemicals are available in several different forms, from liquids to powders, and more recently, pins. The way they work differs in that some rely on direct contact being made between chemical and pest (called "contact" insecticides), while others are absorbed by the plant's roots and are distributed around the plant in its sap (called "systemic" insecticides). Contact chemicals are slightly less effective in a large infestation, as insects underneath leaves may be untouched. Systemic chemicals are effective because they circulate within the plant's whole system, so any insect feeding on the sap of any part of the plant takes up the chemical, too, and is killed. Neither damage the plant in any way.

Dusting
Insecticides can either be applied as a spray (mixed with water according to the instructions) or as a dust (the active chemical is mixed with talc for easier distribution). The dust pack should be used outdoors on a windless day.

Inserting a Plant Pin
Pins are cardboard strips impregnated with systemic chemicals, which are released into the soil for about a month before disintegrating. Place at the edge of the pot (to avoid root scorch) and push down firmly into the soil mix.

Dunking
As an alternative to using chemicals, many pests can be dislodged by spraying with, or inverting the plant into, a bucket of soapy water. Make sure the plant is thoroughly immersed for 2–3 minutes (not the soil), then allow to drain.

Painting the Pest
Pests with a waxy outer coating, such as scale insects, can be painted with rubbing alcohol first, to break down the wax so that the contact chemical is more readily absorbed. Use a fine paintbrush or cotton swab for accuracy.

STEPS TO A HEALTHY PLANT

- Make sure the plant is watered regularly
- Apply plant food when required
- Position the plant so that it receives enough light
- Provide an environment in which the temperature is consistent
- Do not allow the atmosphere to become too dry or too humid
- Leave the plant alone during periods of dormancy
- Keep the plant away from drafts
- Repot when necessary so that the plant's growth is not restricted
- Check soil is sterile and not infected by worms or other pests
- Make sure that leaves are free of dust
- Group plants together to create a microclimate

FORMS OF CONTROL

Pesticides are available in many types and formulations. They are more likely to be safe and effective if the manufacturer's instructions are closely followed.

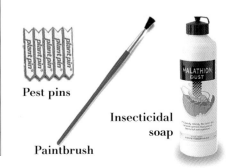

Pest pins

Paintbrush

Insecticidal soap

INDOOR PLANT DIRECTORY

THIS SECTION OF the book is a fully illustrated and up-to-date listing of the most popular (and some of the more unusual) indoor plants available from garden centers. For easy reference, the directory is divided into two parts. On pages 122–141, plants belonging to the same family are listed alphabetically, followed by popular groups of plants, such as bulbs and ferns, which have similar cultivation requirements but do not actually belong to the same family. On pages 142–185 is the main A–Z, in which a wide range of plants is listed in botanical Latin (genus or species) name order. Full cultivation details are given for each entry, including, light, feeding, moisture, and temperature requirements. Where normal room temperature is stated, this should be around 60–70°F (15–21°C).

ABOVE *Freesias are available in a wide range of colors and are easy to grow from dry corms.*

LEFT *The huge, bowl-shaped flowers of* Lilium *'Casa Blanca' have a heady fragrance.*

BROMELIACEAE

Bromeliads

THE BROMELIADS are a large group of tropical and subtropical plants which differ from other plants in that they take in food and water through their leaves, as well as through their roots, hence their common name of airplants. In the wild, they grow as epiphytes on the branches or trunks of trees, in crevices in rocks, or on the ground. They have developed the ability to take in food from the air to such an extent that some have ceased to rely on roots for anything but stability.

Bromeliads are grown variously for their dramatic foliage or for their spectacular flowers, although a few, such as vriesea and aechmea, do well in both categories. The leaves of most of the varieties grown as houseplants tend to be rosette-forming, with a cluster of leathery, straplike leaves surrounding a central, water-filled cup. It is from this cup that the flower arises – some barely rising above the level of the water and others forming at the top of a tall spike. Individual genera are listed below.

Aechmea fasciata

The **urn plant** naturally lives as an epiphyte on the branches of trees in its native Brazil. It roots into accumulated debris, needs little support, and gets all its moisture by catching rain in its rosette of leaves. The arching, spiny leaves are grayish green, with cross markings of powdery white, and can reach to 2 ft. (60 cm) in length. Each rosette produces one flower spike as it matures. This carries pink bracts surrounding the tiny flowers, which are pale blue at first, but rapidly turn red. The flowers are short-lived, but the 6 in. (15 cm) inflorescence can remain decorative for several months. After flowering, the rosette slowly dies, to be replaced by new offsets.

Size Height to 3 ft. (90 cm).

Light Direct sunlight.

Temperature Normal room; minimum 60°F (15°C).

Moisture Water to keep soil moist, but not wet.

Feeding Fertilize every two weeks during spring and summer (into the central cup as well as the soil).

Propagation Detach offsets once they are half the size of the parent plant.

Special needs The central reservoir of water should never be allowed to dry out; it should also be emptied and refilled periodically to prevent the water becoming stagnant. Hard tap water will mark the leaves, so it may be preferable to use rainwater to fill the central cup.

Ananas

Two types of pineapple are commonly grown, although all pineapples will eventually grow into very large plants and are only really suitable for use indoors for a few years. In a heated conservatory, however, they will last until their allotted space is outgrown. ***A. comosus variegatus***, the species, originating from Brazil, is used commercially. It is a dramatic plant with a rosette of long, sharply-toothed leaves. The fruit forms on a 12–18in. (30–45 cm) stalk and is green-brown, surrounded by red bracts. There is a red form, ***A. bracteatus* var. *tricolor***, with leaves striped cream and flushed and edged with pink.Unless the growing conditions are ideal, it may not be edible.

Size Height 3 ft. (90 cm), spread 3–5½ ft. (1–1.6 m).

Light Direct sunlight.

Temperature Needs to be constantly warm to produce edible fruit.

Moisture Keep moist at all times, but not wet.

Feeding Use standard liquid fertilizer

Aechmea fasciata

Ananas comosus variegatus

Billbergia nutans

Cryptanthus bivittatus

at every watering.
Propagation Detach offsets when they are 4–6in. (10–15 cm) long. Rooting should take about 8 weeks.
Special needs Pineapples like high humidity, so place the pot on a tray of damp pebbles and mist on a regular basis.

Billbergia nutans

Also known as **friendship plant** or **queen's tears**, this is one of the easiest of the bromeliads to grow, and is a popular and attractive indoor plant. The arching, olive-green leaves reach about 18 in. (45 cm) long, and form a rosette, although the prolific production of offsets means that the overall appearance is grasslike. Each flower spike carries a cluster of small pink, blue, and yellow-green flowers, backed by long, pink bracts. *Billbergia* comes from South America.
Size Height to 2 ft. (60 cm).
Light Direct sunlight.
Temperature Normal room.
Moisture Keep thoroughly moist all year.
Feeding Provide standard liquid fertilizer every two weeks in spring and summer.
Propagation In the spring, remove

4–6 in. (10–15 cm) offsets, plant shallowly in small pots, and allow to root. Rooting takes 6–8 weeks.
Special needs After a rosette has flowered and the rounding offsets have started to develop, cut it away.

Cryptanthus

This is a genus of ground-dwelling, stemless bromeliads that make their homes amid tree roots and in rock fissures in their native Brazil. They are commonly called **earth stars**. The dramatic foliage is rosette-forming, strongly marked, and highly colored, often with prickly edges. As airplants, they take little through their roots in the way of nutrients, using them chiefly for anchorage. The small, white flowers are usually hidden in the leaves, hence the Latin name, meaning "hidden flower." These plants are ideal for growing in a bottle garden or terrarium. The leaves of *C. bivittatus* form a dense, spreading rosette and can reach 8 in. (20 cm) in length. They are sharply pointed and dark green with two broad, white or pink bands running along their length. Diameter to 1 ft. (30 cm). *C. bromelioides*, known as **rainbow star**, grows upright, rather

than flat, and spreads by stolons with plantlets at the ends. Its leaves are 4–8 in. (10–20 cm) long and olive-green or variegated. The variety *C.b. tricolor* has leaves that are striped lengthwise with light green and cream, flushed rose-pink in bright light. This is not one of the easiest plants to grow since it is inclined to rot at the base. Height to 18 in. (45 cm). *C. fosterianus* is one of the largest species of *Cryptanthus*, with a flat rosette of thick, fleshy leaves that can reach up to 1 ft. (30 cm) in length, in shades of copper-green or purple-brown, banded with gray. Diameter 20 in. (50 cm).
Size See individual species.
Light Direct sunlight.
Temperature Warm.
Moisture Keep barely moist at all times.
Feeding Give only an occasional spray with half-strength foliar fertilizer to improve leaf coloration.
Propagation Use a sharp knife to detach offsets in spring. They root in about 12 weeks. *C. bromelioides* produces plantlets that can be treated as offsets.
Special needs After flowering, cut away the parent plant to allow the new offsets to develop.

Guzmania lingulata

Although its arching, 18 in. (45 cm) long leaves are attractive – shaded from rich dark brown at the base, to green, and sometimes striped with violet – the plant is usually grown for its flowers. More accurately, since the flowers themselves are small and yellow, the attraction is the bracts that surround the flower and form a bright crimson star-shaped cup at the top of a 1 ft. (30 cm) stalk, hence the common name, **scarlet star**. Its home is the West Indies and Brazil.

Size Height 1 ft. (30 cm), spread to 2 ft. (60 cm).

Light Indirect sunlight.

Temperature Warm; above 65°F (18°C).

Moisture Keep thoroughly moist at all times, including the central cup.

Feeding Use half-strength liquid fertilizer once a month on the soil, the leaves, and into the cup.

Propagation Take 3–4 in. (7–10 cm) offsets in spring, using a sharp knife. Rooting should take 3–4 months.

Special needs High humidity is vital. Keep the plant on a tray of damp pebbles and mist the foliage every day.

Tillandsia lindenii

The smooth, loose rosette-forming leaves of the **blue-flowered torch** are dark green above and purple below, arching, and up to 18 in. (45 cm) in length. The flower spike grows to around 16 in. (40 cm) high and consists of a hard, long-lasting head

Guzmania lingulata

10–12 in. (24–30 cm) long, made up of numerous densely overlapping, rose-pink bracts. From between the bracts, the true flowers emerge singly. Each is up to 3 in. (7 cm) long and a rich shade of royal blue with a white throat. This species comes from northwest Peru.

Size Height to 32 in. (80 cm).

Light Indirect sunlight.

Temperature Warm; above 60°F (15°C).

Moisture As the roots serve little purpose in gathering moisture for the plant, mist thoroughly two or three times a week. The water that runs off should suffice for the soil.

Feeding Give half-strength liquid fertilizer once a month using a mister.

Propagation Use a sharp knife to take 3 in. (7 cm) long offsets at any time. Rooting should take 4–6 months.

Special needs High humidity is essential, so place the plant on a tray of moist pebbles.

Vriesea splendens

Also known as **flaming sword**, this plant from Venezuela is grown for both its flowers and foliage. The leaves are 16 in. (40 cm) long and are dark green with broad, dark purple-brown crossbands. The flower spike grows to about 2 ft. (60 cm) high and consists of a flattened, blade-shaped head of tightly-compressed, scarlet bracts, each up to 3 in. (8 cm) long. The yellow flowers, about 2 in. (5 cm) long, emerge from between the bracts. They are fairly short-lived, but the hard flower head and colored bracts persist for several weeks.

Size Height to 3 ft. (1 m) in flower.

Light Direct sunlight, except at noon in summer.

Temperature Normal room.

Moisture Keep the central cup filled.

Feeding Provide half-strength liquid fertilizer once a month, pouring it into both cup and potting soil.

Propagation Detach 3–6 in. (7–15 cm) offsets from the plant's base, not from leaf axils, using a sharp knife. Pot singly and enclose in a plastic bag. Rooting should take about six weeks.

Special needs After flowering, the individual rosette dies, so when taking material for propagation make sure that a replacement for the parent plant is left.

Tillandsia lindenii

Vriesea splendens

CACTACEAE

Cacti

T HE CACTUS family have adapted to the conditions in which they grow by reducing their surface area to a moisture-conserving minimum. They are all succulents (see page 136) in that they store moisture within the main part of the plant itself, but the two types of cactus — desert and rain forest — have differing adaptations. To cope with hot weather and long periods of drought, desert-type cacti have a waxy outer covering (cuticle) and ridges on their stems, and their leaves have become spines or hairs. These spines grow from cushion-shaped, modified sideshoots (areoles), sometimes on wart-like swellings (tubercles). The areoles are the points at which flowers and offsets arise.

Rain-forest cacti establish in places where debris has accumulated, such as on tree branches. Despite the generally humid rain forest atmosphere, these pockets dry out quickly, so moisture needs to be stored within the plant. They do not grow in the upright, cylindrical shape common to many desert cacti, but tend to have long, trailing, modified stems consisting of numerous, leaflike segments.

Cereus peruvianus

This dark green, desert type, columnar cactus, known as **Peruvian apple cactus**, comes from Brazil to Argentina. It has 5–9 thick ribs and few branches. The ribs are rounded, with 8–9 stout yellow or reddish-brown spines growing from brown areoles. Nocturnal, funnel-shaped white flowers are produced in summer, which are up to 6 in. (15 cm) long. Outer petals may be tipped green-brown or red.
Size Height up to 15 ft. (5 m).
Light Direct sunlight.
Temperature Normal room; winter minimum 50°F (10°C).
Moisture Keep moist (but never wet) from spring to fall; in winter apply only enough water to prevent the soil drying out.
Feeding Use half-strength liquid tomato fertilizer once a month in spring and summer.
Propagation Sow seed in spring; take cuttings of young branches in late spring or early summer.
Special needs Give the plant as much direct sun as possible throughout the year to encourage flowering.

Echinocactus grusonii

In its natural desert habitat in southwest USA and northeast Mexico, *Echinocactus*, also known as **barrel cactus**, can live for over 100 years, eventually forming a mound about 6½ ft. (2 m) across. Its shape is like a slightly flattened ball. *E. grusonii*, the golden barrel cactus, has a green stem of 30 ribs and buff-colored spines. The wider crown stems bear straw-colored flowers in summer.
Size Height 5–8 in. (12–20 cm), spread 1 ft. (30 cm).
Light Direct sunlight.
Temperature Normal warm room temperature from spring to fall. During the winter rest period 50°F (10°C). No lower than 40°F (5°C).
Moisture Keep soil moist from spring to fall, in winter apply just enough water to prevent it drying out.
Feeding Use standard liquid tomato fertilizer once a month in spring and summer.

Propagation Sow seed.
Special needs Pot or repot in spring.

Hatiora gaertneri (syn. *Rhipsalidopsis gaertneri*)

The flowers of this rain-forest species, known as **Easter cactus**, are intense red, and are produced either singly or in groups of 2–3, from a cluster of long, brown bristles at the end of new stem segments, over a period of several weeks in spring. Each individual flower may only last two or three days. The segments are thin, flattened, and up to 1¼ in. (3 cm) long, forming stems that are upright at first, drooping down as they get longer. This plant comes

Echinocactus grusonii

Hatiora gaertneri

Mammillaria zeilmanniana

Opuntia brasiliensis

Parodia nivosa

from eastern Brazil. It is ideal for a hanging basket.
Size Spread 12–16 in. (30–40 cm).
Light Indirect sunlight.
Temperature Normal room.
Moisture Keep moist at all times, apart from a 3–4 week rest period after flowering when the soil should only be given enough water to prevent it drying out.
Feeding Use standard liquid tomato fertilizer every two weeks in spring, from the appearance of the flower buds until the last bud has opened. Stop feeding during the rest period, then apply standard liquid fertilizer once a month for the rest of the year.
Propagation Take at least two segments by breaking them carefully from the parent plant. Push deeply enough into a small pot of soil mix to stand upright, then water gently to settle the soil. Several cuttings can be inserted into a larger pot for an immediate effect.
Special needs Repot after the rest period in spring.

Mammillaria zeilmanniana
This desert type is the largest genus of the cactus family, comprising over 300 species. It is different from other cacti in that the species do not have ribs and have spirally arranged tubercles, each with an areole at the tip bearing clusters of spines. *M. zeilmanniana*, or **rose pincushion**, from central Mexico, has clusters of four red-brown main spines surrounded by 15–18 bristly, white radial spines. Initially a solitary plant, it grows to form a cluster of glossy green, globe-shaped stems. The violet-pink or purple flowers are produced in spring in a ring around the top of the plant.

Size Spread 4 in. (10 cm) in four years.
Light Direct sunlight.
Temperature Normal warm room from spring to fall. During winter rest period 50°F (10°C). No lower than 40°F (5°C).
Moisture Keep moist from spring to fall; in winter apply enough water to prevent the soil drying out.
Feeding Use liquid tomato fertilizer once a month in spring and summer.
Propagation Sow seed – allow the pulp from the berries to dry, then pick out the seeds – or take offsets by cutting or pulling them away from the parent plant, drying them for 24 hours, then planting.
Special needs Flowers are produced from part of the stem which grew last year, so a poor growth season means less chance of a good display of flowers the following spring.

Opuntia microdasys
This desert type, Mexican *Opuntia*, takes its common name, **prickly pear**, from its spiny, pear-shaped fruit, and naturally forms shrubby thickets 16–24 in. (40–60 cm) in height. Indoors, however, it tends to remain much more compact. It does not have ridges, but velvety-looking stem segments, reaching $2\frac{1}{2}$–6 in. (6–15 cm) long. These are covered by areoles packed with tiny golden or white, hooked bristles (glochids). It is grown for its shape and appearance, rather than its yellow flowers, which may not appear on indoor specimens. *O. brasiliensis*, from South America ultimately becomes treelike in the wild, growing to 30 ft. (9 m) or more, but it is unlikely to achieve this in the home. It has a cylindrical trunk,

which branches as it grows to produce flattened, oval, leaflike segments and pale yellow flowers.
Size Height and spread 1 ft. (30 cm) in 10 years.
Light Direct sunlight.
Temperature Normal room; winter minimum 50°F (10°C).
Moisture Keep soil moist (but never wet) from spring to fall. In winter, apply only enough water to stop the soil drying out.
Feeding Apply tomato fertilizer every two weeks in spring and summer.
Propagation Detach segments by cutting or pulling from the parent plant in spring or summer, allow to dry for up to three days, then plant into small pots of cactus soil mix.
Special needs The glochids are easily detached, even by the most gentle touch, and quickly penetrate the skin. They are highly irritant if left and should be removed as quickly as possible using adhesive tape.

Parodia
The parodias are mainly small, globe-shaped or elongated desert-type cacti, with colorful or intricately decorative spines bearing crowns of brightly colored flowers. *P. chrysacanthion* from Argentina is covered in spirally arranged tubercles, each topped with an areole bearing 30–40 straight, pale-yellow spines, $\frac{1}{2}$ in. (1 cm) long, and 3–5 golden-yellow spines, up to 1 in. (2.5 cm) long. The very apex of the plant is wooly and tufted with erect spines. The yellow flowers appear in spring and are up to 1 in. (2.5 cm) across. *P. nivosa* is a globe-shaped desert cactus from Brazil, grown for its attractive spines and its display of bright red flowers. It has

many low ribs, set with areoles bearing hairlike spines. The apex of the plant has a white, wooly crown and bears funnel-shaped flowers, 2 in. (5 cm) long and across, which appear around this indentation, each lasting for several days. ***P. crassigibba*** (formerly *Notocactus crassigibbus*) is a flattened dome-shaped plant of up to 7 in. (17 cm) in diameter. It is shiny dark green, with 10-16 low, rounded ribs dotted with chinlike tubercles. The 1 in. (2.5 cm) long spines are off-white to gray or light brown in color. White, yellow, or red-purple flowers are produced in spring and summer.
Size Height to 6 in. (15 cm), spread 4 in. (10 cm).
Light Direct sunlight.
Temperature Normal room; winter minimum 50°F (10°C).
Moisture Keep the soil moist (but never wet) from spring to fall. In winter, apply only enough water to prevent the soil drying out.
Feeding Give liquid tomato fertilizer once a month in spring and summer.
Propagation Remove offsets during summer. Allow to dry for up to three days, then pot into cactus soil mix. If no offsets form, raise from seed.
Special needs Give the plant as much direct sun as possible all year to help it to keep a good shape and encourage flowering. If the roots show signs of rotting when the plant is being repotted, cut damaged tissue back to healthy growth, then repot.

Rebutia chrysacantha

This small, but quick-growing, genus of desert cacti from Argentina easily produces offsets from the base, and flowers while still young. The individual stems are globe-shaped and are covered in tubercles arranged in ridges with bristly, thin, white spines, $\frac{1}{8}$ in. (2–3 mm) long, in clusters of around 20. Pale red flowers appear in late spring around the base of the stems, giving the plant its common name, **red crown cactus**. They are borne over several weeks and each lasts 2–3 days. *R. chrysacantha* is similar to ***R. krainziana***, which has spines in a spiral, and ***R. miniscula***, which has shorter brown spines and masses of flowers.
Size Spread 6 in. (15 cm) in about four years.

Light Direct sunlight, except at noon in summer.
Temperature Normal room; winter minimum 40°F (5°C).
Moisture Keep the soil moist (but never wet) from spring to fall. In winter, apply only enough water to prevent the soil drying out.
Feeding Give liquid tomato fertilizer once a month in spring and summer.
Propagation Offsets can be cut or gently pulled off to ensure the continuation of a particular plant, but rebutias grow readily from seed, often flowering at the end of their first growing season and giving a wide range of flower colors.
Special needs This plant can literally flower itself to death within 5–6 years, so it is wise to propagate a particular favorite from offsets before this happens.

Schlumbergera

There are over 200 named cultivars of the rain-forest type Christmas cactus, all of which flower during winter. They have flowers in shades of purple, pink, white, red, orange, or yellow. The arching stems consist of oblong, flattened segments, the edges of which are scalloped or toothed, with tiny areoles set in the notches along the edges and at the ends of each segment. The tip areoles are slightly elongated and it is from these that the flowers develop, singly or in pairs. Christmas cactus is of garden origin, although its parents are natives of Brazil. *S. truncata* (syn. *Zygocactus truncata*), the **crab** or **lobster cactus**, bears deep pink, red, orange, or white flowers during fall and winter.

Size Spread 12–18 in. (30–45 cm) across in 10 years.
Light Indirect sunlight.
Temperature Normal room.
Moisture Apart from a 3–4 week rest period after flowering (when the soil should only be given enough water to prevent it drying out) keep the soil moist at all times.
Feeding Apply standard liquid tomato fertilizer every two weeks, from the appearance of flower buds until the last bud has opened. Stop feeding during the rest period, then apply standard liquid fertilizer once a month during the rest of the year.
Propagation Carefully break at least two segments from the parent plant. Push into a small pot of potting soil, deep enough so that the cutting can stand upright. Water gently. Several cuttings can be inserted into a larger pot for an immediate effect.
Special needs The buds are likely to drop off if the plant is moved, subjected to a sudden change in temperature, or over- or underwatered once they have started to form. During summer, it may be placed in a shady spot outdoors, but it must be back inside before there is a risk of frost.

Rebutia chrysacantha

Schlumbergera truncata

ORCHIDACEAE

Orchids

ORCHIDS ARE WIDELY recognized for their exotic and beautifully marked flowers, which last on the plant for a long time. They are also often regarded as being, if not difficult to keep alive, then awkward to bring into flower. Some varieties do need more specific conditions in which to thrive, but there are others that are easy to cultivate, and will reward a little care and attention with a regular display of dramatic blooms. In their native habitat, orchids occur in both epiphytic (growing on another plant) and terrestrial forms, and this will affect their requirements indoors, in terms of the medium they are grown in and the amount of light they need to flower. None like cold drafts, but good air circulation is essential to avoid disease problems.

Cymbidium

These semiterrestrial orchids originate in countries from Asia to Australia and are among the easiest to cultivate, especially the miniature hybrids. They have a rhizomatous root system with short pseudobulbs and carry leathery, straplike leaves and upright stalks of waxy flowers in shades of white, yellow, green, pink, red, or maroon. They open along the flower stem over a period of several weeks in winter or spring, each bloom lasting up to six weeks, and each plant, once mature, bearing up to six flowering stems per season. *C.* 'Highland Canary' has maroon-edged lips and speckled columns.
Size Height 18 in. (45 cm).
Light Indirect sunlight.
Temperature Normal room. During the winter rest period, keep at about 60°F (15°C). In fall needs chilling at 40–45°F (5–7°C) to set buds.
Moisture Keep moist from spring to fall. In winter, apply enough water to prevent the soil drying out.
Feeding Give standard liquid fertilizer every two weeks in spring and summer.

Propagation Divide immediately after flowering by washing away the growing medium and cutting the rhizome with a clean, sharp knife. Each piece must have at least two pseudobulbs and some roots.
Special needs Increase the humidity by placing the pot on a tray of moist pebbles and misting regularly in high temperatures.

Paphiopedilum

These are stemless, terrestrial orchids from southeast Asia, which are commonly known as **slipper orchids**. They have thick, fleshy leaves arising from a short rhizome. The waxy flowers are borne, usually singly, at the top of a long, slender stalk, and are in shades of green, pink, maroon, orange, yellow, bronze, and purple. The flowers have a pouch-shaped lip like the front of a slipper, hence the common name. Each lasts from 8 to 12 weeks, and the flowering season is between fall and spring.
Size Height 18 in. (45 cm).
Light Indirect sunlight.
Temperature Keep below 55°F (13°C).
Moisture Keep moist all year, apart from a six-week period after flowering, when only enough water should be applied to stop the soil drying out.
Feeding Give foliar feed once a month, except during the rest period after flowering.
Propagation Divide at the end of the flowering season.
Special needs The roots will rot if the plant is overwatered. If the flower is drooping, tie it to a thin cane inserted into the pot close to the plant.

Cymbidium 'Highland Canary'

Paphiopedilum sp.

Bulbs

IT IS NORMAL to associate bulbs with gardens in springtime, but there are a number of varieties that will grow well indoors, giving color and scent throughout the year. For best results, use bulbs packed and marked as "indoor" varieties, or in the case of hyacinths, labeled "prepared." It is traditional to grow bulbs in bowls of fibrous potting soil, but many will grow happily in glass containers, in water or water-retaining gels. Apart from hippeastrum and lilies, which can be brought indoors again in subsequent years, bulbs are best planted outside after flowering. The word "bulb" often refers to the food-storage organ of plants with a definite dormant season, but these are more accurately divided into bulbs and corms. True bulbs, such as daffodils, are complete plants, with roots emerging from the "basal plate" (a modified stem), above which is a modified bud, containing the leaves and embryonic flower. Corms, such as crocuses, are solid stems from which buds containing the leaves and flowers emerge. Unlike bulbs, corms do not flower a second time, but produce new corms from lateral buds.

IRIDACEAE
Crocus

A corm originating from mid- and southern Europe, North Africa, the Middle East, and central Asia, many species of crocus can be grown indoors, from the smaller-flowered *C. chrysanthus*, which flowers in mid- to late winter, to the slightly later *C. vernus* (late winter) and the large-flowered Dutch hybrids, which flower in late winter to early spring. The cup-shaped flowers come in a variety of colors, and can be plain or striped. All have long, thin, green and white striped leaves.
Size Height to 8 in. (20 cm).
Light Direct sunlight.
Temperature Cool; 65°F (18°C).
Moisture Keep moist.
Feeding Not necessary.
Propagation This plant will reproduce naturally every year.
Special needs None

IRIDACEAE
Freesia

Normally found as cut flowers in the florist's shop, freesias are easy to grow from dry corms and provide a long-lasting display. The funnel-shaped flowers are often highly fragrant and are available in a range of colors, such as red, orange, pink, white, blue, lilac, and yellow. The long, thin, lance-shaped leaves are bright green and arranged in a flat fan shape. Freesias originate from South Africa.

Size Height to 18 in. (45 cm).
Light Mainly indirect sunlight, with some direct sunlight.
Temperature Keep cool; maximum 65°F (18°C).
Moisture Keep moist until flowering has finished, then gradually reduce to dry the corms for winter storage.
Feeding Standard liquid fertilizer every week once buds appear. Propagation and special needs as for Crocus.

AMARYLLIDACEAE
Hippeastrum

The common name of this American native is **amaryllis** or **knight's star lily**. The hybrids produce flowers, 6 in. (15 cm) wide, in spring, in colors ranging from white through shades of pink, orange, and yellow to velvety, deep reds. As well as plain-colored petals, there are varieties with flecks, stripes, and different colored edges.

Freesia hybrid

Hippeastrum cv

Hyacinthus orientalis

Lilium 'Casa Blanca'

Up to four flowers are produced on a single stem: a large bulb may produce two stems. The long, straplike leaves do not start to grow until the flower stalk is well advanced.
Size Height 18 in. (45 cm).
Light Direct sunlight.
Temperature Normal room.
Moisture Keep moist.
Feeding Use high potash fertilizer every two weeks from after the flowers begin to fade until fall when the leaves are dried off.

HYACINTHACEAE
Hyacinthus orientalis
Hyacinths can produce their brightly colored, highly scented flowers at any time from early winter to early spring, according to when they are planted.

Bulbs planted in early fall should flower in time for Christmas. The most commonly available form is the traditional *H. orientalis*, originally from west and central Asia, which has a single flower stem per bulb. Each flower stem carries up to 40 waxy flowers in colors ranging from pure white, through cream, yellow, and orange to pink, red, violet, and blue, over a period of 2–3 weeks. Cultivars include: *H.o* 'Multiflora White,' with multiple stems and white flowers; *H.o* 'Jan Bos,' with red flowers, and *H.o.* 'Delft Blue,' with blue flowers.
Size Height 20–30cm (8–12in).
Light Indirect sunlight.
Temperature Cool; 65°F (18°C).
Moisture Keep moist.
Feeding Not necessary.

LILIACEAE
Lilium
The lily genus is a large one, comprising around 100 bulbous perennial species. These vary considerably in height and flower size, shape, and color, but they share certain characteristics, such as that the bulb is always made up of fleshy, white or yellow scales (these may turn purple when they are exposed to light). Lily bulbs can be bought throughout the winter and spring – choose ones that are plump and glossy, not shriveled or dry. Plant immediately, keeping the "nose" or tip of the bulb just under the surface of the soil. *L. regale*, the **regal lily** from western China, is a fairly tall plant for indoors. In common with other lilies, it prefers a cool

Narcissus papyraceus

Narcissus 'Tête-à-tête'

Tulipa praestans unicum

spot, perhaps a porch or shady conservatory. The trumpet-shaped flowers are produced in summer. They are white with a yellow throat, heavily scented, and up to 6 in. (15 cm) across. The cultivar *L.* **'Casa Blanca'** has a stunning scent to match its huge, pure white flowers. *L. speciosum* originated in China, Japan, and Taiwan, and has highly scented, white bowl-shaped flowers with red markings, 3–5 in. (7–12 cm) across.
Size Height 3–4$\frac{1}{2}$ ft. (1–1.3 m)
Light Indirect sunlight.
Temperature Cool, but above freezing at night in spring.
Moisture Keep soil thoroughly moist as the plant grows and flowers. After flowering, reduce to keep soil just moist as the plant dies down.
Feeding Use high potash fertilizer, such as tomato fertilizer, every two weeks from when the flower begins to fade until the leaves die down, especially if the bulb is to be grown indoors again the following season.
Propagation Break healthy scales from the bulb before planting. Place in a plastic bag of moist soil mix and put in a warm, dark place, such as a n open cupboard. Within 6–8 weeks, tiny new bulblets will begin to form on the lower edges of the scales. These can be potted up and grown on.
Special needs Lily pollen can mark polished surfaces and clothes when brushed against or when it falls, so remove anthers as they develop. Lilies

can be brought into flower the following season by repotting in fall, after the foliage has died down.

AMARYLLIDACEAE
Narcissus
The narcissus genus is enormous and varied in both size and flower form, ranging from tiny, 4 in. (10 cm) high, dwarf types to traditional, tall, garden varieties of 2 ft. (60 cm) high. The species originates from a range of places, including North Africa and the Mediterranean, China and Japan. Many daffodils or narcissi can be brought inside to flower with great success, especially in a cool, well-lit porch or conservatory, away from frosts and high winds. The flowers come in yellow, white, orange, cream, and more recently, pink, and can be single or clustered, with single or double petals. Recommended varieties include: *N.* 'Bridal Crown,' 12–18 in. (30–45 cm) high, cream, double; *N. papyraceus* (also known as the paper-white narcissus), 12–18 in. (30–45 cm) high, white, highly scented; *N.* 'Sundial,' 6–12 in. (15–30 cm) high, yellow, wide-flowered; *N.* 'Tête-à-tête,' 6–12 in. (15–30 cm) high, yellow, multiheaded.
Size See individual species.
Light Indirect sunlight.
Temperature Keep cool; 60–65°F (16–18°C).
Moisture Keep moist.
Feeding Not necessary.

Propagation These bulbs will reproduce naturally.

LILIACEAE
Tulipa
Not as easy as some of the other bulbs to grow indoors, tulips are nevertheless well worth persevering with. Choose varieties that are labeled for indoor growing, such as hybrids of *T. greigii* or *T. kaufmanniana*, as these are less likely to be affected by the warmer conditions and become drawn and weak. Both have a range of flower colors, with either plain or striped petals, and both have attractively marked foliage. Tulip species are from central Asia. Recommended varieties are: *T.* 'Giuseppe Verdi,' a *T. kaufmanniana* form, which is 6–12 in. (15–30 cm) high, with yellow and red striped flowers and *T.* 'Red Riding Hood,' a *T. greigii* form with red flowers. *T. praestans unicum* has leaves which are broadly edged with white and up to five flowers per stem, each red with a yellow base and black anthers.
Size See individual species.
Light Indirect sunlight.
Temperature Keep cool; 60–65°F (16–18°C).
Moisture Keep moist.
Feeding Not necessary.
Special needs After flowering, the bulbs will often recover and flower again in subsequent years if they are planted outdoors.

Ferns

FERNS ARE FOUND throughout the world, in a variety of habitats. Many favor wooded positions, thriving in shade and high humidity, and may grow on the forest floor or as epiphytes high in the trees. Some are not suited to being brought indoors because they dislike the artificial, dry atmosphere caused by central heating; the ones that fare best tend to have originated in warmer areas. Unlike other groupings, such as the cacti, ferns do not belong to a single family: they are categorized because of their means of reproduction, which is different to other plants in that they do not produce flowers and seeds, but spores. Their leaves, or fronds, vary widely, from entire and straplike to feathery and finely divided, and the mature fronds carry neatly arranged, brown spore cases (sori) on their undersides. All make lush, attractive foliage plants in the right conditions.

ADIANTACEAE
Adiantum
From North America and eastern Asia, adiantums are among the most loved ferns. They are known as **maidenhair ferns** because their shiny, dark leaf stalks resemble human hair.

A. pedatum
The **five-fingered maidenhair fern** or **Northern maidenhair fern** is extremely attractive. It differs from other maidenhair ferns in the almost palmate shape of its 1 ft. (30 cm) frond blades, carried on leafstalks up to 20 in. (50 cm) long. The small leaflets (pinnules) are oblong and pale green. All maidenhair ferns need warmth and humidity to thrive. *A.p.* 'Japonicum' (**early red maidenhair**) has purple-pink fronds. *A.p.* 'Laciniatum' has fronds to 8 in. (20 cm) and deeply divided pinnules.
Size Height to 2 ft. (60 cm).
Light Indirect sunlight.
Temperature Normal to warm room; minimum 50°F (10°C).
Moisture Keep moist at all times.
Feeding Give half-strength liquid fertilizer once a month in spring and summer.
Propagation Divide older clumps or remove a small piece of rhizome with 1–2 fronds attached.

Special needs Adiantums like high humidity, but not wet roots (which will quickly rot), and they should never be allowed to dry out. Drafts and dry air will shrivel and eventually kill the leaves.

A. raddianum
Originating from South America, the **delta maidenhair fern** is a pretty, delicate plant in its own right, but can be used to complement and soften other arrangments. The dark green, triangular fronds are semierect at first, drooping gracefully with age, and can be up to 8 in. (20 cm) long x 6 in. (15 cm) wide. To grow well, it needs moist air, warmth, and shade, preferring a conservatory or bathroom to a living room or hallway.
Size Height 18 in. (45 cm), spread to 2 ft. (60 cm).
Light Bright, but indirect.
Temperature 60–70°F (15–21°C).
Moisture Keep moist, but do not allow to become waterlogged.
Feeding Benefits from monthly feeding throughout the growing season.
Propagation Divide in spring, or break off new clumps from the rhizome with one or two fronds attached.
Special needs Ferns cannot thrive if they are neglected. They need both moist air and soil; dry air, gas fumes, and cold drafts will harm them, as will allowing the soil to dry out and then soaking it. Remove older fronds as their appearance deteriorates, a few at a time, from right at their base in spring each year to allow space for new shoots to develop.

Adiantum sp.

Adiantum raddianum

ASPLENIACEAE
Asplenium nidus

This true fern from tropical Asia takes its common name of **bird's-nest fern** from the arrangement of its leathery, apple-green leaves, which form an open rosette. Unlike many ferns, the leaves are uncut, and may reach $4^1/_2$ ft. (1.3 m) long, although usually they are about 18 in. (45 cm) long x 2–3 in. (5–7cm) wide. New leaves uncurl from the fibrous, brown central core and are delicate for the first few weeks so should not be handled. Brown blotches on the reverse of older fronds are likely to be spore cases rather than insects, particularly if arranged in a regular pattern.
Size Height 2 ft. (60 cm), spread 3 ft. (90 cm).
Light Medium light at all times, never direct sun.
Temperature Keep warm; not below 60°F (15°C).
Moisture Keep thoroughly moist.
Feeding Apply standard liquid fertilizer once a month from spring until fall.
Propagation By spores (difficult to achieve) as offsets are not formed.
Special needs Mature fronds benefit from having dust gently wiped away.

Asplenium nidus

BLECHNACEAE
Blechnum gibbum

The large, so-called **miniature tree fern** from Fiji will tolerate a certain amount of dry air indoors. The fronds are carried in a rosette and can be either sterile or fertile, reaching 3 ft. (90 cm) long x 1 ft. (30 cm) wide. The shiny, green leaflets are slightly drooping. As it grows, a scaly black trunk develops, up to 3 ft. (90 cm).
Size Height 4 ft. (1.2 m), spread 3 ft. (90 cm).
Light Indirect sunlight.
Temperature Warm; preferably above 60°F (15°C).
Moisture Keep very moist. If the temperature falls below 55°F (12°C), reduce watering to a minimum.
Feeding Give half-strength liquid fertilizer once a month in spring and summer.
Propagation Remove offsets, if they are produced; otherwise use spores.
Special needs To maintain adequate humidity, place the pot on a tray of moist pebbles.

DENNSTAEDTIACEAE
Microlepia strigosa

This is a fern in the traditional sense, with creeping rhizomes that send up graceful, deeply divided fronds, which can be as long as 30 x 12 in. (75 x 30 cm wide). Each is divided into 2–3 oval to lance-shaped pinnae, which have short, coarse hairs on the veins. The pinnae are divided into 8 x $1^1/_2$ in. (20 x 4 cm) pinnules, which are oblong with a notch at the tip, and toothed or lobed along the edges. The leafstalks are up to 14 in. (35 cm) long and covered with coarse hairs. Microlepia comes from tropical Asia. *M.s.* 'Cristata' has fronds with lobed pinnae, crested at the tips, giving an unusual effect.
Size Height to 3 ft. (90 cm).
Light Indirect sunlight or partial shade.
Temperature Normal room.
Moisture Keep moist from spring to fall, drier in winter.
Feeding Use standard liquid fertilizer once a month from spring to fall.

Blechnum gibbum

Propagation Divide rhizomes in spring or sow spores at 70°F (20°C).
Special needs To maintain the high humidity this plant requires, mist regularly or place the pot on a tray of moist pebbles.

Nephrolepis exaltata 'Bostoniensis'

Pellaea rotundifolia

OLEANDRACEAE
Nephrolepis exaltata 'Bostoniensis'

The **Boston fern** is widespread in tropical regions. It is a lush, graceful fern with long, arching fronds, and makes a lovely specimen plant on a pedestal or in a hanging basket. In the right conditions, the fronds can reach 4 ft. (1.2 m) long, and are rich mid-green with numerous pinnae occurring alternately on each side of the midrib. As the plant matures, two rows of brown spore cases appear on the underside of each pinna, either side of the central vein.

Size Spread 3 ft. (90 cm) at five years.
Light Indirect sunlight or warm partial shade (not deep shade).
Temperature Normal room.
Moisture Keep moist at all times.
Feeding Give standard liquid fertilizer every two weeks from spring to fall.

Propagation Furry runners grow from the rhizome and plantlets develop at their tips. Remove plantlet once it has rooted by severing the runner with a knife. Spore propagation is not easy, as viability is variable.
Special needs In higher temperatures, dry air will cause browning of the pinnae. Place the pot on a tray of moist pebbles to increase humidity.

SINOPTERIDACEAE
Pellaea rotundifolia

Unusually for a fern, the **button fern** from New Zealand and Australia prefers a dry environment. Its stout, creeping rhizomes give rise to red-brown, scaly leafstalks. The low, arching, and spreading fronds are up to 1 ft. (30 cm) long, and dull dark green with pairs of glossy minutely-toothed pinnae that are round at first, becoming oval with age. The shape of this plant makes it ideal as a filler in a larger display to soften the outline.

Size Spread 18 in. (45 cm).
Light Indirect sunlight or partial shade.
Temperature Normal room.
Moisture Keep thoroughly moist.
Feeding Give standard liquid fertilizer once a month from spring until fall.
Propagation Divide in spring, or sow spores.
Special needs Reduce watering if the temperature is low in winter, mist daily if it rises in summer.

POLYPODIACEAE
Polypodium

Arching fronds grown from a creeping rhizome make polypodiums the most architectural of ferns. The rhizome is covered with furry orange-brown or white scales and has a diameter of about 1 in. (2.5 cm). The fronds are mid-green, turning brown with age. These are attractive ferns grown in a conservatory border, or when smaller, in a hanging basket. *P. aureum* from tropical America, is a large creeping fern, known as **hare's foot fern** with long, arching fronds up to 39 x 20 in. (1 m x 50 cm), which are deeply cut. *P. vulgare*, also known as **common polypody**, comes from North America, Europe, Africa, and East Asia, and is a smaller fern, with delicate fronds up to 12 x 6 in. (30 x 15 cm). They can be entire or toothed with a 4 in. (10 cm) stalk.

Size See individual species.
Light Indirect sunlight, partial shade.
Temperature Normal room.
Moisture Keep thoroughly moist all year round.
Feeding Standard liquid fertilizer once a month from spring to fall.
Propagation Divide in spring, or sow spores.
Special needs Reduce watering if the temperature is low in winter, mist once a day if it rises in summer.

DRYOPTERIDACEAE
Polystichum tsussimense

This evergreen fern from Northeast Asia is commonly known as **Holly fern** or **Korean rock fern** and grows into a shuttlecock-shaped plant, up to 18 in. (45 cm) high, with broad, dark-green fronds. Each frond is lance-shaped, with spiny-toothed and pointed pinnae.

Cultivation details as for *Polypodium* above.

POLYPODIACEAE
Pteris cretica

A neat, small plant that forms a clump of fronds from a short underground rhizome, the **table fern** or **Cretan brake** is found in tropical and subtropical regions. Each frond has a slender stalk of 8–10 in. (20–25 cm) long, arching pinnae that can be striped, variegated, or plain, according to variety, and carried singly or in forked pairs. *P.c.* 'Albolineata' has leaf segments with a broad white stripe, *P.c.* 'Parkeri' is larger, with glossy fronds and finely toothed leaflets.

Size Height 1 ft. (30 cm).
Light Indirect sunlight or warm, partial shade (not deep shade).
Temperature Normal room.
Moisture Keep thoroughly moist.
Feeding Give half-strength liquid fertilizer once a month from spring until fall.
Propagation Divide larger plants in spring, or sow spores.
Special needs Cut out older fronds as they fade to make room for new ones. In higher temperatures, increase the humidity by placing the pot on a tray of moist pebbles.

Herbs

H ERBS ARE GROWN to add flavor and interest to food, as well as for their medicinal value. Those chosen (below) for indoor growing, have also been selected for their culinary and visual appeal. As sun-lovers, they will do best on a bright windowsill – ideally in the kitchen so that they are handy when needed – or perhaps in a well-lit living room or sunroom. Individual pots may be grouped together to maintain humidity (important for soft-leaved herbs, such as basil), or planted in groups in larger containers. The herbs listed all have similar cultivation requirements.

LAURACEAE
Laurus nobilis
A slow-growing, woody plant, which originally comes from the Mediterranean, **bay** may grow to a 30 ft. (9 m) tree, but often stays short and stubby. It responds well to clipping to shape and grows well in a tub. The aromatic, oval leaves are a glossy mid-green and clusters of small yellow flowers often appear in spring.

LABIATAE
Mentha spicata
Originally from southern and central Europe, many varieties of **spearmint** or **garden mint** can be grown indoors. Try also peppermint, *M.* x *piperata*, or apple mint, *M. suaveolens*, which has a pale green and cream variegated form. Outdoors, these hardy perennials grow up to 2 ft. (60 cm) high and become invasive. Indoor plants will quickly fill a small pot, so prepare new plants by rooting cuttings.

LABIATAE
Ocimum basilicum
Originally from India, **basil** grows to about 20 in. (50 cm) high and has bright green, soft leaves and spikes of small white or purple-tinged flowers in summer – prick these out to encourage a bushier plant. *O.b.* 'Dark Opal' is purple-leaved.

UMBELLIFERAE
Petroselinum crispum
A hardy biennial, **parsley** should be treated as an annual indoors to maintain a fresh supply of its crinkled, fresh, green leaves. In its second year, it produces a tall flowering stem up to 3 ft. (90 cm) high.

LABIATAE
Thymus x citriordorus
A twiggy, upright shrub, **lemon thyme** forms a compact cushion of masses of oval leaves and pale purple flowers up to 30cm (12in) high. When crushed, the leaves give off a sharp lemon scent and have a warming flavor.
Size Given under individual species.
Light At least six hours of direct sunlight every day.
Temperature Warm room; 60–70°F (15–21°C).
Moisture Keep moist at all times.
Feeding Use standard liquid fertilizer every two weeks in spring, once a month in summer.
Propagation Sow basil and parsley; take cuttings of bay and mint; sow, divide roots, or layer thyme.
Special needs Basil and thyme enjoy lots of direct sunlight, while chives and parsley like a bright position but a cooler atmosphere of about 60°F (15°C). Mint does not like hot sun at noon, and needs cool, moist soil. Turn the plants daily indoors to prevent them from becoming one-sided. These herbs enjoy fresh air, but should be kept out of drafts.

Mentha spicata

Ocimum basilicum

Petroselinum crispum

Succulents

SUCCULENTS ARE PLANTS from a wide range of families with specially adapted leaves and/or stems that allow them to store water within the tissue. They tend to originate in areas where the water supply is erratic – the succulent tissue enables water to be stored when it is plentiful for use when it is scarce. Many of these plants have also developed a waxy outer covering to their leaves, or a rosette-forming habit to cut down on the amount of moisture lost. Some have adapted even more, and reduced their leaves to a bare minimum as spines. Succulents are fairly easy to cultivate because they can withstand a degree of neglect, but they do need conditions to mimic their natural habitat: free-draining growing medium, good light, water during the growing season, and a cool, dry rest period.

ALOEACEAE
Aloe

Aloes are native to the Mediterranean, West Indies, and South America. *A. vera* is often used in cosmetic and medical preparations: juice applied from a snapped-off leaf can help relieve the pain of a burn. It grows as a rosette of gray-green succulent leaves, usually tinged red, sometimes spotted. The edges leaf edges are pale pink and toothed. The flower spike grows to 3 ft. (90 cm) and the tubular yellow flowers are $1^1/_4$ in. (3 cm) long. *A. arborescens* is similar, with red flowers, and has a variegated form.
Size Height 2 ft. (60 cm)
Light Direct sun.
Temperature Normal room.
Moisture Water plentifully from spring to fall, sparingly in winter.
Feeding Give full strength liquid fertilizer every two weeks from spring until fall.
Propagation Detach suckers with a knife close to the parent plant when they start to open into a rosette shape.
Special needs Mealybugs tend to hide in the folds of the rosette.

Aloe vera

CRASSULACEAE
Crassula ovata
(syn. C. argentea)

The common names of this many-branched shrub from South Africa are **dollar plant**, **jade plant**, and **jade tree**. Its fleshy stems are covered with peeling bark and the spoon-shaped leaves are shiny, mid- to dark-green, often edged with red or pale green markings. The small, star-shaped flowers are white, tinged pink, with purple anthers, produced in fall in clusters up to 2 in. (5 cm) across. *C.o.* 'Basutoland' has pure white flowers.
Size Height 3–4 ft. (90–120 cm).
Light Some direct sunlight.
Temperature Cool to normal room. In winter, keep at 45–55°F (7–12°C).
Moisture Allow to dry slightly between waterings, from spring to fall. In winter, apply only enough water to prevent the soil drying out.
Feeding Use standard liquid fertilizer once a month from spring to fall.
Propagation Remove individual leaves or take 2 in. (5 cm) tip cuttings and root in water or soil, in spring or summer.
Special needs No crassula will flower without sunshine.

Crassula ovata

CRASSULACEAE
Echeveria

The echeverias are succulent evergreen plants originating from dry, semidesert regions where they have adapted to make full use of all the available water. *E. agavoides*, from Mexico, has fleshy, mid-green, triangular leaves arranged in a rosette around the short stem. They are sharply pointed and waxy, with transparent margins. The flower head has two branches with small flowers which open successively from the base of the curled spike to the tip. Each is bell-shaped, pink-orange outside, yellow within, and about $1/_2$ in. (12 mm) across. If the plant is grown in full sunlight, the edges of the leaves will take on a reddish tint.

Echeveria agavoides

E.a. 'Metallica' has purple-lilac leaves, turning olive-bronze. **E. secunda** has short stems, forming clumps as it produces offsets. The rounded, succulent leaves are tipped with a bristle and feel waxy. They are up to 2 in. (5 cm) long and pale green, tipped and edged with red. Red flowers with a yellow center may be produced in early summer on 12 in. (30 cm) long stems.
Size Spread 6 in. (15 cm).
Light Direct sunlight.
Temperature Normal room. Keep at 55–60°F (12–15°C) for winter rest.
Moisture Keep barely moist.
Feeding Use standard liquid fertilizer once a month from spring to fall.
Propagation Take leaf cuttings or remove offsets.
Special needs Overwatering, even to a small extent, will cause soft growth, which is likely to rot.

ALOEACEAE
Haworthia margaritifera
An unusual clump-forming, stemless plant from the Western Cape, South Africa, the **pearl haworthia** has a rosette of around 50 tightly packed, fat, rigid, dark green or purple-green leaves, with sharp, red-brown tips covered in rough, pearly white, lumps. Branched stems, to 16 in. (40 cm) long, form in summer, bearing tube-shaped, brown to yellow-green flowers in clusters up to 6 in. (15 cm) long. They are best grown like cacti, in individual pots, or in groups in a larger container
Size Spread 4–7 in. (10–18 cm).
Light Indirect sunlight.
Temperature Keep cool at all times.
Moisture Keep moist from spring to fall. In winter, apply only enough water to prevent the soil drying out.
Feeding Give low-nitrogen liquid fertilizer once a month from spring to fall.
Propagation Sow seed, remove offsets, or divide, in spring.
Special needs Do not allow the soil to become wet or the roots will rot.

CRASSULACEAE
Kalanchoe blossfeldiana
Flaming katy is an attractive, compact little plant from Madagascar. It normally flowers in the late winter and early spring for a period of about three months, but new hybrid varieties mean they can now be bought in flower almost all year. A perennial, although frequently discarded after the blooms have faded, it has crowded bunches of small, tubular flowers in shades of red, orange, pink, or yellow, surrounded by rounded, glossy green leaves with slightly toothed edges.
Size Height 15 in. (38 cm).
Light Direct sunlight.
Temperature Normal room.
Moisture Keep barely moist.
Feeding Use standard liquid fertilizer every two weeks while in flower.
Propagation Not usually done at home because it can be difficult to bring into flower and is so easy to buy.
Special needs To keep the plant, allow it six weeks rest after flowering, giving minimum water and no fertilizer, and then resume. The subsequent flowering will be erratic, but the foliage is still attractive.

CRASSULACEAE
Sedum morganianum
From Mexico, this evergreen perennial has floppy, woody-based stems, which lie along the soil or trail over the sides of a container. Commonly known as **lamb's tail** or **donkey's tail**, it has small, succulent, green-blue leaves clustered around the stems in a spiral arrangement. Small, deep pink flowers are produced in spring and summer if conditions are good.
Size Stems to 12 in. (30 cm) long.
Light Direct sunlight.
Temperature Normal room; cooler in winter.
Moisture Keep thoroughly moist from spring to fall. In winter, apply only enough water to prevent the soil drying out.
Feeding Not necessary.
Propagation Take 2–3 in. (5–7cm) tip cuttings in spring or summer.
Special needs The leaves are easily knocked off this plant, so position it where it is unlikely to be damaged.

ASTERACEAE
Senecio macroglossus
From South Africa, this slender, twining plant, known as **Natal ivy** or **wax vine**, resembles ivy, but has softer, more fleshy, almost succulent-looking leaves. The stems and leafstalks are

Kalanchoe blossfeldiana

Senecio macroglossus

purple and the leaves are mid-green. The form *S. m.* 'Variegatus' is most often grown. Irregularly marked with cream, a few shoots are almost entirely cream-colored. Left to themselves, the stems trail gracefully, making it ideal for a hanging basket.
Size Spread 6–7 ft. (2–2.2 m).
Light Direct sunlight, indirect sunlight, or partial shade.
Temperature Normal room; for the winter rest keep at 50–55°F (10–12°C).
Moisture Keep moist from spring to fall. In winter, apply only enough water to prevent the soil drying out.
Feeding Give liquid fertilizer every two weeks, from spring to fall.
Propagation Take 3 in. (7 cm) tip cuttings in spring or summer.
Special needs The daisy-like flowers will only appear if the plant receives 2–3 hours of direct sunlight every day. If shade is too deep, the cream variegation will revert to green.

Palmlike Plants

WITH THEIR EXOTIC, architectural foliage, palms make wonderful specimen plants. They can be used on their own as a dramatic focal point or in a group of other plants to give height and structure to the arrangement. Although they seldom flower or fruit indoors, unless conditions are ideal, the glossy leaves are so attractive that this is not important. They enjoy warm growing conditions, as they originate in countries with a hot (or even tropical) climate, and need good indirect light, although the amount of humidity varies from species to species. The leaves (fronds) are either pinnate, with many small leaflets arising from a long central midrib, or palmate, where the leaflets fan out from the leafstalk. Only a few new fronds are produced each year, and older ones tend to be shed from the base, leaving an attractive textured or scarred trunk.

PALMAE
Chamaedorea elegans
The **parlor palm** from Mexico has graceful, arching leaves, up to 2 ft. (60 cm) long, from a short central stem. These darken with age, from mid- to glossy, dark green, and the mature plant occasionally produces sprays of small, yellow flowers. The variety *C. elegans* 'Bella' reaches only half the height of the species, and is often the plant offered for sale.

Size Height to 3 ft. (90 cm).
Light Indirect sunlight.
Temperature Preferably warm, 65–75°F (18–25°C); winter minimum 55°F (12°C).
Moisture Keep thoroughly moist from spring to fall. During winter, apply only enough water to prevent the soil drying out.
Feeding Apply half-strength liquid fertilizer once a month from spring until fall.

Propagation Not practical. Buy small new plants and grow on.
Special needs Humidity is important, so place the pot on a tray of damp pebbles.

PALMAE
Chrysalidocarpus lutescens
The waxy stems of the dramatic **areca palm** or **yellow palm** grow in clusters, producing yellowish green fronds that are first upright, then arching over as the feathery green leaflets unfurl. Mature fronds can be up to $6^1/_2$ ft. (2 m) long, with up to 60 leaflets (pinnae) on on either side of the midrib (rachis). Growth is relatively slow, with only about 8 in. (20 cm) added each year. The remains of old fronds leave the stem marked like a bamboo cane. This plant needs some space, but gives an instant rainforest effect in a warm conservatory or sunroom. It originates from the Indian Ocean islands, such as Madagascar, Comoros, and Pemba.
Size Height to 5 ft. (1.5 m) in about 10 years.
Light Indirect sunlight.
Temperature Normal room.
Moisture Keep thoroughly moist .
Feeding Standard liquid fertilizer every two weeks from spring to fall.
Propagation Remove suckers in spring, ideally about 1 ft. (30 cm) long, with plenty of roots.
Special needs Reduce watering to a bare minimum if the temperature falls below 55°F (12°C).

Chamaedorea elegans

PALMAE
Cocos nucifera

The **coconut palm**, from the western Pacific and islands of the Indian Ocean, makes an interesting and unusual feature plant, either as a solitary specimen or as a high point in a grouping. The trunk grows directly from the nut itself, and in indoor specimens this sits on top of the soil. The leaves consist of arching fronds, each with a sheath of woven, light brown fibers.

Size Height 5 ft. (1.5 m) or more.
Light Indirect sunlight.
Temperature Warm.
Moisture Keep moist at all times.
Feeding Give half-strength liquid fertilizer every two weeks in spring and summer.
Propagation Not applicable.
Special needs This plant has a limited life in the home because it resents root disturbance and, to grow well, needs an intensity of both heat and high humidity, which are usually difficult to maintain.

PALMAE
Howea fosteriana

The **Kentia palm** originates from the Lord Howe Islands in the Pacific Ocean, off eastern Australia. It is a tolerant plant, which seems to thrive in a wide range of indoor conditions, and makes a very attractive specimen, particularly as it grows taller, but it does need plenty of room to grow well. The graceful, dark green foliage, borne on tall, straight leaf-stalks, is almost flat in appearance, with the many long leaflets drooping only slightly on each side of the raised midrib.

Size Height 8 ft. (2.5 m).
Light Any, except deep shade.
Temperature Normal room; winter minimum 55°F (12°C).
Moisture Keep soil thoroughly moist from spring to fall. During the winter, apply only enough water to prevent the soil from drying out.
Feeding Use standard liquid fertilizer once a month from spring to fall.
Propagation Sow fresh seed (rarely produced on indoor plants) at a temperature of 80°F (25°C).
Special needs Wipe the leaves periodically with tepid water to remove build-up of dust.

Chrysalidocarpus lutescens

Cocos nucifera

Howea fosteriana

Licuala grandis

PALMAE
Licuala grandis

A small palm from the New Hebrides, the **licuala** has an upright trunk of up to 10 ft. (3 m) high, which is covered in fibrous leaf bases. The long-stalked leaf blades are arranged spirally around the upper part of the stem. Each blade is rounded and glossy, reaching up to 3 ft. (90 cm) across on a mature plant. They are pale to mid-green with wavy edges and divided into three wedge-shaped segments. The green-white flowers are produced on long, drooping spikes in summer. This is a good plant for a warm conservatory where it can be grown in a border.
Size Height 10 ft. (3 m).
Light Indirect sunlight or partial shade.
Temperature Keep warm; minimum 60°F (15°C).
Moisture Keep thoroughly moist from spring to fall, drier during the winter.
Feeding Use standard liquid fertilizer once a month from spring to fall.
Propagation Sow seed in spring at 80°F (25°C) or take suckers from an established plant
Special needs Mist regularly during summer, especially if temperatures are high.

AGAVACEAE
Nolina recurvata (syn. Beaucarnea recurvata)

An unusual plant, also known as **elephant foot tree** or **bottle palm**, this species eventually becomes a large tree in its native southeast Mexico. Its flask-shaped trunk is swollen at the base and branches only rarely as it ages. Clusters of long, dark green leaves are borne in terminal rosettes, each leaf curving downward, with a pronounced channel and slightly toothed edges. It is this plume of foliage that gives the plant another of its common names, **pony tail**.
Size Height to 6–7 ft. (2–2.2 m).
Light Direct sunlight.
Temperature Normal room; winter minimum 50°F (10°C).
Moisture Keep moist from spring to fall. In winter, apply only enough water to prevent the soil mix from drying out.
Feeding Use standard liquid fertilizer once a month in spring and summer.
Propagation Detach offsets in spring.
Special needs The swollen base is used for storing water, so this is one plant which can cope quite well with occasional neglect.

PALMAE
Phoenix canariensis

The **Canary Island date palm** is a decorative palm tree with a single, bulbous stem marked with oblong leaf scars. The finely divided fronds are emerald-green and arch gracefully, with stiff pinnae arranged along a lighter green midrib. This is one of the hardiest of the palms, being tolerant of temperature variations and direct sunlight, and not easily damaged. It is slow-growing, with fronds up to 3 ft. (90 cm) long, making it a particularly good plant to use as a specimen in a conservatory.
Size Height 6½ ft. (2 m).
Light Direct sunlight.
Temperature Normal room, but needs a winter rest period at 50–55°F (10–12°C).
Moisture Keep thoroughly moist from spring to fall. In winter, apply only enough water to prevent the soil from drying out.
Feeding Give standard liquid fertilizer once a month in spring and summer.

Propagation Sow seed at around 80°F (25°C).

Special needs Avoid overwatering; never allow the pot to stand in water or the roots will rot.

Rhapis excelsa

The **lady palm**, **ground rattan**, or **bamboo palm** from China and Japan is a graceful, slow-growing tree that looks spectacular as an individual specimen. The leafstalk is equal in length to the blade, which is dark green and divided up to 10 times to within an inch or two of the midrib (rachis), giving it a fanlike appearance. The leaves are borne on reed-like stems, clothed with coarse, brown fibers. As the lower leaves age and fall off, they take some of the fiber with them, leaving scars on the now-smooth stem. *R.e.* 'Variegata' has palmate leaves with leathery, white-striped segments and the leaf segments of *R.e.* 'Zuikonishiki' are edged with yellow.

Size Height 5 ft. (1.5 m).

Light Indirect sunlight or cool light. Direct sunlight in winter.

Temperature Normal room temperature or cooler; minimum 45°F (7°C).

Moisture Keep moist from spring to fall, drier in winter.

Feeding Give standard liquid fertilizer once a month in spring and summer.

Propagation Remove basal suckers in spring or summer.

Special needs Avoid overwatering and never allow the pot to stand in water or the roots will rot.

AGAVACEAE
Yucca filamentosa

Called **spoonleaf yucca**, **Adam's needle**, and **needle palm**, this is the typical yucca from the USA with a stout, woody stem and stiff, sword-shaped leaves in loose rosettes at the tips of each branch. The edges of the leaves have long, thin threadlike hairs hanging from them. Although it is slow-growing, it is capable of reaching a height of 5 ft. (1.5 m), and looks best where it has room to develop to the full, such as in a cool conservatory, sunroom, or hallway. *Y.f.* 'Bright Edge' is only 2 ft. (60 cm) high and

Nolina recurvata

has leaves broadly edged butter-yellow. *Y.f.* 'Variegata' has leaves edged with white, becoming pink tinted.

Size Height 5 ft. (1.5 m).

Light Direct sunlight.

Temperature Normal room.

Moisture Keep thoroughly moist from spring to fall. In winter, apply only enough water to prevent the soil drying out.

Feeding Feed with standard liquid fertilizer every two weeks from spring until fall.

Propagation Take cane cuttings or remove offsets.

Special needs The plant can be placed outdoors during the summer months, in a position that receives at least three hours of direct sunlight every day, to encourage growth. The yucca is tolerant of a range of temperatures as well as dry air, and will thrive in conditions that would be unsuitable for many plants.

Yucca filamentosa

A–Z Plant Directory

IF YOUR NEW PLANT is to be a temporary visitor for a few weeks, then the information on its plant care label will be enough to keep it alive until you discard it. If, on the other hand, it is to become an integral part of your home, then this A–Z aims to give you more detail about many of the plants in garden centers. The information given includes each plant's place of origin, to give an indication of the growing conditions it will require, and its common name; although, as this may vary from place to place, the Latin name (which does not change) is a better guide. There are photographs to show the sheer variety of plants available, details of where and how each plant likes to grow, and how it will reward your devotion with a glorious, lasting display.

GESNERIACEAE
Achimenes
The species in this genus, commonly known as **cupid's bower, nut orchid**, or **magic flower**, come from the West Indies and Central America. They vary from $^1/_2$–2 ft. (15–60 cm), with the larger ones tending to have a more trailing habit. All have a rhizomatous root system, which sends up many individual stems carrying heart-shaped, velvety, dark green leaves. The short-stalked flowers are short-lived, but produced over a long period. Once flowering is over, the plant starts to shrivel and dry out. At this point, stems can be removed at soil level and the plant set aside to rest until growth restarts in spring. Despite its name, *A. erecta* (**syn. A. coccinea**), is a trailing plant up to 18 in. (45 cm) tall which, in the right conditions, produces spectacular flowers and foliage. Each small rhizome produces a reddish green stem carrying pairs of heart-shaped, dark green, hairy leaves. The bright red flowers are borne from early summer to mid-fall. It prefers a warm, well-lit place, and can be grown in a hanging basket. *A. longiflora* has trailing stems, up to 2 ft. (60 cm) long, growing from small rhizomes. The hairy leaves, to 3 in. (8 cm) long and $1^1/_4$ in. (3 cm) wide, have sawtoothed edges. The flowers, up to 2 in. (5 cm) long and 3 in. (8 cm) across, produced from early summer to mid-fall, are blue with a white throat. There is a white form, *A.l.* 'Alba' and *A.l.* 'Ambroise Verschaffelt' has white flowers with purple lines down the throat. *A.* 'Tango' has glowing pink flowers with pink-streaked throats.
Size Height to $1^1/_2$–2 ft. (45-60 cm).
Light Indirect sunlight.
Temperature 60–80°F.(15–25°C)
Moisture Keep thoroughly moist from spring to fall, then gradually reduce. Do not water in winter.
Feeding Apply standard liquid fertilizer every two weeks from spring until fall.
Propagation Take tip cuttings or cut up pieces of rhizome in spring or summer.
Special needs Tolerates temperatures as low as 55°F (12°C), but above 80°F (25°C) the buds will shrivel and die.

Adiantum see *Ferns* p. 132
Aechmea fasciata see *Bromeliads* p.122

GESNERIACEAE
Aeschynanthus
This genus from Malaysia, commonly known as **lipstick plant** or **vine**, has long, trailing stems and large, fleshy, dark green leaves, up to 4 in. (10 cm) long and $1^1/_2$ in. (4 cm) wide. The leaves are arranged in threes along the stems; at the end of the stems there tends to be 4–8 leaves around the base of a cluster of 6–20 flowers. *A. speciosus* has flowers shaded from orange-yellow, in the lower part, to orange-red at the tip, blotched dark red inside, with a yellow-streaked throat. Each is surrounded by a short,

Achimenes 'Tango'

Aeschynanthus speciosus

Aglaonema crispum

Allamanda cathartica

Anthurium scherzerianum

yellow-green calyx. *A. marmoratus* has tubular, greenish flowers There are many species of *Aeschynanthus*, with bright red, pink, or orange flowers up to 4 in. (10 cm) long.
Size Trailing stems to 2 ft. (60 cm).
Light Indirect sunlight.
Temperature Normal room.
Moisture Water plentifully during flowering; at other times keep moist.
Feeding Use a standard liquid fertilizer at one-eighth strength at every watering.
Propagation Take tip cuttings, 4–6 in. (10–15 cm) long, at any time.
Special needs High humidity is vital, so mist daily, especially when in flower. If conditions are warm and moist, the plant will not have a rest period, so watering should be constant. Prefers an acid soil mix.

Ananas comosus see *Bromeliads* p. 122

ARACEAE
Aglaonema crispum (syn. A. roebelinii)
The attractive and long-lived **painted drop-tongue** or **Chinese evergreen** comes from the Philippines and it can eventually make a large specimen plant. The leaves are thick and leathery, grow to 1 ft. (30 cm) long and are gray-green, edged olive-green. The variety *A.c* 'Silver Queen' has dark

gray-green leaves, heavily marked with silvery white and cream. The flowers, which are not particularly showy, consist of a spathe, 2 in. (5 cm) long, with a central spadix and are produced in summer or early fall.
Size Height to 3 ft. (90 cm).
Light Cool light.
Temperature Normal room; minimum 60°F (15°C).
Moisture Keep thoroughly moist from spring to fall, slightly drier in winter.
Feeding Give standard liquid fertilizer monthly in spring and summer.
Propagation Using a knife, sever a basal shoot (bearing 3–4 leaves and preferably some roots), just below soil level in spring. Pot up and enclose in a plastic bag. Rooting should take 6–8 weeks.
Special needs As the plant ages, it tends to form a stout trunk, scarred by old leafstalks, with a cluster of 10–15 leaves at the top. This can be disguised by grouping with other plants.

APOCYNACEAE
Allamanda cathartica
This vigorous climber from South America is best suited to a warm conservatory where it can grow to its full height or be trained against a wall. The leaves are glossy, dark green, oval, and 4–6 in. (10–15 cm) long. The spectacular flowers are produced

throughout summer. They are golden yellow, marked white in the throat, and earn it its common name, **golden trumpet**. Varieties of *A. cathartica* include: 'Grandiflora,' more compact with large flowers; 'Hendersonii,' with bronze-tinged buds and orange-yellow flowers; and 'Nobilis,' which has large, bright gold flowers.
Size Height to 20 ft. (6 m).
Light Direct sunlight.
Temperature Warm; minimum 60°F (15°C).
Moisture Keep moist from spring to fall; allow to dry slightly in winter.
Feeding Give standard liquid fertilizer every two weeks in spring and summer.
Propagation Take tip cuttings, 3–4 in. (8–10 cm) long, in spring. Cover with a plastic bag or propagator and keep at 70°F (21°C) in bright light, but not direct sun.
Special needs Strong-growing, so can be cut down by two-thirds in winter.

Aloe sp. see *Succulents* p. 136

ARACEAE
Anthurium scherzerianum
The flowers (or inflorescences) are the most striking feature of this anthurium, called **flamingo flower** or **tail flower** and from Costa Rica. They are long-lasting and consist of a thin, twisted, orange-red spadix, 2–3 in. (5–7.5 cm) long, surrounded by a flat, scarlet spathe, 3–4 in. (7.5–10 cm) long. The flowers usually appear from late winter to midsummer, although plants growing in good conditions may produce more throughout the year. The leaves are dark green, leathery, lance-shaped, and up to 8 in. (20 cm) long. Varieties

Aphelandra squarrosa 'Louisae'

Argyranthemum foeniculaceum

of *Anthurium scherzerianum* include: 'Atrosanguineum,' with a deep red spathe; 'Rothschildianum,' with a white-spotted, red spathe and a yellow spadix; and 'Wardii,' with red stems and large, dark burgundy spathes with long red spadices.

Size Height to 2 ft. (60 cm), spread 18 in. (45 cm).

Light Indirect sun.

Temperature Warm; prefers 65–70°F (18–20°C).

Moisture Keep thoroughly moist from spring to fall. Allow to dry slightly between waterings in winter.

Feeding Give liquid fertilizer every two weeks from spring to fall.

Propagation Divide large clumps in spring. Each section will need a growing point and some roots. Pot up and keep at a steady 70°F (20°C) until growth starts.

Special needs High humidity aids flowering, so mist regularly. If the flower stems begin to flop, tie them to thin stakes pushed in around the sides of the pot.

Aphelandra squarrosa 'Louisae'

Originating in Brazil, the **zebra plant**, as it is commonly known, could be grown for its foliage alone, so the bright yellow flowers are a bonus. The glossy, dark green leaves have vivid white markings along the midrib and veins and are 8–10 in. (20–25 cm) long. The flowers, which are usually on the plant when it is bought, are brilliant golden yellow, earning the plant its other common name, **saffron-spike**. The flowers are fairly short-lived, but the bracts surrounding them last long after.

Size Height 12–18 in. (30–45 cm), spread 1 ft. (30 cm).

Light Indirect sunlight.

Temperature Normal room; minimum 55°F (12°C) in winter.

Moisture Keep thoroughly moist from spring to fall. During the winter rest allow the top half of the soil mix to dry between waterings.

Feeding Apply standard liquid fertilizer weekly in spring and summer.

Propagation Take tip cuttings, 4–6 in. (10–15 cm) long, in spring or summer.

Special needs Aphelandras like high humidity, so place the pot in a tray of moist pebbles.

Argyranthemum

Marguerites can reach 3 ft. (90 cm) tall when left to grow naturally, such as *A foeniculaceum* (syn. *Chrysanthemum foeniculaceum*), which originated as a garden plant. The argyranthemums available for indoors have usually had their growing tips pinched out, or have been treated with a growth-restricting chemical to keep them at about 18 in. (45 cm). They form bushy plants, some with deeply cut, blue-gray leaves, covered with masses of yellow or white flowers throughout summer. Once the plant has finished flowering, it can be planted outside. *A. frutescens* (syn. *Chrysanthemum frutescens*) is another half-hardy, white-flowered species from the Canary Islands.

Size Height 18 in. (45 cm).

Light Direct sunlight.

Temperature Keep cool; 55–65°F (12–18°C).

Moisture Water plentifully to keep the soil thoroughly moist.

Feeding Give standard liquid fertilizer every two weeks from spring to fall, or while in flower.

Propagation: Take tip cuttings, 4 in. (10 cm) long, in spring.

Special needs Higher temperatures will shorten the flowering period.

LILIACEAE (ASPARAGACEAE)
Asparagus

Indoors, the members of this genus are grown for their wonderful, graceful foliage, which consists of finely divided, modified branchlets. They bear a close resemblance to fern fronds, giving rise to the common names, but are generally easier to cultivate than ferns. The flowers are small, often fragrant, and followed by purple, orange, or red berries. *A. densiflorus* **'Sprengeri'** is a coarse, fern-like plant, also known as **emerald fern**, with woody stems that can reach 3 ft. (90 cm) long and be erect or trailing. The feathery, emerald-green foliage is much prized by flower arrangers; it is also useful among a group of other indoor plants to soften the display and add contrast. The flowers are small and inconspicuous, but are sometimes followed by

bright red fruits. This species is from South Africa. *A. setaceus* (syn. *A. plumosus*) has the common name **asparagus fern**, but this plant is not a true fern, although its delicate foliage does resemble that of a fern and is often used in bouquets. The stems are green and wiry and can be up to 4$\frac{1}{2}$ ft. (1.3m) long. They will naturally climb or scramble as the plant matures. The bright green "leaves" form flattened triangular-shaped sprays. The misty effect of the foliage means this is an ideal plant for softening and filling in an arrangement of indoor plants, particularly where it has room to follow its natural growth pattern. The species comes from South and East Africa.

Size See individual species.

Light Indirect sunlight.

Temperature Normal room.

Moisture Keep thoroughly moist from spring to fall. During the winter, apply only enough water to prevent the soil from drying out.

Feeding Use standard liquid fertilizer every two weeks from spring until fall.

Propagation Divide larger plants in spring.

Special needs Do not place in direct sunlight because this may scorch the foliage.

LILIACEAE (CONVALLARIACEAE
Aspidistra elatior

The **cast-iron plant** from China is one of the most resilient houseplants ever introduced. It grows as a clump, producing many single dark green leaves, which reach up to 2 ft. (60 cm) long. Cream and purple flowers, $\frac{3}{4}$–1$\frac{1}{4}$ in. (2–3 cm) across, are produced in spring, but may not be seen among the foliage. Varieties include: *A.e.* 'Milky Way,' with leaves speckled white, and *A.e.* 'Variegata,' with cream-variegated leaves.

Size Height 18 in. (45 cm), spread 2 ft. (60 cm).

Light Partial shade.

Temperature Tolerates a wide range.

Moisture Keep barely moist.

Feeding Give standard fertilizer at each watering.

Propagation Divide large plants in spring. Each piece should have leaves and some roots.

Special needs Overwatering causes brown blotches on the surface of the leaves.

Asplenium nidus see *Ferns* p.132
Azalea indica see *Rhododendron simsii*
Basil see *Herbs* p.135
Beaucarnea recurvata see *Nolina recurvata*

Asparagus densiflorus 'Sprengeri'

Asparagus setaceus

Aspidistra elatior

BEGONIACEAE
Begonia

The begonia genus is a huge one, covering climbers, shrubs, and herbaceous plants, which range in size from tiny, ground-covering creepers to woody giants of up to 6½ ft. (2 m) tall. Their root systems (by which they are usually categorized) can be fibrous, tuberous, or rhizomatous, and some also have aerial roots, which can vary from woody to succulent. Other characteristics are common to all the plants throughout the genus. For example, the leaves might vary considerably in color, pattern, and texture, but all are produced alternately from stipules (sheaths that surround the new leaves), and are asymmetric in appearance. The waxy flowers are carried in clusters of a single sex, although both sexes are borne on the same plant. The female flowers are less showy than the male, and have a characteristic 3-winged ovary behind the petals. Begonias are from the tropics and subtropics, especially the Americas, and make good indoor plants, either in the house or a conservatory, especially as many do not require direct sunlight.

B. bowerae
This bushy, stemless plant from Mexico is grown for its foliage rather than its flowers, which are small and pale pink. It has attractive heart-shaped, light green leaves with irregular darker markings around their edges. The common name of **eyelash**

begonia is derived from the short hairs that fringe the leaf edges.
Size Height 6–9 in. (15–23 cm).
Light Indirect sunlight.
Temperature Normal room.
Moisture Keep moist from spring to fall; water sparingly in winter.
Feeding Use standard liquid fertilizer every two weeks from spring to fall.
Propagation Divide at any time, or take leaf cuttings in spring.
Special needs High humidity is important, so place the pot on a tray of moist pebbles and mist regularly. Good hygiene is also critical where humidity is high because gray mold thrives in such conditions. Remove damaged and dying leaves.

B. x elatior (syn. B. x hiemalis, B. Elatior Group)
Although the common name of this plant, **winter-flowering begonia**, suggests that it flowers only in the winter, improvements in breeding mean that it is now available in flower all year round. It is fibrous-rooted, with flowers that can be single or double, and can range in color from white to pink, yellow, orange, or red. The leaves are usually glossy, pale green, but plants with darker flowers also tend to have darker, more bronzy foliage. This group of begonias is of garden origin.
Size Height 18 in. (45cm), spread 2 ft. (30 cm).
Light Indirect sunlight.
Temperature Normal room.

Moisture Keep the soil mix moist, but not wet.
Feeding Use standard liquid fertilizer every two weeks in spring and summer.
Propagation Take tip cuttings, 3–4 in. (7–10 cm) long, from non-flowering shoots.
Special needs Direct sunlight may cause scorching to the leaves. Overwatering can cause rotting.

B. rex
Known as the **painted-leaf begonia**, B. rex is originally from Assam and, with its closely-related hybrids in the Rex Cultorum Group, has the most dramatic foliage of any of the begonias. They are rhizomatous with red, hairy stems bearing large, puckered leaves that can be hairy both on top and underneath. The leaves are rich, metallic green, splashed with silvery white above and dull red beneath. The winter-borne flowers are pink. The Rex Cultorum Group of hybrids is large, with most plants being grown for their foliage rather than their flowers. The leaves are heart-shaped, up to 2 ft. (30 cm) in length, and have striking patterns in a range of colors, including wine-red, and shades of green, bronze, and silver.
Size Height 1 ft. (30 cm), spread to 3 ft. (90 cm).
Light Indirect sunlight.
Temperature Normal room.
Moisture Keep the soil mix moist, but not wet.
Feeding Use standard liquid fertilizer every two weeks in spring and summer.
Propagation Cut 2–3 in. (5–7 cm) sections of rhizome, each with a growing point, plant shallowly, and cover with a plastic bag. Alternatively, cut a healthy leaf with 1–2 in. (2–3 cm) of leafstalk, plant it at an angle of 45° in a pot or tray of soil, and enclose it all in a plastic bag. Pot up when the small new plantlets have 2–3 leaves.
Special needs Direct sunlight may scorch the leaves. Overwatering can cause rotting.

Beloperone guttata see *Justicia brandegeeana*
Billbergia nutans see *Bromeliads* p.122
Blechnum gibbum see *Ferns* p.132

Begonia x *elatior* (syn. *B.* x *hiemalis*)

Begonia rex hybrid

Bougainvillea glabra

Browallia speciosa

Brunfelsia pauciflora 'Macrantha'

NYCTAGINACEAE
Bougainvillea glabra
A woody, spiny plant that originates in subtropical Brazil, **paper flower** needs quite high levels of both warmth and light in order to flourish. It is a vigorous grower, and regular pruning and training will keep it smaller and more bushy. Given good conditions, it will produce clusters of 10–20 vividly colored bracts (which surround the inconspicuous cream flowers) in shades of white, pink, red, or purple, throughout spring and summer. Varieties include: *B.g.* 'Magnifica,' with vivid purple bracts; *B.g.* 'Sanderiana,' with long-lasting, magenta bracts; and *B.g.* 'Harrisii,' which has gray-green leaves, splashed with cream.
Size Height to 10 ft. (3 m).
Light Direct sunlight.
Temperature Not less than 50°F (10°C) in winter.
Moisture Keep the soil mix thoroughly moist from spring to fall; during the winter apply only enough water to prevent the soil mix from drying out.
Feeding Use standard liquid fertilizer every two weeks in spring and summer.
Propagation Take tip cuttings, 6 in. (15 cm) long, in spring and place in a heated propagator. Rooting should take 6–8 weeks.
Special needs Leaf loss in winter is normal, but at any other time it indicates that growing conditions are not ideal. To reduce excessive growth, cut

long shoots back to 2–3 buds in early spring, and reduce the rest of the growth by one-third.

SOLANACEAE
Browallia speciosa
A glorious display of large, sapphire-blue flowers in fall and winter make the **bush violet** from Colombia an impressive and attractive pot plant. The trailing stems lend themselves to use in a hanging basket. Removing the flowers as they fade can prolong the display for several weeks. It is best treated as an annual and discarded once flowering is over. Varieties include: *B.s.* 'Major' (**sapphire flower**), which has a more upright habit, bright green leaves, and large, violet-blue flowers with a white throat and deep blue veining on the petals, and *B.s.* 'Silver Bells,' which is a white cultivar.
Size Height 18–24 in. (45–60 cm).
Light Direct sunlight, except noon in summer.
Temperature 55–60°F (12–15°C).
Moisture Keep moist at all times.
Feeding Give standard liquid fertilizer every two weeks while the plant is in flower.
Propagation Sow seed in spring or summer. Pinch the tips of the shoots as they grow to make them bush.
Special needs The thin branches need tying to stakes if the plant is to be grown as a bush. Higher than recommended temperatures will lead to the flowers fading quickly.

SOLANACEAE
Brunfelsia pauciflora 'Macrantha'
The fascinating common name of this Brazilian shrub – **yesterday, today, and tomorrow** – comes from the coloration of the flowers, which open purple, change to violet, and finally turn white over a period of about three days. They are flat, five-lobed, often fragrant and up to 3 in. (7 cm) across, produced in clusters of up to 10. Leaves are lance-shaped, leathery, but also glossy. Grown in the right conditions, brunfelsia can become a bushy plant, producing flowers throughout the year, but to achieve this it needs to be protected from sudden temperature changes.
Size Height to 2 ft. (60 cm), spread 1 ft. (30 cm).
Light Direct sunlight, except at noon in summer.
Temperature Normal room all year to maintain flowering.
Moisture Keep thoroughly moist at all times.
Feeding Use standard liquid fertilizer every two weeks.
Propagation Tip cuttings, 3–4 in. (7–10 cm) long, in spring and summer.
Special needs High humidity is important, so place the pot on a tray of moist pebbles and mist regularly. Old plants can be pruned hard in spring, taking off up to half of the existing stems. The resultant new growth should be pinched to make the plant bush out.

Caladium bicolor

Calathea makoyana

ARACEAE
Caladium bicolor

The caladiums, also called **angel wings** or **elephant's ears**, are a large group of tuberous-rooted plants from northern South America with strikingly colored, paper-thin, heart-shaped leaves, which rise on long, fleshy stalks directly from the base. The color of the leaves varies considerably between the different hybrids and they can be up to 18 in. (45 cm) long. They look particularly striking when they are grouped together or mixed with other foliage plants. Suggested hybrids: *C.b.* 'Carolyn Whorton,' which has pink leaves with green-black marbling and red ribs; *C.b.* 'Gingerland,' whose gray leaves have white ribs, maroon spots, and dark green edges; *C.b.* 'Miss Muffet,' a dwarf type with white-ribbed, sage-green leaves with soft red centers; and *C.b.* 'White Queen,' which bears white leaves with crimson veins and green edges.
Size Height up to 2 ft. (60 cm), leaves to 18 in. (45 cm) long.
Light Indirect sunlight.
Temperature Warm; at least 65–75°F (18–23°C).
Moisture Keep thoroughly moist through spring and summer. Reduce watering to a minimum over the rest period, only to prevent the potting soil from drying out severely.
Feeding Give half-strength liquid fertilizer every two weeks during spring and summer.
Propagation As the plant emerges from its rest period, small tubers can be detached from the parent plant and potted up.
Special needs To thrive, caladiums need a five month rest period from when the leaves die down in fall until the following spring.

MARANTACEAE
Calathea makoyana

Although this tropical plant from Brazil produces white flowers, surrounded by green bracts, they are of minor importance compared to the dramatic foliage, which earns it its common names – **peacock plant**, **cathedral windows**, and **brain plant**. The oval leaves can be as long as 13 in. (32 cm), and are pale green, feathered cream, with dark green blotches along the veins, and dark green borders. Underneath, they have a repeat of the pattern, but shaded with purple.
Size Height 3 ft. (90 cm), spread 2 ft. (60 cm).
Light Indirect sunlight.
Temperature Keep warm; 60–70°F (15–21°C).
Moisture Keep thoroughly moist from spring to fall, slightly drier in winter.
Feeding Apply standard liquid fertilizer every two weeks during spring and summer.
Propagation Divide in spring: each clump needs roots and shoots to grow. Enclose the new plant in a plastic bag to keep the humidity high until it has established.
Special needs In warmer temperatures, increase the humidity by misting daily with rainwater (to avoid marking the foliage). Bright light will make the leaf markings fade.

SCROPHULARIACEAE
Calceolaria
Herbeohybrida Group

Known as **pocketbook plant** or **pouch flower**, this plant blooms gloriously for several weeks in spring, but is best regarded as short-term decoration for indoors, and discarded once flowering has finished. The inflated, pouch-shaped flowers come in shades of white, yellow, orange, copper, and red, and most are blotched with other colors. The leaves are soft and bushy, clustered at the base of the plant, and up to 8 in. (20 cm) across. The Herbeohybrida Group is of garden origin with its parents originating in South America.
Size Height 18 in. (45 cm).
Light Indirect sunlight.
Temperature Cool; prefers 50–60°F (10–15°C).
Moisture Keep thoroughly moist.

Feeding Not necessary.

Propagation Sow seed in summer in a cool environment for flowering the following year. Not easy, and probably best left to the nurseryman.

Special needs Watch for aphids, which love the lush growth, and keep shaded from bright sun, which will scorch the leaves.

THEACEAE
Camellia japonica

This **camellia** from Japan makes a large shrub or small tree, which, in temperate climates, will survive all but the harshest of winters outdoors, as long as it is growing in the acid conditions it prefers. It can be grown under cover, but needs a cool, light, airy position, such as an unheated conservatory, sunroom, or porch. A number of cultivars are available. All have leaves of glossy, dark green and flowers in a range of colors from white through to dark red. These may be single, semidouble, and double, and are produced from late winter until summer, according to variety.

Size Variable, up to 50 ft. (15 m) high.

Light Indirect sunlight.

Temperature Keep cool; 45–60°F (7–15°C). Avoid frost.

Moisture Keep thoroughly moist at all times.

Feeding Give standard liquid fertilizer every two weeks over spring and summer.

Propagation In summer, take semiripe cuttings, with at least ³/₄ in. (2 cm) of brown woody stem at the base. They need rooting hormone and bottom heat – from an electric propagator, for example.

Special needs As essentially outdoor plants, it is preferable to bring camellias indoors only while they are in flower, unless they can be kept cool.

CAMPANULACEAE
Campanula isophylla

A pretty, trailing form, also called **star-of-Bethlehem**, **falling stars**, or **Italian bellflower**, this campanula from northern Italy looks good tumbling from a pot or a hanging basket. The star-shaped flowers are produced throughout summer and fall, and are usually violet-blue, although white (*C. isophylla* 'Alba') and variegated (*C.* 'Balchiniana') are also available.

Calceolaria Herbeohybrida Group

There is also a double cultivar, 'Flore Pleno.' The stems and leaves are bright green and slightly brittle. If they are broken, they exude a distinctive smell and a milky white sap.

Size Height to 1 ft. (30 cm).

Light Indirect sunlight.

Temperature Normal room or cooler; winter minimum 45°F (7°C).

Moisture Keep thoroughly moist during spring and fall, slightly drier in winter.

Feeding Give standard liquid fertilizer every two weeks during late spring and fall.

Propagation Take tip cuttings, 2 in. (5 cm) long, in spring. Root them in potting soil or water.

Special needs Remove flowers as they fade to prolong the flowering period. In fall, when flowering is over, cut stems back close to the base.

Campanula isophylla

Canna 'Wyoming'

Capsicum annuum

CANNACEAE
Canna

Canna lilies have tall, erect flower spikes, carrying exotic blooms in a variety of colors, from white to red, through yellow and pink, which can also be plain, striped, or spotted. They make a cheerful addition to an indoor display, particularly in a warm position. The leaves, arising from the rhizomatous root system, are long, straplike, and range from gray and leathery to chocolate-red and thin. *C.* 'Wyoming' has brownish-purple leaves and stunning orange flowers. *C.* 'Black Knight' has brown leaves and red flowers. *C.* 'Lucifer' is a dwarf variety bearing crimson flowers with yellow borders. These are hybrids of garden origin whose parents are natives of the West Indies and Central America.

Size Height 2–4 ft. (60–120 cm).
Light Indirect sunlight with some direct sunlight.
Temperature Keep warm; 70–80°F (21–25°C).
Moisture Keep thoroughly moist in spring and fall. Reduce watering to a minimum in winter, to prevent the soil from drying out severely.
Feeding Give standard liquid fertilizer every two weeks from summer until fall.
Propagation Division of rhizomes in spring.
Special needs If the temperature is very high, mist regularly.

SOLANACEAE
Capsicum annuum

Known as **ornamental pepper**, from tropical America, this is among the few indoor plants grown for its fruits rather than flowers or leaves. The tiny, white flowers in summer or fall are followed by the fruits, which are green, turning to orange, red, or purple over a period of weeks as they ripen. There are a various different fruit shapes, including the **cherry pepper**, which is ball-shaped, and the **cone pepper**, which is conical and upright. Both are popular at Christmas.
Size Height 1 ft. (30 cm).
Light Indirect sunlight with some direct sunlight.
Temperature Normal room.
Moisture Keep thoroughly moist at all times.
Feeding Give standard liquid fertilizer every two weeks.
Propagation Sow seed in early spring.
Special needs Wash hands thoroughly after touching the fruit — these relatives of chili and cayenne peppers are extremely hot and the juice will sting the eyes and mouth.

Chaemaedorea elegans see *Palmlike Plants* p.138

LILIACEAE (ANTHERICACEAE)
Chlorophytum comosum

When set in a hanging basket or on a pedestal where it can grow unhindered, the **spider plant** or **ribbon plant** from South Africa makes a dramatic trailing plant. As well as having long, curved, straplike leaves, the display is enhanced by long, arching stems bearing tiny white flowers or the numerous small plantlets. Attractive cultivars include: *C.c.* 'Picturatum,' with a yellow central stripe; *C.c.* 'Variegatum,' which is green at the center and white or cream at the edges; and *C.c.* 'Vittatum,' which has green leaves with a broad white stripe running lengthwise down the center.

Size Spread to 2 ft. (60 cm).
Light Indirect sunlight.
Temperature Normal room.
Moisture Keep the soil mix thoroughly moist from spring to fall; slightly drier in winter.
Feeding Feed with standard liquid fertilizer every two weeks from spring to fall.
Propagation Young plantlets can be rooted into water or soil before or after being detached from the parent. If they are in water, pot up as soon as the roots are $^3/_4$ in. (2 cm) long.
Special needs If the plant is allowed to dry out, it will develop permanent brown tips on the leaves.

Chrysalidocarpus lutescens see *Palmlike Plants* p.138

VITACAEAE
Cissus
Cissus is a genus of some 350 climbers, shrubs, and evergreen perennials originating in tropical and subtropical regions, so the species grown for cooler climates are ideally suited to growing indoors or in a frost-free conservatory. The climbers share characteristics with their near relative, the grape, in that they have attractive leaves and twining tendrils to support themselves as they grow.

C. antarctica
The long trailing stems of the **kangaroo vine** from Australasia allow the plant to be used in a wide variety of ways, from being trained up a wall or trellis to cascading out of a large hanging basket. The glossy, heart-shaped leaves are 3–4 in. (7–10 cm) long, toothed, and pointed, and produced on red-tinted petioles. *C.a.* 'Minima' is a dwarf, slow-growing form with spreading branches.
Size Height to 10 ft. (3 m).

Light Indirect sunlight.
Temperature Normal room.
Moisture Keep the potting soil just moist from spring to fall. In winter, apply only enough water to prevent drying out.
Feeding Feed standard liquid fertilizer every two weeks from spring until fall.
Propagation Take tip cuttings, 4–6 in. (10–15 cm) long, in spring. Use rooting hormone.
Special needs Regularly pinching out the growing tips will produce a more bushy plant.

C. rhombifolia
From tropical America, **grape ivy** or **Venezuela treebine** is a quick-growing vine with lush, glossy foliage on trailing stems that support themselves by forked tendrils. It makes a striking feature grown up a wall or trellis or trailed from a hanging basket. The glossy, toothed leaves consist of three leaflets shaped like rhomboids. Fine white hairs cover the new growth, giving it a silvery sheen; older leaves are covered underneath with fine brown hairs. *C.r.* 'Ellen Danica' has more deeply lobed leaflets.
Size Height to 10 ft. (3 m).
Light Indirect sunlight.
Temperature Normal room.
Moisture Keep the soil just moist from spring to fall. In winter, apply

only enough water to prevent the plant from drying out.
Feeding Use standard liquid fertilizer every two weeks from spring until fall.
Propagation Take tip cuttings, 4–6 in. (10–15 cm) long, in spring. Use rooting hormone.
Special needs Regularly pinch out the growing tips to produce a more bushy plant.

Chlorophytum comosum

Cissus rhombifolia

RUTACEAE
Citrus

The citrus genus includes some interesting indoor plants, which produce flowers and fruit intermittently all year when conditions are right. They have glossy, deep green foliage, spiny stems, and white, fragrant flowers. Each fruit ripens slowly from green to orange or yellow, so that there will be fruit of each color on the plant at the same time. *C. limon*, from Southeast Asia and better known as **lemon**, will ultimately grow into a small tree up to 6 ft. (2 m) high, but while small, makes an attractive indoor plant. Its flowers are tinged purple. To grow edible fruit, choose a named variety. *C.l.* 'Variegata' has leaves variegated cream and fruit striped green, becoming fully yellow. x *Citrofortunella microcarpa* (formerly *Citrus mitis*) is an ornamental orange, called **calamondin orange**, which produces fruits when still quite young. Its unripe green fruits, although bitter, are useful for making marmalade. x *C.m.* 'Tiger' has leaves edged and streaked with white.
Size Height 4 ft. (1.2 m).
Light Direct sunlight.
Temperature Normal room; winter minimum 50°F (10°C).
Moisture Keep moist from spring to fall. In winter, apply enough water to prevent the soil from drying out.
Feeding Provide with standard liquid tomato fertilizer every two weeks from spring through to fall.
Propagation Take 4 in. (10 cm) tip cuttings, preferably semiripe with a heel, in spring or summer, and dip in hormone rooting powder. Seed will take longer to grow to flowering size.
Special needs Increase humidity by placing the pot on a tray of moist pebbles. In warm regions, the plants can be placed outdoors in summer. Pinch out the growing tips at regular intervals to produce bushy growth.

VERBENACEAE
Clerodendrum thomsoniae

This vigorous, twining shrub is from tropical West Africa and is commonly called **bleeding-heart** vine or **glory bower**. It has long, weak stems that rapidly become straggly if not trained against a support or pinched regularly to make the plant more bushy. The large, coarse leaves are heart-shaped and dark green with pronounced, paler veins. Clusters of up to 20 flowers are produced in summer, each consisting of a white, bell-shaped calyx over a red, star-shaped corolla.
Size Height to 10 ft. (3 m).
Light Indirect sunlight.
Temperature Normal room; cooler in winter at 50–55°F (10–12°C).
Moisture Keep thoroughly moist from spring to fall. In winter, apply only enough water to prevent the soil from drying out.
Feeding Provide standard liquid fertilizer every two weeks from spring through to fall.
Propagation Take tip cuttings 4–6 in. (10–15 cm) long in spring; use hormone rooting powder. Keep enclosed in a plastic bag or heated propagator at a temperature of 70°F (21°C). Rooting will take 4–6 weeks.
Special needs Extra humidity in summer will help flowering, so place the pot on a tray of moist pebbles. To keep the plant under control, cut the stems back by up to two-thirds as growth starts in spring.

AMARYLLIDACEAE
Clivia miniata

Dark green leaves that grow to 2 ft. (60 cm) long, make this native of South Africa an impressive indoor plant, even when it is not in flower. It needs space to grow and should not be moved while the flowers are developing or when they open. The 18 in. (45 cm) flower stalk appears in spring, carrying up to 15 broadly funnel-shaped flowers, 3 in. (7 cm) long and scarlet with a yellow throat.
Size Spread 3 ft. (90 cm).
Light Indirect sunlight.
Temperature Normal room. The plant must have a winter rest period of 6–8 weeks at 40–50°F (5–10°C).
Moisture Keep moist from spring to fall. In winter keep almost dry until the flower stalk appears, then increase watering.

x *Citrofortunella microcarpa*

Clerodendrum thomsoniae

Feeding Feed with standard liquid fertilizer every two weeks from when the flower stalk is 4–6 in. (10–15 cm) high until fall.

Propagation Divide, or detach offsets, immediately after flowering, taking care not to damage fleshy roots.

Special needs Not observing the winter rest period results in short, premature flowers or a shortened flower life. Clivias need repotting only when they have entirely filled their pot and the roots appear on the surface of the soil (every 3–4 years). Remove fruits because these will sap much of the plant's energy and reduce flowering the following year.

Cocos nucifera see *Palmlike Plants* p.138

EUPHORBIACEAE
Codiaeum variegatum var. pictum
Known as **croton** or **Joseph's coat**, this tropical shrub from the Pacific islands has upward-pointing leaves which are always glossy, leathery, and heavily patterned, but vary widely in their size, shape, and color. They can be long and thin, or broad and rounded, straight or twisted, entire or lobed. The color is in combinations of yellow, orange, pink, and red with dark green, becoming more pronounced with age, when small, inconspicuous cream flowers are also produced.

Size Height to 3 ft. (90 cm).

Light Indirect sunlight, some direct sunlight (not noon in summer)

Temperature Normal room.

Moisture Keep thoroughly moist from spring to fall. In winter, apply just enough water to prevent the soil drying out.

Feeding Feed standard liquid fertilizer every two weeks from spring through to fall.

Propagation Take tip cuttings in spring or summer; use rooting hormone.

Special needs Increase humidity by placing the pot on a tray of moist pebbles. The stems exude milky sap when cut, so if a large plant needs trimming back, do it in early spring and put a small piece of paper towel over the cut to absorb the latex.

Coleus blumei see *Solenostemon scutellarioides*

Clivia miniata

Codiaeum variegatum var. *pictum*

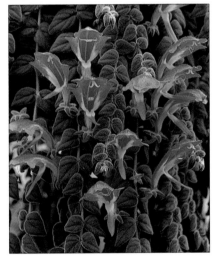

Columnea gloriosa 'Purpurea'

GESNERIACEAE
Columnea gloriosa
From Central America, the **goldfish plant** makes a dramatic specimen for a high position or hanging basket where the trailing stems can fully develop. In the right spot, the stems, which branch only at the lower ends, can reach to 3 ft. (90 cm) long. Oval, green leaves, up to $1^1/_4$ in. (3 cm) long, are carried in pairs and have a dense covering of red-purple hairs. The 3 in. (7 cm) flowers are borne singly and are scarlet with a yellow throat. *C.g.* 'Purpurea' has purple-red leaves and deep scarlet flowers.

Size Stems to 3 ft. (90 cm) long.

Light Indirect sunlight.

Temperature 65–85°F (18–30°C).

Moisture Water sparingly at all times, only enough to keep the soil barely moist.

Feeding Give liquid tomato fertilizer at quarter strength with every watering from spring to fall.

Propagation Take tip cuttings, 4 in. (10 cm) long, in spring.

Special needs Columneas are very susceptible to root rot, so both mature plants and cuttings need an open, free-draining soil mix. The foliage, however, needs high humidity, so mist regularly with warm water – cold water will mark the leaves.

Crassula ovata see *Succulents* p.136
Crocus see *Bulbs* p.129
Cryptanthus see *Bromeliads* p.122

Ctenanthe oppenheimiana

MARANTACEAE
Ctenanthe oppenheimiana

From East Brazil, ctenanthe is also known as the **never-never plant.** Grown for its rosettes of beautifully marked foliage, rather than its inconspicuous white flowers, it is robust and bushy with leathery, lance-shaped leaves up to 18 in. (45 cm) long and dark green with silvery gray feathering above and wine-red to purple below. Closely related to maranta and calathea, which are also grown for their leaves, it is more compact in habit. *C.o.* 'Tricolor' has leaves blotched with cream.

Size Height to 3 ft. (90 cm).
Light Indirect sunlight.
Temperature Normal room.
Moisture Keep moist from spring to fall. In winter, apply water only to prevent soil from drying out.
Feeding Apply standard liquid fertilizer every two weeks from spring through to fall.
Propagation Remove basal offsets from the rhizomatous roots (detach them as close to the parent plant as possible) or take tip cuttings of 3–4 leaves. With tip cuttings, use hormone rooting preparation and bottom heat if possible.
Special needs To increase humidity, place pot on a tray of moist pebbles.

PRIMULACEAE
Cyclamen persicum

This plant, known as the **florist's cyclamen,** comes in a variety of shapes and sizes and is originally from the Mediterranean. The nodding flowers can be ruffled, twisted, or speckled. They are sometimes scented and may be in shades of pure white to purple, through a range of reds and pinks. The fleshy leaves can be large or tiny, and usually have silver patterning. Often seen at Christmas, cyclamen flowers should last several weeks, but do not buy plants from an outdoor vendor, because being chilled will shorten their flowering period.

Size Height 4–8 in. (10–20 cm).
Light Cool light.
Temperature Keep cool; 55–65°F (12–18°C).
Moisture Keep the soil moist. Always water from below, as the tuber is only half buried in the potting soil and watering from above may cause it to rot.
Feeding Give standard liquid fertilizer every two weeks.
Propagation Small plants can be raised from seed, but these cyclamen are usually bought as mature flowering plants.
Special needs Hygiene is critical to prevent gray mold, so as flowers fade or leaves die, remove them immediately by twisting them off as close as possible to the base.

Cymbidium see *Orchids* p.128

CYPERACEAE
Cyperus

These are grasslike plants, originating in tropical, subtropical, and temperate regions of the world, but almost always in a wet habitat. Cyperus species have lush foliage and dramatic, umbrella-shaped flowerheads where leaflike bracts accompany the spiky flowers. They need moist, humid conditions to thrive and

Cyclamen persicum

are suited to positioning at the edge
of a pool in a warm conservatory,
where they can be kept thoroughly
moist. *C. albostriatus* is a thickly
tufted perennial plant from Southern
Africa which forms thin rhizomes as
it grows. The stems, up to 2 ft. (60
cm) high, are thin and topped with
up to 24 narrow, radiating bracts and
pale brown flowers. The narrow, pur-
ple-sheathed leaves form a cluster at
the base. *C.a.* 'Variegatus' has stems,
leaves, and bracts striped white.
C. involucratus, from Africa, is also
called **umbrella grass** and is a perennial tuft-forming plant with short
basal leaves. It grows to a height of
2-2¹/₂ ft. (60-75 cm) and produces yellow flowers in summer on top of long,
three-sided stems, surrounded by
12–28 long bracts arranged spirally
like the spokes of an umbrella.
C. papyrus, used for paper making
since ancient times, is also known as
papyrus or **Egyptian paper reed**. It
is a large, clump-forming plant from
Africa that needs plenty of space to
grow to full size of 10 ft. (3 m) or
more. It also needs a very moist environment and will thrive in boggy
conditions, although it should not be
completely submerged. The dark
green "leaves" at the top of the tall,
triangular stems are actually bracts
above which the flowers are carried in
grasslike clusters.
Size See individual species.
Light Direct or indirect sunlight.
Temperature Normal to warm; minimum 60°F (15°C).
Moisture Keep moist at all times.

Cyperus papyrus

Overwatering this plant is almost
impossible.
Feeding Fertilize with standard liquid fertilizer once a month, from
spring to fall.
Propagation Divide in spring.
Special needs The high requirement
for water and humidity can be
catered to by placing the pot in a tray
or saucer full of water. Dry air or drying out of the root ball will result in
brown tips on the bracts.

ARACEAE
Dieffenbachia seguine (syn. *D. picta*, *D. maculata*)
Grown primarily for its decorative
foliage, dieffenbachia or **dumb cane**,
from Central America, makes a striking feature plant, either on its own or
in a massed arrangement. The large,
downward-pointing leaves are soft,
fleshy, and marked with white or
cream. The thick, woody, unbranched
stem is inclined to become bare at the
base as the plant ages. *D.m.* 'Tropic

White' has large leaves blotched with
white. *D. m.* 'Veerie' has green-yellow
leaves with white blotches.
Size Height to 5 ft. (1.5 m).
Light Mainly indirect sunlight; direct
sunlight in winter.
Temperature Warm and humid;
minimum 60°F (15°C).
Moisture Keep moist at all times.
Feeding Give standard liquid fertilizer every two weeks from spring
through to fall.
Propagation Take tip cuttings,
4–6 in. (10–15 cm) long, in spring.
Dip them in rooting hormone and
keep warm (70°F/21°C) in a plastic
bag or heated propagator. Alternatively, take a 4 in. (10 cm) section of
main stem with a growth bud and lay
it horizontally on the potting soil,
then treat as for a tip cutting.
Special needs The common name is
derived from the effect of the poisonous sap on the mouth and tongue (it
causes painful swelling), so always
wash your hands thoroughly after
touching this plant.

Dieffenbachia seguine

DROSERACEAE
Dionaea muscipula

In its natural environment in south-eastern America, this carnivorous plant, called the **Venus fly trap**, supplements its nutrient intake by trapping insects with a fascinating mechanism. It grows as a low rosette of leaves with broad-winged, leafy stalks and two rounded, hinged blades that turn glossy, bright red in sunlight. The leaves, fringed with spines, have touch-sensitive hairs in the middle, so that when a fly touches, it triggers the mechanism to snap the leaves shut.

Size Height to 18 in. (45 cm) in flower.
Light Direct sunlight (not noon in summer).
Temperature Warm and humid.
Moisture Keep thoroughly moist.
Feeding Give extra flies or tiny pieces of meat occasionally.
Propagation Bought as small plants.
Special needs Not usually long-lived indoors, but interesting while it lasts.

Dizygotheca elegantissima see *Schefflera elegantissima*

AGAVACEAE
Dracaena

The dracaenas are shrubby plants, which often resemble palms with arching leaves and bare, woody stems. They are grown for their striking leaves, which are usually long and lance-shaped, and striped or blotched with white, cream, and/or red. Some mature dracaenas can grow to heights of 4 ft. (1.2 m) or more and are ideal within arrangements of other plants or as single specimens. *D. cincta* **'Tricolor'** comes from Africa and the variety 'Tricolor' is also known as **rainbow plant** because of its dramatic leaf coloration – green, striped cream, and edged red. As the plant ages, the lower leaves turn down and fall, leaving a tuft of leaves at the top of a gradually lengthening, thin, bare stem. It will ultimately reach a height of about 5 ft. (1.5 m). The plants in *D. fragrans* **Deremensis Group** have long, arching, lance-shaped leaves overlapping each other all the way up and around the stem. They are slow-growing, and ultimately reach 4 ft. (1.2 m) or more

high. The species originates in tropical East Africa. Recommended varieties: *D.f.* 'Lemon Lime,' with leaves of lime-green with pale yellow edges and a central stripe; *D.f.* 'Warneckei,' with green leaves that have two white stripes near the edge; and *D. f.* 'Yellow Stripe,' which has green leaves with rich yellow edges and a central stripe. There is some confusion over the naming of different plants within the *Dracaena* genus and *D. marginata* **'Colorama'** bears a strong resemblance to *D. cincta* 'Tricolor,' differing in that the leaves are broadly red-edged. The species is from Africa. *D. reflexa* **'Variegata'** is also known as **song of India** and needs a warm position with high humidity to grow well. Originating from Madagascar and Mauritius, it is less woody and more graceful than most of its relatives and is beautifully marked with deep cream edges to the leaves.

Light Indirect sunlight.
Temperature Warm; minimum 65°F (18°C).
Moisture Keep thoroughly moist from spring to fall. In winter, apply only enough water to prevent the soil from drying out.
Feeding Give standard liquid fertilizer every two weeks from spring to fall.
Propagation Take tip cuttings, 4–6 in. (10–15 cm) long, from the soft basal shoots in spring or early summer. Alternatively, longer pieces of mature woody stem can be inserted upright (the same way up as they were growing originally) into pots

Dionaea muscipula

Dracaena fragrans 'Warneckei'

156

Dracaena fragrans Deremensis Group

Dracaena marginata 'Tricolor'

Elatostema repens var. *pulchrum*

of soil, providing an instant "tree" effect, or 2 in. (5 cm) pieces of mature stem, each with at least one growth bud (a slight swelling under the bark), can be laid horizontally onto the soil, with the bud facing up. **Special needs** High humidity is important, so place the pot on a tray of moist pebbles.

Echeveria agavoides see *Succulents* p.136
Echinocactus texensis see *Cacti* p.125

URTICACEAE
Elatostema repens var. *pulchrum*

A low, spreading plant, **rainbow vine** or **satin pellionia** from Vietnam is grown for its fleshy, purple-tinted stems and striking leaves, which are $^3/_4$–2 in. (2–5 cm) long, and emerald-green marked with a dull black-green along the midrib and veins above, light purple below. While small, it is a useful plant in a terrarium or bottle garden. It is also effective at the front of an arrangement to disguise the container and soften the outline, or in a hanging basket. As it grows, it will form roots wherever the stems are in contact with the soil.
Size Stems to 18 in. (45 cm) long.
Light Indirect sunlight.
Temperature Normal room all year; minimum 55°F (12°C).
Moisture Keep thoroughly moist

from spring to fall. In winter, apply only enough water to prevent the soil from drying out.
Feeding Give standard liquid fertilizer once a month during spring and summer.
Propagation Take tip cuttings in spring or summer. Lift layers at any time.
Special needs Mist occasionally in high temperatures, shelter from drafts, and do not allow direct sunlight to scorch the leaves.

ARACEAE
Epipremnum aureum

The angular stems of this woody vine from the Solomon Islands in the Pacific, which is also known as **devil's ivy** or **golden pothos**, can be trained to climb up a moist moss pole or cascade down from a high planter or hanging basket. They are striped with yellow or white, and have aerial roots. The heart-shaped leaves are large – 6–12 in. (15–30 cm) long – and are green with yellow or white stripes. Good varieties include: *E.a.* 'Marble Queen,' with white leafstalks bearing green leaves streaked white and moss-green, and white stems streaked with green, and *E.a.* 'Tricolor,' which has leaves boldly variegated with white and off-white stems and leafstalks.
Size Height 5 ft. (1.5 m) or more.
Light Indirect sunlight.
Temperature Keep warm; minimum

Epipremnum aureum

65°F (18°C).
Moisture Keep moist from spring to fall. In winter, apply only enough water to prevent the soil from drying out.
Feeding Provide standard liquid fertilizer every two weeks from spring to summer.
Propagation Take tip cuttings, 4 in. (10 cm) long, in spring or early summer.
Special needs To maintain high humidity, place the pot on a tray of moist pebbles. Overwatering will cause root rot, and drafts will damage the foliage. Too little light will eventually make the leaf colors revert to green.

EUPHORBIACEAE
Euphorbia pulcherrima

With its cheerful, brightly colored display, the **poinsettia** from Mexico has become an essential element of decoration at Christmas time. The long-lasting, scarlet, pink, or cream "flowers" are, in fact, large bracts surrounding tiny, short-lived, yellow true flowers. It is normal to discard the plant once the bracts fade, as bringing it back into color in subsequent years is not easy.

Size Height 12–18 in. (30–45 cm).
Light Indirect sunlight.
Temperature Normal room.
Moisture Water thoroughly, but allow to dry slightly before watering again.
Feeding Not necessary unless the plant is kept after the bracts fade.

Euphorbia pulcherrima

Eustoma grandiflorum

Propagation Take tip cuttings, 3 in. (7 cm) long, once growth starts in spring. The plant exudes an irritant milky latex from cut surfaces, so the cuttings should be sealed by placing them in water.
Special needs When purchasing a poinsettia, look for small, unopened flower buds in the center of the bracts, and ensure that it has been kept indoors (unless your climate is very hot, never buy one that has been placed outside for any length of time). The plant will only form flowers or colored bracts if it is lit for less than 12 hours per day from the autumnal equinox on. Ensure that the plant is not in a well-lit room from then until flowering begins.

GENTIANACEAE
Eustoma grandiflorum

The **prairie gentian** from the USA and Mexico is an upright annual or biennial, grown for its foliage and attractive flowers, which last well when cut. The pointed-oval, thinly fleshy leaves, 3 in. (8 cm) long, are gray-green and thickly covered with a fine, powdery, bluish bloom, which can be rubbed off with the fingers. The bell-shaped flowers are borne in summer on $2\frac{1}{2}$ in. (6 cm) stalks, either singly or in clusters. Each is satiny, $2–2\frac{1}{2}$ in. (5–6 cm) across, in white, blue, pink, or purple with a darker central patch, and the short tube is paler than the lobes. Smaller plants are now popular as pot plants.
Size Height 8 in.–2 ft. (20–60 cm).

Light Indirect sunlight.
Temperature Cool.
Moisture Keep moist from spring to fall. In winter, apply only enough water to prevent the plant drying out.
Feeding Use standard liquid fertilizer every two weeks from spring through to fall.
Propagation Sow seed in fall or late winter.
Special needs In milder areas, eustomas can be grown outdoors, otherwise, they will thrive in a cool conservatory. The plant will need supporting because its stems are not particularly strong.

GENTIANACEAE
Exacum affine

This short-lived perennial plant from South Yemen is generally treated as an annual and discarded after flowering. Also called **Persian violet** or **German violet**, it has glossy green leaves and an abundance of fragrant, sky-blue to pale violet or rich purple flowers with prominent, golden stamens. If the plant is in bud when bought, it will flower throughout summer and fall. *E.a.* 'Blue Gem' is compact (to 8 in./20 cm) with lavender-blue flowers.
Size Height 1 ft. (30 cm).
Light Indirect sunlight.
Temperature Normal room, but avoid drafts.
Moisture Keep thoroughly moist.
Feeding Use standard liquid fertilizer every two weeks while the plant is in flower.
Propagation Sow seed in late summer for the following year, or in spring for a slightly later flowering in the same year.
Special needs Pick off fading flowers to extend the flowering period. Exacums like high humidity, so place the pot on a tray of moist pebbles.

GRAMINAE
Fargesia nitida

This pretty, slow-growing bamboo, also called **fountain bamboo**, will gradually form a dense thicket of purple-green canes, each marked with powdery white under the leaf nodes. The canes do not branch until they are in their second year of growth, when the upper part of the

Exacum affine 'Blue Gem'

stems produces a cluster of purple branchlets. Narrow, tapering, mid-green leaves are produced in abundance on all stems. This plant will eventually grow too high to be considered as a long-term houseplant, but there are dwarf forms available, which are generally labeled miniature bamboo or house bamboo.

Size Height 6–15 ft. (2–5 m) Dwarf forms from 1 ft (30 cm).

Light Indirect sunlight.

Temperature Tolerates a wide range.

Moisture Keep moist at all times.

Feeding Give standard liquid fertilizer once a month from spring through to fall.

Propagation Divide clumps or cuttings of rhizomes in spring.

Special needs This is a hardy bamboo in all but the coldest of regions, so it may be planted outdoors once it has outgrown its position inside.

x *Fatshedera lizei*

ARALIACEAE
x *Fatshedera lizei*

This is the offspring of a breeding cross between *Fatsia japonica* 'Moseri' and *Hedera hibernica*, two distinct genera within the same plant family. Also called **ivy tree**, it is an attractive, evergreen plant bearing characteristics from both parents and inheriting their ease of cultivation. From fatsia comes the wide-spreading glossy leaves, from hedera the sprawling stems, which can be trained up canes or pinched to produce a more bushy effect. The young leaves are covered in rust-colored hairs. Cultivars include: x *F.l.* 'Annemieke' with leaves marked yellow; x *F.l.* 'Pia,' with wavy green leaves; and x *F.l.* 'Variegata,' which has white marks on the leaves.

Size Height 4 ft. (1.2 m).

Light Cool light. Variegated forms need more light than green ones.

Temperature Keep variegated forms above 60°F (15°C) at all times; green forms tolerate a much cooler position, even an unheated conservatory.

Moisture Keep moist from spring to fall. Apply only enough water in winter to prevent the soil mix from drying out.

Feeding Apply standard liquid fertilizer every two weeks in spring and summer.

Propagation Take tip cuttings, 4 in. (10 cm) long, or stem cuttings, 2 in. (5 cm) long, in spring or summer. Dip in rooting hormone, enclose in a plastic bag, and then put in a warm, bright place.

Special needs In warmer positions, increase humidity by placing the pot on a tray of moist pebbles

ARALIACEAE
Fatsia japonica

This is a wide-spreading, evergreen shrub from Japan (hence the common name, **Japanese fatsia**) and it can be grown either indoors or out. It has large, leathery, many-fingered leaves that leave prominent scars on the woody stem as they fall. Making an impressive specimen plant, it grows quickly and needs plenty of room. The foliage tends to be a lighter color when grown indoors; the white flowers are only produced on a mature plant that is kept in cool conditions.

Size Height 5 ft. (1.5 m) high in 2–3 years.

Light Cool light.

Temperature Preferably cool; below 60°F (15°C) in summer and below 45°F (7°C) in winter.

Moisture Keep thoroughly moist from spring to fall and just moist during winter.

Fatsia japonica

Feeding Apply standard liquid fertilizer every two weeks from spring through to fall.

Propagation Take stem cuttings, 2 in. (5 cm) long, in spring or summer. Remove the lower leaves and dip the end in rooting hormone. Enclose in a plastic bag or propagator at a temperature of around 60°F (15°C) in a well-lit position.

Special needs Large plants can be pruned hard in spring to remove up to half the growth.

MORACEAE
Ficus

The ficus (or fig) genus encompasses some 800 species of trees (many of which contain a milky latex), shrubs, and woody root-climbing or strangling vines. They originate in tropical and subtropical areas and make good indoor plants because they are not particularly demanding. The leaves are usually entire (one whole shape, with no lobes or teeth), and the tiny flowers are borne within a hollow, fleshy receptacle (a syconium or fig). They are pollinated by insects entering the receptacle through a minute opening in the end.

F. benjamina

Also called the **weeping fig**, this is a graceful tree originating in countries from southeast Asia to the southwest Pacific. It will grow to 6 ft. (1.8 m) or more and makes a beautiful specimen tree, or can be used as a centerpiece for a mixed planting. The branches droop downward as they grow, dripping with shiny, thinly leathery leaves, which change from mid- to dark green as they age. The little figs are borne in pairs and, if pollinated, mature to orange-red, scarlet, and finally purplish black.
Size Height 6 ft. (1.8 m).
Light Partial shade.
Temperature Normal warm room.
Moisture Keep just moist at all times.

Feeding Provide standard liquid fertilizer every two weeks in spring and summer.
Propagation Take tip cuttings, 4 in. (10 cm) long, in spring. The cutting will root better if the bottom $\frac{1}{2}$ in. (1 cm) has become light brown and woody. To prevent the latex forming a cap on the base of the cutting, strip the leaves from the lower third and place in water for 30 minutes. Remove, shake off the water, and dip the cut surface only in rooting hormone, then insert into potting soil and seal into a plastic bag in a bright place, out of direct sun.
Special needs All fig species will benefit from having their leaves cleaned at intervals to remove dust. Be careful not to damage young foliage because any marks inflicted will never disappear. Wounds to most figs result in the oozing of milky latex, often in large quantities. Applying powdered charcoal, a cotton ball, or a piece of paper towel to the wound will help the latex coagulate.

F. binnendijkii (syn. F. longifolia)
This fig grows into an attractive, glossy shrub or small tree, making it both an attractive feature plant or an ideal foil in a mixed arrangement. Known as the **narrow-leaf fig**, it has graceful, drooping, pointed-tipped foliage, which changes size and shape as the plant ages. When young, the

leaves are long and lance-shaped (8 x $1\frac{1}{2}$ in./20 x 4 cm) developing a more oblong shape in a mature specimen (9 x 3–3.5 cm/$3\frac{1}{2}$ x $1\frac{1}{4}$–$1\frac{1}{2}$ in.). The egg-shaped figs, $\frac{1}{2}$ in. (10 mm) across, are borne singly or in pairs. This species originates in areas from southeast Asia to the Philippines.
Size Height 6 ft. (1.8 m).
For cultivation see *F. benjamina*.
Propagation Take tip cuttings, 4 in. (10 cm) long, in spring. The cutting will root better if the bottom 1/2 in. (1 cm) has become light brown and woody. To prevent latex forming a cap on the base of the cutting, strip the leaves from the lower third and place in water for 30 minutes. Remove, shake off water, and dip the cut surface only in rooting hormone, then insert in soil and seal in a plastic bag in a bright place, out of direct sun.

F. deltoidea (syn. F.d. var. diversifolia)
This twiggy shrub from southern Thailand to Borneo has small, rounded-triangular leaves that are bright green on top and olive-brown beneath. Known as the **mistletoe fig**, from a young age it regularly produces pairs of inedible, round, pea-size, yellow fruit in the leaf axils.
Size Height 3 ft. (90 cm).
For cultivation and propagation see *F. benjamina*.

Ficus benjamina

Ficus binnendijkii

Ficus deltoidea

Ficus elastica 'Doescheri'

Ficus pumila 'Variegata'

Fittonia albivenis Verschaffeltii Group

F. elastica

The original **rubber plant**, which hails from the eastern Himalayas to Java, has been popular as an indoor plant for many years, although it has now been largely superseded by newer cultivars with a more compact habit or with colored leaf markings. The glossy leaves are large and leathery with prominent midribs and pointed tips. They arise from a single tall stem that rarely produces sideshoots, unless the top is removed. Cultivars include: *F.e.* 'Decora,' which bears broad, shiny leaves with white midribs; *F.e.* 'Doescheri,' with green, gray-green, creamy yellow, or white on its leaves; *F.e.* 'Tricolor,' whose gray-green leaves are variegated pink and cream; and *F.e.* 'Variegata,' which has pale green leaves with a white or yellow margin.
Size Height $6^{1}/_{2}$ ft. (2 m).
For cultivation see *F. benjamina*.
Propagation Take 3–4 in. (7–10 cm) stem cuttings with two nodes, remove the lower leaf, and roll up the top leaf, upper surface facing out, and secure with a rubber band to form a tube. To prevent the latex forming a cap on the base of the cutting, place in water for 30 minutes. Remove, shake off the water, and then dip the cut surface only in rooting hormone. Support the cutting with a short cane passing down through the rolled leaf, then insert into potting soil and seal into a

plastic bag in a bright place, out of direct sun. Alternatively, this plant can be air-layered.

F. pumila

This plant from eastern Asia is a complete contrast to the taller treelike figs in that it is a low-growing, small-leaved trailer or climber; hence its common name, **creeping fig**. It has small, slightly puckered, green leaves and many aerial roots; these will root easily into a moist surface such as a moss pole, but it is equally attractive as a trailing plant or as ground cover. Varieties include the small, slender, slow-growing *F.p.* 'Minima' and the vigorous *F.p.* 'Variegata' whose leaves are marbled with white or cream.
Size Height to 2 ft. (60 cm) – named varieties are smaller.
For cultivation see *F. benjamina*.
Propagation Take tip cuttings, to 4 in. (10 cm) long, in spring or summer. Roots easily, even in water. Pot several rooted cuttings together to give an instant bushy effect.

ACANTHACEAE
Fittonia albivenis
Verschaffeltii Group

Fittonias are creeping, stem-rooting, evergreen plants that grow naturally in the warm, moist conditions of the tropical rain forests of Peru. Commonly known as the **mosaic plant**, this group

comprises attractive, small plants that have downy, deep olive-green leaves, $2^{1}/_{2}$–4 in. (6–10 cm) long, with a dense network of rose-pink veins. The leaves are oval and are carried on stems 3 in. (8 cm) long. The white flowers are borne in slender 4-angled spikes, up to 3 in. (8 cm) long, but they are largely concealed by bracts. *F.a.* Argyroneura Group, known as **silver net plant**, has slightly larger leaves that are emerald-green, closely net-veined with silver-white.
Size Height 6 in. (15 cm).
Light Partial shade.
Temperature Preferably a constant 65°F (18°C).
Moisture Careful watering is vital: too much and the roots will rot; too little and the leaves will shrivel and drop. Keep barely moist at all times.
Feeding Provide half-strength liquid fertilizer every two weeks in spring and summer.
Propagation Take 2 in. (5 cm) tip cuttings in spring, or layer by placing the pot inside a larger one filled with soil mix. Pin the tip of a shoot down onto the soil with a wire hoop until it roots, then gently sever it from the parent and pot it up.
Special needs Fittonias are ideally suited to planting in a bottle garden or terrarium as they need high humidity to really grow well.

Freesia see *Bulbs* p.129

Gardenia augusta 'Veitchiana'

Gerbera jamesonii

RUBIACEAE
Gardenia augusta (syn. G. jasminoides)

The gardenia is a bushy, evergreen, acid-loving shrub from Japan, China, and Taiwan grown for its attractive, waxy flowers which are up to 3 in. (7 cm) across, white, and intensely fragrant. They are usually double, but also occur as semidouble. The leaves are 2–4 in. (5–10 cm) long, lance-shaped, glossy dark green, and leathery. *G.a.* 'Radicans Variegata' has a miniature, mound-forming habit, small white flowers, and glossy leaves tinted gray and edged white. *G.a.* 'Veitchiana' is upright and compact with bright green leaves and small, pure white, fully double, very fragrant flowers.

Size Height 18 in. (45 cm).
Light Indirect sunlight.
Temperature While flower buds are forming, a constant, draft-free 63°F (17°C) is needed to prevent bud loss. Otherwise, keep at normal room temperature.
Moisture Keep moist from spring to fall using soft water or rainwater. During the winter, apply only enough water to prevent the soil drying out.
Feeding Use acid fertilizer every two weeks from spring to fall.
Propagation Take 3 in. (7 cm) tip cuttings in spring, dip in rooting hormone, and push into pots of an acidic, peat moss-enriched soil. Cover, and give bottom heat, if possible, and place in a bright position, out of direct sun.
Special needs High humidity is vital while the flower buds are forming, so place the pot on a tray of moist pebbles and mist frequently. Prune after flowering, to an outward-facing bud.

ASTERACEAE
Gerbera jamesonii

There are a wide range of seed selections of this popular flowering pot plant, known as **Transvaal daisy** or **Barberton daisy** and originating from South Africa. They occur in a range of heights, and flowers can be single or double in colors from red to orange, yellow, pink, and white. The flowers appear from late spring to late summer, from rosettes of hairy, lobed, mid-green leaves. For single flowers choose 'California Mixed,' tall and multicolored, or 'Parade Mixed,' which is shorter with early, long-lasting flowers. Double flowered varieties include: 'Festival Mixture,' with early flowers; 'Fantasia Double Strain,' whose flowers, to 5 in. (12 cm) across, have a quilled center and 'Sunburst Mixture,' which has large flowers to 4 in. (10 cm) across.

Size Height 1–2 ft. (30–60 cm), depending on variety.
Light Indirect sunlight with some direct sunlight, not noon in summer.
Temperature Normal room.
Moisture Keep moist at all times.
Feeding Give standard liquid fertilizer every two weeks.
Propagation Sow seed in spring.
Special needs The taller strains need staking to support the weight of the flower head. Discard after flowering.

LILIACEAE (COLCHICACEAE)
Gloriosa superba 'Rothschildiana'

A tuberous perennial, the **glory lily** from tropical Africa and Asia climbs using tendrils at the tips of the leaves. Each tuber produces 1–4 stems, 4 ft. (1.2 m) or more in length. The flowers are produced in midsummer and have strongly swept-back petals of scarlet or ruby red with a yellow base.

Size Height 4 ft. (1.2 m).
Light Indirect sunlight with some direct sunlight, but not at noon in summer.
Temperature Normal room.
Moisture Keep thoroughly moist from spring to fall.
Feeding Use standard liquid fertilizer every two weeks in spring and summer.
Propagation Plant new tubers upright in a pot, with the tip 1 in. (2.5 cm) below the surface. As the plant

matures, offsets can be severed and potted separately in spring.

Special needs The stems are weak and need support. As the flower buds start to swell, keep the plant warm and well watered, and mist in high temperatures. In winter, store the tuber in the pot in a frost-free position and keep the soil barely moist.

PROTEACEAE
Grevillea robusta

This native of eastern Australia has graceful, 1 ft. (30 cm) long, arching foliage making it an ideal mixer for a large arrangement. The leaves are bronze to dark green, ferny, and covered on the underside with silky hairs, hence the common name, **silky oak**. As a young plant it makes a good subject for a table centerpiece, quickly growing to 1 ft. (30 cm) in its first year; after 4–5 years it may be up to 6 ft. (2 m), making it more useful in a conservatory or on a large porch.

Size Height to 6½ ft. (2 m).
Light Direct sunlight, except at noon in summer.
Temperature Tolerates a wide range; winter minimum 65°F (18°C).
Moisture Keep moist from spring to fall, barely moist in winter.
Feeding Apply standard liquid fertilizer every two weeks in spring and summer.
Propagation Sow seed in spring or summer in an acidic, peat moss-enriched soil. Position in a bright spot, out of direct sun, at a temperature of 55–60°F (12–15°C).
Special needs The leaves tend to lose their ferny appearance as the plant ages, so it may be better to start again with a young plant after 3–4 years.

Guzmania lingulata see *Bromeliads* p.122
Hatiora gaertneri see *Cacti* p.125
Haworthia margaritifera see *Succulents* p.136

ARALIACEAE
Hedera

Ivies are evergreen, woody-stemmed climbers or creeping plants found all over the world. They are unusual in that their juvenile foliage is different to the mature leaves in shape and often also color. The juvenile stage is self-clinging by means of aerial roots, but these disappear in older stems. The flowers are borne in clusters, followed by black, cream, yellow, or orange fruits. **H. canariensis** from Europe is a vigorous, large-leaved ivy that is also called **Algerian ivy** or **Canary Island ivy**. Up to 6½ ft. (2 m) high, it thrives in cooler positions indoors and is useful for climbing, trailing, for weaving around posts or bannisters, or as a ground cover. The stems and undersides of young leaves are covered with small red hairs, and until the plant reaches its adult phase (when the leaves change shape and texture), they are lobed, thick, matte, and leathery. *H.c.* 'Gloire de Marengo' has light green leaves edged and splashed creamy white. **H. helix** is the best-known of all the ivies, with distinctively shaped, 3–5-lobed leaves. Known as **English ivy,** from Europe, Scandinavia, and Russia, it is a fully hardy bushy, densely-leaved plant, ideal for trailing and ground cover. Within the grouping, there are many variations in coloring and leaf shape; for indoors the less vigorous, decorative cultivars are most suitable. The stems are stiff, but only self-supporting where the aerial roots can grip. They branch regularly, so the foliage fans out as it grows, and can be used to trail from a shelf or from the front of a container.

Size Height 3–6½ ft. (1–2 m)
Light Indirect sunlight.

Temperature Tolerates a wide range.
Moisture Keep moist from spring to fall. In winter, apply only enough water to prevent drying out.
Feeding Give standard liquid fertilizer every two weeks from spring through to fall.
Propagation Layer adventitious roots, which are produced at leaf nodes along each stem, or take tip cuttings and root in water or soil.
Special needs In high temperatures, increase the humidity by misting or placing the pot on a tray of moist pebbles. Variegated plants will lose their leaf markings if they are placed in a position that is too dark.

Hedera canariensis 'Gloire de Marengo'

Hedera helix

Hibiscus rosa-sinensis

Hoya lanceolata subsp. *bella*

Feeding Give high potash liquid fertilizer (tomato fertilizer) every two weeks from spring to summer, once a month in fall.
Propagation Take 4 in. (10 cm) tip or heel cuttings in spring.
Special needs If it begins to outgrow its position, it can be pruned hard in early spring.

Hippeastrum see *Bulbs* p.129
Howea fosteriana see *Palmlike Plants* p.138

ASCLEPIADACEAE
Hoya lanceolata subsp. *bella*

A trailing plant with thick, fleshy leaves and fragrant flowers, the **miniature wax plant** from the Himalayas to northern Burma, looks wonderful in a hanging basket where the scent and the detail of the flowers can be appreciated. The stems are initially upright, arching only as they grow longer, and the dull green leaves are borne in pairs. The star-shaped flowers appear in clusters of up to 10, with waxy, white outer "petals" and a purple-red center. These are produced intermittently throughout the summer and fall. Hoyas benefit from the extra humidity of a kitchen or bathroom, as long as it is a warm and well-lit position.
Size Stems can reach 18 in. (45 cm) long.
Light Indirect sunlight, with some direct sunlight.
Temperature Normal room.
Moisture Keep moist from spring to fall. In winter, apply only enough water to prevent the soil mix from drying out.
Feeding Give a high potash fertilizer (tomato fertilizer) every two weeks from spring to fall.
Propagation Take 3 in. (7 cm) tip cuttings in spring or summer and group 3–5 to a pot.
Special needs The plant exudes a milky latex when the stem is cut, although loss should not be excessive. Do not repot until absolutely necessary, and do not disturb once the flower buds begin to swell or remove the flower spur (as the next flowers will also arise here). Allow the flowers to fall naturally.

MALVACEAE
Hibiscus rosa-sinensis

From tropical Asia, this is one of the few flowering plants that really enjoys a sunny windowsill. Known as **Rose of China** or **Chinese hibiscus**, it is a long-lived shrub, even indoors, and with care will last up to 20 years. The leaves are large and glossy, but the main attraction is the profusion of 4–5 in. (10–12 cm) flowers, produced mainly in spring and summer, although more can appear throughout the year if the plant is growing well. They vary in color, but are chiefly mid- to deep red with a long, prominent, central column.
Size Height $6^{1}/_{2}$ ft. (2 m).
Light Direct sunlight, except noon in summer.
Temperature Normal room; winter minimum 55°F (12°C).
Moisture Keep moist from spring to fall. In winter, apply only enough water to prevent the soil mix from drying out.

Hyacinthus see *Bulbs* p.129

HYDRANGACEAE
Hydrangea macrophylla
The varieties grown for indoors are the **mop-headed hydrangeas** from Japan, as these tolerate being under cover. To grow well, they need cool, light, and airy conditions; they are well-suited to growing in a cool conservatory. They form short, woody shrubs bearing large, oval leaves. The flowers are green in bud, opening blue, red, pink, or white in a rounded cluster. The blues need to be kept in an acid soil mix or they change color to pink or red. They are ideal for use in a large container, because they will flower year after year. Once they have outgrown their allotted space, they can be planted outdoors.
Size Height 2 ft. (60 cm).
Light Indirect sunlight.
Temperature Cool; preferably below 60°F (15°C).
Moisture Keep thoroughly moist from spring to fall.
Feeding Provide standard liquid fertilizer every two weeks.
Propagation Only really viable on a plant for outdoors. Take 4 in. (10 cm) tip cuttings in spring or summer.
Special needs After flowering, either discard the hydrangea or plant it outside, as it is unlikely to bloom indoors a second time.

ACANTHACEAE
Hypoestes phyllostachya
From South Africa, the **polka dot plant** is small and shrublike. It is usually grown for a year for its foliage and then discarded as it becomes too tall and woody. When it is young, the foliage is bushy and the leaves are dark or olive-green, conspicuously spotted with pink. Small, lilac-colored flowers may be produced in spring; these will take energy from the leaves so may be pinched out. These can be bought as quite tiny plants, ideal for planting into a bottle garden or terrarium. *H.p.* 'Splash' has larger, showier pink leaf spots.
Size Limit to 1 ft. (30 cm) by pinching, to keep the plant bushy.
Light Indirect sunlight.
Temperature Normal room.
Moisture Keep moist from spring to fall. In winter, apply only enough water to prevent the soil mix from drying out.
Feeding Give standard liquid fertilizer every two weeks from spring through to fall.
Propagation Sow seed in spring, or take 4 in. (10 cm) tip cuttings in spring or summer.
Special needs Too little light will eventually cause the pink markings to become green.

BALSAMINACEAE
Impatiens New Guinea Hybrids
Larger than the traditional busy lizzy and almost shrubby in habit, the dramatic **New Guinea or "busy lizzies"** bear the same characteristics of constant flowering from a young age, brittle, succulent-looking stems, and lush, fleshy foliage. However, they are more bold and colorful, with leaves that may be bright green, green splashed with yellow, or bronze-red. The flowers are larger, generally single, with a prominent spur, and come in many shades of red, pink, mauve, and white.
Size Height to 14 in. (35 cm).
Light Indirect sunlight.
Temperature Normal room.
Moisture Keep moist from spring to fall. In winter, apply only enough water to prevent the soil mix from drying out.
Feeding Use standard liquid fertilizer every two weeks from spring to fall.
Propagation Take 4 in. (10 cm) tip cuttings in spring or summer, and root in water or soil.
Special needs A position that is too warm will cause rapid wilting, so place pots on a tray of moist pebbles to increase humidity.

Hydrangea macrophylla

Hypoestes phyllostachya

Impatiens New Guinea Hybrids

Jasminum polyanthum

OLEACEAE
Jasminum polyanthum

A graceful, but vigorous climber, which branches profusely as it ages, **jasmine** is easily trained. It will thrive in a pot, where it can be grown around a hoop or over a small trellis, or in a conservatory border, where it can be trained to cover a wall, larger trellis or arch. The heavily-scented, tubular flowers are produced in clusters in winter and spring, and are pink on the outside and white within. The glossy green leaves have 5–7 small leaflets. Jasmine comes from southwest China.

Size Spread 10 ft. (3 m), or more if left unpruned.

Light Indirect sunlight, with some direct sunlight.

Temperature Cool. Stand outdoors in summer.

Moisture Keep moist at all times.

Feeding Apply standard liquid fertilizer once a month in summer and fall.

Propagation Take 4 in. (10 cm) tip or heel cuttings in summer.

Special needs Keep jasmine under control by regular pruning and pinching out growing tips to encourage a bushy plant. It can be pruned hard after flowering if necessary.

ACANTHACEAE
Justicia brandegeeana (syn. *Beloperone guttata*)

This is a shrubby plant from Mexico. The common name **shrimp plant** comes from the arching, 4 in. (10 cm) long, shrimplike flowers, which are produced almost all year round. They are composed of many overlapping bracts in shades of yellow to brown, brick-red or rose, surrounding a red- or purple-tipped, white inner corolla. The stems are upright and woody, and the oval leaves are slightly downy. *J.b.* 'Yellow Queen' has bright yellow bracts.

Size Height 2 ft. (60 cm).

Light Indirect sunlight, with some direct sunlight to ensure good color in the bracts. Cool light.

Temperature Normal to cool room.

Moisture Keep barely moist all year.

Feeding Use standard liquid fertilizer once a month in spring and summer.

Propagation Take tip cuttings, 2–3 in. (5–7 cm) long, in spring or summer.

Special needs Pinch regularly to encourage bushy growth, and cut the whole plant back by half in spring to prevent it becoming straggly.

Kalanchoe blossfeldiana see *Succulents* p.136

VERBENACEAE
Lantana camara

From tropical America, this small shrubby plant, known as **shrubby verbena** or **yellow sage**, has coarse-textured, dull, mid-green leaves and bristly stems, but erupts into color when it flowers throughout spring and summer. The numerous tubular flowers are produced in clusters on short stalks; they open progressively from the outside of the circle to the middle. An individual flower may be white, yellow, orange, pink, or red,

Justicia brandegeeana

usually with a brighter colored eye, but the color changes and darkens as the flower ages, so that each cluster contains flowers of several different shades at once. *L.c.* 'Brasier' has bright red flowers.

Size Height 18–24 in. (45–60 cm).

Light Some direct sunlight every day is essential throughout the year or the plant will not flower.

Temperature Normal room; winter minimum 55°F (12°C).

Moisture Keep thoroughly moist from spring to fall. In winter, apply only enough water to prevent the soil drying out.

Feeding Apply standard liquid fertilizer every two weeks in spring and summer.

Propagation Sow seed in spring, or take 4 in. (10 cm) tip cuttings in spring or summer.

Special needs Cut back after flowering. Young plants produce more flowers, so it is worth replacing the plant with cuttings every 2–3 years.

MYRTACEAE
Leptospermum scoparium
The **Manuka** or **tea tree** from New Zealand, Australia, and Tasmania, is a pretty-flowered, woody, evergreen shrub with glossy, aromatic leaves, which are covered with a sheen of fine, silky hairs as they emerge. The 5-petaled flowers are usually white, but see the cultivars below. It is almost hardy outdoors in milder temperate regions, and will thrive in a cool conservatory. Cultivars include: *L.s.* 'Burgundy Queen,' with deep red flowers; *L.s.* 'Cherry Brandy,' with cerise flowers and deep red-bronze leaves; and *L.s.* var. *incanum* 'Keatleyi,' which has red new shoots and large, silky, pink flowers.

Size Height up to 10 ft. (3 m).

Light Direct sunlight, but not noon sun in summer. Cool light.

Temperature Tolerates a wide range; winter minimum 40°F (4°C)

Moisture Keep moist from spring to fall, drier in winter.

Feeding Standard liquid fertilizer once a month in spring and summer.

Propagation Take 4 in. (10 cm) tip or heel cuttings in spring or summer.

Special needs Keep the plant bushy by pinching the tips of the shoots after flowering.

Lantana camara

Licuala grandis see *Palmlike Plants* p.138
Lilium see *Bulbs* p.129

PAPILIONACEAE
Lotus berthelotii
This perennial subshrub comes from the Canary Islands and the Cape Verde Islands and has brightly colored, beak- or clawlike flowers, giving rise to the common names of **coral gem**, **parrot's beak**, and **pelican's beak**. It has trailing, gray stems covered with deeply-divided, silvery gray leaves. The 1½ in. (4 cm) long flowers are produced in spring and summer, either singly or in pairs, and are orange-red to scarlet. Although hardy outdoors in some milder temperate regions, lotus may still need winter protection. It is a particularly good plant for a sunroom or conservatory, where it will thrive and where the beautiful flowers can be fully appreciated.

Size Stems to 2 ft. (60 cm).

Light Indirect sunlight, with some direct sunlight.

Temperature Tolerates a range of temperatures from spring to fall; winter minimum 50°F (10°C).

Moisture Keep moist from spring to fall, drier in winter.

Feeding Apply standard liquid

Lotus berthelotii

fertilizer once a month from spring through to fall.

Propagation Sow seed in spring at 65–75°F (18–23°C). Take 4 in. (10 cm) tip or heel cuttings in late spring or summer.

Special needs Cut back, if necessary, immediately after flowering. Some direct sunlight is essential to ripen the shoots ready for flowering.

Mammillaria zeilmanniana see *Cacti* p.125

Mandevilla x *amoena* 'Alice du Pont'

Maranta leuconeura

Temperature Normal room.
Moisture Keep moist from spring to fall. In winter, apply only enough water to prevent the soil mix from drying out.
Feeding Give standard liquid fertilizer every two weeks in spring and summer.
Propagation Take tip cuttings, 4 in. (10 cm) long, from new growth in spring. Root at 75–80°F (23–25°C).
Special needs Flowers are only produced on the current year's growth, so do not prune until fall, then cut back most of the newest shoots to encourage the production of more the following spring.

APOCYNACEAE
Mandevilla (syn. *Dipladenia*)
This genus of woody climbers, known as **Brazilian jasmine**, support themselves by winding their stems around a support. The leathery, glossy, mid-green leaves, borne in pairs, are up to 2 in. (5 cm) long. Throughout late spring, summer, and early fall, clusters of 3–5 flowers appear on the new growth. They are large and showy, being trumpet-shaped, up to 3 in. (7 cm) across. *M.* x *amoena* 'Alice du Pont' is rose pink and *M. sanderi* is also rose-pink with a yellow throat. *M. s.* 'Rosea' has larger leaves, bronze beneath, and flowers, to 3½ in. (8 cm) across, of salmon-pink with yellow throats. The flowers are produced when the plant is still young, and regular pinching can be used to encourage a bushy plant rather than a tall one.
Size Spread up to 10 ft. (3 m) if left unpruned.
Light Indirect sunlight.

MARANTACEAE
Maranta leuconeura
This Brazilian plant is grown primarily for its striking foliage. The common name of **prayer plant** is derived from its habit of folding its leaves together at night. The leaves are oval, up to 5 in. (12 cm) long, and lustrous dark green, marked with gray or maroon, veined silver, red, or purple above and gray-green or maroon below. The white or violet flowers are inconspicuous. *M.l.* var. *erythroneura*, called **herringbone plan**t, has green-black leaves with scarlet veins and a lime-green zone along the midrib. *M.l.* var. *kerchoveana*, also called **rabbit's foot**, has gray-green leaves with a row of purple-brown to olive blotches along each side of the midrib.
Size Height 2 ft. (30 cm).
Light Partial shade.
Temperature Normal room.
Moisture Keep soil thoroughly moist from spring to fall, drier during the winter.
Feeding Apply standard liquid fertilizer once a month in spring and summer.
Propagation Divide large clumps in spring, or take 4 in. (10 cm) cuttings with 3–4 leaves in spring or summer.
Special needs Do not allow water to splash onto the leaves because it will cause discoloration. It is important to keep marantas out of bright light or the leaves will fade.

Mentha spicata (spearmint) see *Herbs* p.135
Microlepia strigosa see *Ferns* p.132

168

ARACEAE
Monstera deliciosa

In its native habitat from Mexico to Panama, the **Swiss cheese plant** will scramble up the trunks and along the branches of large trees, anchoring itself by means of strong aerial roots, which also take in moisture and nutrients. It matures into a large plant with heart-shaped leaves, up to 18 in. (45 cm) across, on 1 ft. (30 cm) stalks. The common name arises from the leaves, which are undivided on a young plant, but which gradually become deeply incised between the veins, with holes in the remaining sections.

Size Height 10 ft. (3 m) or more.
Light Indirect sunlight.
Temperature Normal room.
Moisture Keep barely moist all year round.
Feeding Apply standard liquid fertilizer once a month from spring through to fall.
Propagation Take tip cuttings with two leaves in spring, or stem cuttings of a single node with a short length of stem. Alternatively, layer or air-layer.
Special needs Train the stem against a moss pole – this will allow the aerial roots to anchor and take in moisture in the same way that they would in the wild.

RUTACEAE
Murraya

These evergreen plants, originating in China and India to Australia, grow to become large shrubs or small trees, ideal for a conservatory. *M. koenigii* is called **curry leaf or karapincha** and has pungently aromatic foliage used for flavoring curries. Each leaf has 5-10 finely toothed leaflets and white flowers followed by dark blue-black fruits. *M. paniculata*, also known as **orange jasmine**, **satinwood**, and **Chinese box**, has glossy, smooth, dark green leaves, divided into three or more leaflets, each up to 2 in (5 cm) long. Small, fragrant, white flowers are produced in dense terminal clusters all year, followed by oval, orange-red fruit.

Size Height 10–12 ft. (3–4 m).
Light Direct sunlight, indirect sunlight, or partial shade.
Temperature Keep warm; minimum 55–60°F (12–15°C).
Moisture Keep thoroughly moist from spring to fall, drier in winter.
Feeding Apply standard liquid fertilizer once a month in spring and summer.
Propagation Sow seed in spring, or take semiripe tip cuttings in summer.
Special needs Prune in late winter, if necessary.

MUSACEAE
Musa acuminata

Many varieties of the **banana**, from southeast Asia, grow much too big for even a large conservatory, but *M.a.* 'Dwarf Cavendish' is a more compact form, often producing small, edible fruits. The green-brown, suckering, pseudostems are formed from overlapping leaf sheaths and the palmlike leaves grow to 3 ft. (90 cm) or more. Tubular flowers with red-purple bracts are borne on brown-haired, central stems, from which young fruit curve upward. This plant will grow in a conservatory border or large container.

Size Height 6½–7 ft. (2–2.2 m).
Light Direct sunlight, indirect sunlight, or partial shade.
Temperature Tolerates a wide range; winter minimum 55°F (12°C).
Moisture Keep thoroughly moist from spring to fall; moist in winter.
Feeding Use standard liquid fertilizer once a month in spring and summer.
Propagation Detach rooted suckers in summer.
Special needs For fruit production, keep the temperature above 65°F (18°C), even at night.

Narcissus see *Bulbs* p.129
Nephrolepsis exaltata 'Bostoniensis' see *Ferns* p.132

Monstera deliciosa

Musa acuminata

Nerium oleander

Passiflora 'Amethyst'

APOCYNACEAE
Nerium oleander

Originating from the Mediterranean to western China, **oleander** is a large evergreen shrub with leathery, dark green leaves, grown for its display of beautiful, often fragrant, funnel-shaped flowers. These are produced in terminal clusters and can be single, semidouble or fully double, according to the variety, in shades of white, cream, yellow, apricot, salmon, copper, pink, red, carmine, and purple. Individual flowers can be up to 2 in. (5 cm) across and are borne in groups of 6–8. This is an ideal plant for a sunny windowsill while it is small, and for a well-lit conservatory or sunroom as it grows.

Size Height up to 6½–7ft. (2–2.2 m).
Light Direct sunlight.
Temperature Normal room from spring to fall, but below 60°F (15°C) in winter for the rest period; winter minimum 45°F (7°C).

Moisture Keep thoroughly moist from spring to fall, barely moist in winter. Allowing the plant to dry out as the flowers form will result in the buds being shed.
Feeding Provide standard liquid fertilizer every two weeks in spring and summer.
Propagation Take tip cuttings, to 6 in. (15 cm) long, in summer, rooted in either soil or water.
Special needs *The whole plant – sap, flowers, and seeds – is very poisonous, so handle with extreme caution, and wash hands thoroughly after contact.*

Nolina recurvata see *Palmlike Plants* p.138
Notocactus see *Cacti* p.125
Ocimum basilicum (basil) see *Herbs* p.135
Opuntia microdasys see *Cacti* p.125
Paphiopedilum see *Orchids* p.128
Parodia see *Cacti* p.125

PASSIFLORACEAE
Passiflora caerulea

A vigorous plant from Brazil and Argentina, the **passion flower** or **blue passion flower** has deep green, angular stems and climbs by using twisting tendrils. It flowers while still quite young, producing fat green buds along the stems from which uncurl the characteristic flowers, each of which grows to 4 in. (10 cm) across. The flowers are complex in appearance, consisting of five white sepals and five white petals of equal length, surrounding a circle of filaments shaded blue-purple, with a white band in the middle. Held prominently within this arrangement are five golden-yellow anthers and three brown stigmas. The flowers are followed by egg-shaped, orange-yellow fruits. *P.* 'Amethyst' has pinkish-mauve flowers and dark filaments; *P. c.* 'Constance Elliott' has ivory-white flowers.

Size Spread up to 20 ft. (6 m) if left unchecked.
Light Direct sunlight.
Temperature Normal room from spring to fall, with a winter rest period at around 50°F (10°C).
Moisture Keep thoroughly moist from spring to fall. In winter, apply only enough water to prevent the soil drying out.
Feeding Use standard liquid fertilizer every two weeks in spring and summer.
Propagation Take 4 in. (10 cm) tip cuttings in summer.
Special needs Older plants can be pruned hard in spring if necessary.

GERANIACEAE
Pelargonium

Better known as geraniums, the pelargoniums tend to be the varieties of the family grown for indoors. Being closely related to their outdoor counterparts, they bear a strong resemblance, but have pointed rather than rounded leaf lobes. Pelargonium is a large group, covering plants grown for their bright flowers and others for their scented foliage. They are bushy subshrubs with rounded or divided leaves and a long flowering season. Most originate from South Africa, with a few from tropical Africa, Australia, and the Middle East. **P. crispum,** also called **lemon geranium**, is a scented-leaf pelargonium, grown for its aromatic foliage rather than its small pink flowers. The stems are stiffly upright, but regular pinching can be used to control the shape of the plant. Its rough-textured leaves are $^1/_2$ in. (1.5 cm) across, rounded, and strongly lemon scented. Varieties include: *P.c.* 'Major,' which has larger leaves; *P.c.* 'Minor,' with small, crisped leaves, and *P.c.* 'Peach Cream,' with pink flowers and smelling of peaches. Height up to 2 ft. (60 cm) if left unchecked. **Regal geraniums (P. x domesticum hybrids)** are a large group of hybrids of complicated origins. All have thick, branching stems and hairy, toothed leaves up to 4 in. (10 cm) across. The flowers are large and showy, and are borne in upright clusters, in single or combined shades of white, pink, salmon, orange, red, or purple; the upper petals are often blotched with a darker color. They are usually single. *P.* 'Carisbrooke' has large, pink flowers, marked wine-red. *P.* 'Pompeii' is a compact plant bearing flowers with nearly black petals and narrow pink-white edges. Height 18 in. (45 cm). **Ivy-leafed geraniums (P. peltatum)** are a trailing or climbing variety of evergreen pelargonium with fleshy, bright green leaves with a darker central zone. The flowers are single to double, with colors including white, pink, red, mauve, and purple, often with darker veins. They are excellent plants for hanging baskets. **Zonal geraniums (P. x hortorum)** are hybrids with smooth, succulent stems and large, rounded leaves, up to 4 in. (10 cm) in diameter, sometimes varie-gated or marked with a darker horse-shoe-shaped zone. The flowers may be single, semidouble, or double, in shades of white, orange, pink, red, purple, and occasionally yellow. Height 2 ft. (60 cm). The group can be divided into various new and traditional categories:

Cactus-flowered: single or double flowers with narrow, twisted petals.
Single-flowered: flowers with five petals or less.
Double- and semidouble-flowered: flowers with six or more open petals.
Stellar: small plants with irregularly star-shaped flowers, and often zoned leaves.
Rosebuds: flowers with many small petals packed tightly in the center.
Fancy-leaved: grown for foliage which may be gold, silver, green, white, black, or bronze in combination.
Irenes: fast-growing, free-flowering, with large flower heads.
Miniatures and dwarfs: compact and free-flowering; miniatures reach 5 in. (13 cm) and dwarfs up to 8 in. (20 cm) in height.

Many zonal geraniums will not breed true from seed and must be propagated by taking cuttings; usually these are the more showy varieties, ideal for the house or conservatory.
Size See individual groups or species.
Light Direct or indirect sunlight.
Temperature Normal room.
Moisture Keep moist from spring to fall. In winter, apply enough water to prevent soil drying out.
Feeding Give half-strength liquid fertilizer once a month in spring and summer
Propagation Take tip or stem cuttings in spring or summer; remove small stipules and leaves from the nodes on the lower third of the stem. Allow cuttings to wilt for 30 minutes before inserting into soil mix or water for rooting.
Special needs Do not use rooting hormone when taking cuttings of any pelargonium, as they naturally contain high levels of hormone, so adding extra will make the stem rot.

Pellaea rotundifolia see **Ferns** p.132

Pelargonium 'Henry Cox' (Zonal)

Regal geranium

Pentas lanceolata
RUBIACEAE

This species, also known as **Egyptian star cluster**, originates in countries from East Africa to Yemen. It is an attractive and unusual, soft-wooded shrub with 4 in. (10 cm) long, hairy, lance-shaped leaves. The flowers are borne in 4 in. (10 cm) clusters, each individual, tubular bloom opening out in a 5-pointed star shape, measuring 1/2 in. (1 cm) across, usually in fall and winter, but also at other times. The flowers can be in shades of magenta, red, mauve, pink, or white, according to the variety.
Size Height 18 in. (45 cm).
Light: Direct sunlight.
Temperature Normal room temperature; minimum 50°F (10°C).
Moisture Keep moist throughout the year, apart from a 6–8 week period immediately after flowering, when only enough water should be applied to prevent the soil mix from drying out severely.
Feeding Give standard liquid fertilizer once a month all year, except during the rest period.

Propagation Take 3–4 in. (7–10 cm) tip cuttings from nonflowering shoots in spring or summer.
Special needs Pinch out the shoot tips on a regular basis to produce a bushy plant.

Peperomia
PIPERACEAE

There is a wide range of peperomias, all grown for their foliage. They vary in size, shape, and color, but all have fleshy, waxy leaves, and a long, thin, upright "rat's tail" of a flower spike, bearing tiny, green-white flowers. They are popular plants for terrariums and bottle gardens, although their slightly brittle nature means that they are not easily maneuvered into position. A peperomia can be found for almost every growing position – trailing, bushy, or upright – and many have attractive, deeply ridged or highly colored leaves. *P. caperata* is a small plant from Brazil, commonly called **emerald-ripple pepper**. It has heart-shaped, glossy, emerald-green, deeply rippled leaves, up to 1 1/2 in. (3 cm) long. Between the ridges, the leaf looks almost black. The leafstalks are green to dull red and up to 3 in. (7 cm) long. *P.c.* 'Emerald Ripple' is more compact with smaller leaves. *P.c.* 'Little Fantasy' is a dwarf form. **P. glabella** is an erect or sprawling species from Central and South America and the West Indies. Also called the **radiator plant**, it has softly fleshy, glossy, red stems and mid-green, oval, fleshy leaves, on 1/2 in. (9 mm) red stalks. The thin, green-white flower stalks reach up to 6 in. (15 cm) high. This is an attractive plant to use as a foil to brighter colors within a mixed arrangement of plants. *P. g.* 'Variegata' has pale green leaves, edged or variegated off-white. **P. obtusifolia** comes from regions from Mexico to northern South America and the West Indies. Also known as **baby rubber plant**, **American rubber plant**, and **pepper face**, it is stoloniferous, sending up purplish stems and rooting as it spreads. The rounded, fleshy leaves are deep purple-green, and short, white flower stalks are produced in the spring and fall. Varieties include: *P.o.* 'Alba,' which has cream-colored new growth and stems spotted red; *P.o.* 'Albo-marginata,' which has small, gray-green leaves edged cream; *P.o.* 'Minima,' which is a dwarf plant with glossy, densely packed leaves; and *P.o.* 'Variegata,' which has pointed, pale green leaves with cream markings and scarlet stems.

Pentas lanceolata

Peperomia caperata

Size Height 8–12 in. (20–30 cm).

Light Indirect sunlight.

Temperature Normal room.

Moisture Keep barely moist at all times.

Feeding Give half-strength liquid fertilizer once a month from spring through to fall.

Propagation For *P. caperata*, take leaf cuttings in spring or summer. Use the whole leaf with 1 in. (2.5 cm) of stalk attached, and insert it until the edge of the leaf is in contact with the soil. For *P. glabella* and *P. obtusifolia*, take 3 in. (7 cm) tip cuttings in spring or summer.

Special needs High humidity is important, but if the pot is standing on a tray of moist pebbles make sure that the plant cannot take up the extra water.

Peperomia glabella 'Variegata'

Peperomia obtusifolia 'Variegata'

ASTERACEAE

Pericallis x hybrida (syn. Cineraria cruentus)

This is the **florist's cineraria**, which originates in Tenerife in the Canary Islands. Although actually a perennial plant, it is usually grown as an annual to be discarded after flowering. The large, dome-shaped cluster of daisylike flowers is set within a circle of hairy, heart-shaped, mid-green leaves, and can be white, pink, terracotta, red, maroon, purple, violet, or blue, according to the variety, often with a white base to the petals. Many different flower forms are available – single, double, or star-shaped – in either large or more compact forms.

Size Height up to 18 in. (45 cm).

Light Indirect sunlight. Cool light.

Temperature Cool.

Moisture Keep thoroughly moist, but do not allow to stand in water.

Feeding Unnecessary for the period that it is indoors.

Propagation Sow seed in late spring or summer. Not easy.

Special needs For the maximum flowering period, buy a plant with only a few open flowers (just showing the color) and plenty of buds. Given the right conditions, cinerarias will continue to flower for several weeks indoors.

Petroselinum crispum (parsley) see *Herbs* p.135

Pericallis x *hybrida*

ARACEAE

Philodendron

The philodendrons grown for indoors are evergreen, mainly climbing plants, which support themselves by means of aerial roots. They have glossy, leathery leaves which may be heart-, arrow-, or lance-shaped, and which change shape as the plant ages. Growing a philodendron against a moss pole will allow it to use its aerial roots to anchor it in the same way it would use a tree in its native habitat.

P. bipinnatifidum (syn. P. selloum)

This treelike shrub from southeast Brazil is also known as **tree philodendron**. It usually has a single, sturdy, upright stem, which is inclined to fall over and lie horizontally as it ages, with only the tip pointing upward. The downward-pointing leaves grow to 3 ft. (1 m) long, half of which is the stalk. They are heart-shaped, bright green, and deeply cut, with many narrow, wavy-edged lobes. The flower is a spathe 12 in. (30 cm) long and cream with a red margin. *P.b.* 'German Selloum' has finely cut leaves with wavy, graceful lobes. *P.b.* 'Painted Lady' has golden-colored new leaves, turning green. *P.b.* 'Variegatum' has leaves with light green to yellow blotches.

Size Height eventually 15 ft. (5 m).
Light Indirect sunlight or partial shade.
Temperature Normal room.
Moisture Keep moist from spring to fall. In winter, apply enough water to prevent the soil mix from drying out.
Feeding Apply standard liquid fertilizer once a month from spring through to summer.
Propagation Sow fresh seed in spring, or take tip cuttings from shoots at the base of the plant.
Special needs Variegated plants always need more light than green forms, otherwise the plant compensates for the low light by converting the yellow leaf areas to green and any distinctive markings will fade or be lost altogether.

Philodendron bipinnatifidum

P. 'Emerald Queen'

This is a vigorous hybrid philodendron whose parents originated in tropical America. It is ideal for growing on a moss pole because the foliage is a uniform size. The glossy, bright green leaves are medium-size, arrow-shaped, on short stalks and closely spaced along the stems. It is a plant grown particularly for its resistance to both cold and disease.

Size Height up to 10 ft. (3 m) if left unchecked.
Light Indirect sunlight or partial shade.
Temperature Normal room.
Moisture Keep moist from spring to fall. In winter, apply only enough water to prevent soil drying out.
Feeding Give standard liquid fertilizer once a month from spring to summer.
Propagation Take 4 in. (10 cm) tip cuttings in spring or summer.
Special needs For the aerial roots to cling to the moss pole, it should be kept moist at all times. Once the roots attach themselves, the plant should become self-supporting, with no need for unsightly ties or string.

Phoenix canariensis see *Palmlike Plants* p.138

URTICACEAE

Pilea cadierei

This is an easily-grown, upright species, originating in Vietnam and commonly called **aluminum plant** because of its unusual, metallic-silver markings on the leaves. The slender branchlets are green, tinted pink, but are inclined to become bare at the base and straggly as the plant ages. The leaves are oval, toothed around the edges, and marked with silver on a dark green background, sometimes to the extent that the whole leaf

Philodendron b. 'Painted Lady'

Pilea cadierei

appears metallic silver. The markings are caused by tiny pockets of air between the veins within the leaf, raising the surface slightly and giving an opalescent effect. *P.c.* 'Minima' is a dwarf cultivar with densely branched, pink stems and small, scalloped, deep olive green leaves with raised silver patches.

Size Height 18 in. (45 cm).
Light Indirect sunlight or partial shade.
Temperature Keep warm; minimum 55°F (12°C).
Moisture Keep barely moist.
Feeding Give half-strength liquid fertilizer every two weeks in spring and summer.
Propagation Take 3 in. (7 cm) tip cuttings in spring or summer.
Special needs Regular pinching out of growing tips will encourage a bushy plant that will not become straggly as quickly.

Plumbago auriculata

PLUMBAGINACEAE
Plumbago auriculata (syn. P. capensis)
This evergreen shrub from South Africa has long, arching stems that need tying to supports to prevent them straggling. Also called **Cape leadwort**, it has pretty sky-blue flowers borne in clusters of up to 20 throughout spring, summer, and fall amid the long-oval, mid-green leaves. The individual flowers are tubular, flaring out into five petals, each of which is marked with a darker blue central stripe. *P.a.* var. *albu* has pure white flowers.
Size Height up to 10 ft. (3 m) if left unchecked.
Light Direct sunlight.
Temperature Normal room. The winter rest period should be at 45–50°F (7–10°C).
Moisture Keep thoroughly moist from spring to fall. In winter, apply only enough water to prevent the soil drying out.
Feeding Give high potash fertilizer (tomato fertilizer) every two weeks in spring and summer.
Propagation Take 3–4 in. (7–10 cm) cuttings in spring or summer, or layer or sow seed.
Special needs Remove the flowers as they fade to promote the production of more buds. Flowers are produced on current season's growth, so pruning should be done in early spring to give the maximum flowering time. Reduce growth by up to two-thirds.

Polypodium see *Ferns* p.132

ARALIACEAE
Polyscias guilfoylei
An evergreen shrub or small tree from the western Pacific, **geranium aralia** or **wild coffee** has upright, sparsely branched stems, usually bearing its attractive foliage only at the tips. The leaves are 12–18 in. (30–45 cm) long, divided into 5–9 leaflets, each deeply toothed and mid-green with a creamy white margin. This plant is ideal for a warm conservatory, but may be too large as a houseplant. Its forms would be more appropriate: *P.g.* 'Crispa' is compact with sharply-toothed, bronze-tinted leaves; *P.g.* 'Laciniata' has drooping, doubly-pinnate leaves with white, toothed margins; and *P.g.* 'Victoriae' (**lace aralia**) is compact, to 3 ft. (1 m) with finely dissected leaves, each leaflet having a pure white margin.
Size Height up to 10 ft. (3 m).
Light Indirect sunlight.
Temperature Keep warm; minimum 65°F (18°C).

Polyscias guilfoylei

Moisture Keep moist all year.
Feeding Apply standard liquid fertilizer every two weeks from spring to fall.
Propagation Take 4 in. (10 cm) tip cuttings in spring.
Special needs To increase humidity, place the pot on a tray of moist pebbles. Polyscias do not have a rest period; growth merely slows down in winter, so maintain a moist soil.

Polystichum tsussimense see *Ferns* p.132

PLUMBAGINACEAE
Primula
Many members of the primula family can be grown as indoor plants. Although most are treated as annuals and discarded after flowering, some are actually quite frost-hardy and can be planted outdoors afterward to be enjoyed for years to come. Polyanthus fall into this hardy category and they are ideal for containers or hanging baskets in a cool conservatory or on a cool windowsill. Some primulas are hardy, but many require warmth to flower well.

P. obconica
This pretty plant from China, which is also known as **German primrose** or

Primula obconica

Radermachera sinica

poison primrose, produces masses of large, fragrant blooms during the early months of the year, in shades of white, pink, salmon, lilac, magenta, or red, each with a distinctive apple-green eye. Several specimens can be grouped together for instant effect, or individuals can be used to add short-term color to a more permanent foliage arrangement. The flowers are borne in clusters on 1 ft. (30 cm) stalks emerging from amid leaves that are roughly circular, coarse, and covered with fine hairs.
Size Height 1 ft. (30 cm).
Light Cool light.
Temperature Keep cool; 50–55°F (10–12°C).
Moisture Keep thoroughly moist.
Feeding Provide standard liquid fertilizer every two weeks.
Propagation Commercially, primulas are grown from seed but this is not recommended in the home.
Special needs *The fine hairs that cover the leaves may cause skin irritation.* Picking off flowers as they fade will prolong the flowering period. *P. obconica* is usually treated as an annual and discarded after flowering, but it can be brought back for a second year if kept cool and barely moist after flowering until the fall, when it can be repotted and the watering increased.

P. Pruhonicensis Hybrids
This group covers a vast number of hybrids of garden origin, produced by interbreeding several species, including *P. elatior*, *P. juliae*, *P. veris*, and *P. vulgaris*. The flowers may be primrose-type with single blooms on short stalks, or polyanthus-type with clusters of flowers on longer, stout, hairy stalks. All have a rosette of oval, heavily-veined, mid-green leaves, and the flowers are produced in shades of white, yellow, pink, orange, red, or blue, usually with a yellow eye, in late winter and spring. They can be placed individually, grouped together for a splash of color, or used to add short-term color to a more permanent foliage arrangement.
Size Height up to 8 in. (20 cm).
Light Cool light.
Temperature Keep cool; 50–55°F (10–12°C).
Moisture Keep thoroughly moist.
Feeding Provide standard liquid

fertilizer every two weeks.
Propagation Sow seed in summer.
Special needs Unlike the tender indoor primulas, the polyanthus group can be planted outdoors when flowering has finished: most are frost-hardy and will continue flowering for many years. Choose a lightly shaded position and keep well watered until they are established.

Pteris cretica see *Ferns* p.132

BIGNONIACEAE
Radermachera sinica
This species is relatively new to the indoor plant selection, having been introduced in the early 1980s from Taiwan, and owes its popularity to its tolerance of dry, centrally-heated air. It is an evergreen shrub with large, graceful, compound leaves, up to 30 in. (75 cm) long, with glossy, deeply-veined leaflets. The fragrant, deep yellow flowers are produced only on mature plants. It is ideal for creating a softening effect in a large arrangement or for framing flowering plants.
Size Height 3 ft. (1 m).
Light Indirect sunlight.
Temperature Normal room.
Moisture Keep moist at all times.
Feeding Use standard liquid fertilizer every two weeks from spring to fall.
Propagation Take 4 in. (10 cm) tip cuttings in spring or summer.
Special needs Do not allow soil to become waterlogged or to dry out, because both will cause the lower leaves to drop prematurely.

Rhapis excelsa see *Palmlike Plants* p.138
Rebutia minuscula see *Cacti* p.125

ERICACEAE
Rhododendron simsii (syn. Azalea indica)
Found in large quantities and a wide range of colors throughout winter and spring, this is the **florist's azalea**, also called **Indian azalea**. It gives a spectacular display, with a succession of flowers over a period of about six weeks. They are in shades of white, pink, red, or purple, or a combination. Individual blooms last several days and should be removed as they fade to

ensure continued production. Buy a plant with only a few open blooms (to ascertain the color) but plenty of buds as this will ensure the maximum display. *R. simsii* originates in northeast Burma, China and Taiwan.

Size Height 12–18 in. (30–45 cm).

Light Cool light.

Temperature Keep cool; 45–60°F (7–15°C).

Moisture In order to thrive this plant needs to be kept wet, not just moist.

Feeding Provide standard liquid fertilizer every two weeks in spring and summer, then once a month in fall.

Propagation Take 2 in. (5 cm) tip cuttings in late spring from the new growth. Use rooting hormone and an acidic, peat moss-enriched soil mix.

Special needs Remove only the petals of the faded flower when deadheading, as the new shoots that follow the flowers arise from the same point on the stem – cutting off the whole flower head will remove the shoot buds too. This is an acid-loving plant which may suffer if watered with hard tap water. Using rainwater will help if the leaves start to turn yellow (chlorosis), as will repotting, after flowering, into an acidic, peat moss-enriched soil.

Rhoeo discolor see *Tradescantia spathacea*

ROSACEAE
Rosa 'Rouletii' (syn. R. chinensis 'Minima')

There is a tendency to view roses as outdoor plants, but the miniature varieties make excellent indoor flowering specimens, giving color and fragrance throughout the summer. This variety from China has double, deep pink flowers, borne freely from summer to fall. The colors of other miniature roses include red, pink, yellow, white, and a range of shades in-between. After flowering, these roses can be planted in the garden or, with a little attention, kept for future use indoors.

Size Height up to 1 ft. (30 cm).

Light Direct sunlight.

Temperature Normal room. If the plant is to be kept, it will need a winter rest period of eight weeks at 45°F (7°C) or lower.

Moisture Keep moist from spring to fall. In winter, apply enough water to prevent soil drying out.

Feeding Use standard liquid fertilizer every two weeks during spring and summer.

Propagation Take tip cuttings, 2 in. (5 cm) long, in spring. Use rooting hormone.

Special needs High humidity is important, so place the pot on a tray of moist pebbles. To bring the plant into flower indoors for a second year, repot in fall and place it outside. Bring indoors in late winter, acclimatizing it gradually, rather than putting it straight into a warm room. Prune to outward-facing buds to shorten each stem by half, increase watering and feeding, and the plant could be in flower by early spring.

Rhododendron simsii

Rosa 'Rouletii'

Ruellia makoyana and *R. devosiana*

Saintpaulia ionanthe

Sansevieria trifasciata

ACANTHACEAE
Ruellia

This genus covers a range of evergreen perennials and soft-stemmed or woody shrubs, from tropical America, Africa, and Asia. **R. makoyana** is a spreading plant from Brazil, also known as **monkey plant** or **trailing velvet plant**. Its weak stems can be allowed to trail gracefully from a hanging basket or tied to a support and pinched regularly to encourage bushiness. The pointed-oval leaves are velvety, olive-green, tinted violet above, purple beneath, and veined in silvery gray. Masses of single, trumpet-shaped, rose-carmine flowers, up to 2 in. (5 cm) across, are borne in winter and early spring. **R.devosiana** is a hairy shrub with soft, purplish stems and funnel-shaped pale lavender flowers from spring to summer.

Size Stems to 2 ft. (60 cm) long.
Light Indirect sunlight.
Temperature Warm; minimum 55°F (12°C).
Moisture Keep moist all year, apart from the six week rest period immediately after flowering, when only enough water should be applied to prevent the soil drying out.
Feeding Use standard liquid fertilizer every two weeks, apart from during the rest period.
Propagation Take 3–4 in. (7–10 cm) tip cuttings in summer.
Special needs High humidity is essential, so place the pot on a tray of moist pebbles.

GESNERIACEAE
Saintpaulia ionanthe

Hybrids of the **African violet** from Tanzania make ever-popular indoor plants, due both to their compact size and long flowering period. The velvety leaves are up to $1\frac{1}{2}$ in. (4 cm) across, slightly scalloped around the edges, with erect hairs on the upper surface, and colored red-maroon beneath. Clusters of flowers are produced on upright stalks, to 2 in. (5 cm) long, in shades of purple, violet, blue, mauve, and white.

Size Up to 1 ft. (30 cm) across.
Light Indirect sunlight.
Temperature Normal room; protect from drafts and temperature changes or growth will be checked.
Moisture Keep moist, but not wet.

Feeding Use standard liquid fertilizer every two weeks from spring through to fall.
Propagation Take whole leafstalk cuttings.
Special needs The leaves and flowers are easily damaged by water falling on them, so always water from below and never mist. Increase humidity by placing the pot on a tray of moist pebbles instead. Saintpaulias grow best slightly pot-bound in plastic pots.

AGAVACEAE
Sansevieria trifasciata

This plant is known as **mother in law's tongue** or **snake plant** and originates from Nigeria. It seems to survive where no others can, and is tolerant of sunshine and shade, dry air, drafts, and even some neglect in terms of watering. Each rhizomatous plant can last for many years, as the rate of growth is slow, and seldom needs repotting. The stiffly erect leaves are narrow, flat, long, and pointed, and banded light and dark green. *S.t.* 'Laurentii,' has bright yellow leaf margins.

Size Height 2 ft. (60 cm).
Light Direct sunlight, indirect sunlight, or partial shade.
Temperature Normal room; minimum 55°F (12°C).
Moisture Keep moist from spring to fall. In winter, apply enough water to prevent soil drying out.
Feeding Give half-strength liquid fertilizer once a month in spring and summer.
Propagation Divide clumps so each new piece has both leaves and roots. Or, take leaf cuttings by cutting one leaf into short pieces and inserting them, base downward, into a pot or tray of soil mix. Plants propagated by leaf cuttings will be all-green.
Special needs Sanseverias grow best when slightly pot-bound, so do not repot each year.

SAXIFRAGACEAE
Saxifraga stolonifera

This small evergreen plant from China and Japan spreads by means of long, thin red stolons which bear plantlets at their tips: the common name **mother of thousands** arises from the copious quantities of these small plants that are produced. It is also known as **strawberry geranium**. The leaves are round, bristly, long-stalked, and mid-green with silvery veins above, flushed red beneath. Branched flowering stems up to 16 in. (40 cm) long are produced in late summer and early fall, bearing clusters of white flowers. *S.s.* 'Tricolor' is less vigorous with its leaves edged cream with a pink flush.

Size Height 8 in. (20 cm).

Light Indirect sunlight or partial shade. *S.s.* 'Tricolor' needs direct sunlight for at least part of each day to ensure good coloration.

Temperature Cool. *S.s.* 'Tricolor' needs normal room temperature.

Moisture Keep thoroughly moist from spring to fall. In winter, apply only enough water to prevent the soil drying out.

Feeding Use standard liquid fertilizer once a month in spring and summer.

Propagation Root plantlets into small pots of soil before or after detaching from the parent plant.

Special needs In higher temperatures, increase the humidity using a tray of moist pebbles, but do not allow to stand in water or the roots will rot.

ARALIACEAE
Schefflera
With their delicate, umbrella-like leaf formation, these are some of the most attractive indoor foliage plants. They are easy to grow, provided the atmosphere is kept humid rather than dry (which will cause brown edges to the leaves) and will add height and structure to a massed arrangement.

S. actinophylla
In its native habitat of Australia and New Guinea, this plant can become a tree up to 40 ft. (12 m) high, but indoors it is more usual to see it as a pretty, bushy shrub with leaves borne in terminal rosettes resembling the spokes of an umbrella, hence the common name, **umbrella plant**. The upright stalks can reach as long as 32 in. (80 cm), bearing 7–16 glossy, bright green leaflets, which grow to 12 x 4 in. (30 x 10 cm). It looks equally attractive as an individual specimen or in a group display, where the lush foliage softens outlines.

Saxifraga stolonifera

Size Height eventually 6¹⁄₂–7 ft. (2–2.2 m).

Light Indirect sunlight.

Temperature Normal room.

Moisture Keep moist from spring to fall. In winter, apply only enough water to prevent soil drying out.

Feeding Apply standard liquid fertilizer once a month from spring through to fall.

Propagation Take tip cuttings in summer, use rooting hormone, and seal in a plastic bag at 70°F (21°C).

Special needs Increase humidity by placing the pot on a tray of moist pebbles and by misting when temperatures are high.

S. elegantissima (syn. Dizygotheca elegantissima)
One of the most graceful and delicate plants available for indoors, the **false aralia** or **finger aralia** forms an elegant specimen with lacy, coppery green foliage. Each leaf comprises 7–10 narrow, toothed leaflets borne at the end of slim, 4 in. (10 cm) stalks. Both the stems and leafstalks are mottled with white, which makes an interesting color contrast.

Size Height 3 ft. (1 m).

Light Indirect sunlight.

Temperature Normal room.

Moisture See *S. actinophylla* above.

Feeding Use standard liquid fertilizer every two weeks during spring and summer.

Propagation Difficult. Young plants are readily available to buy.

Special needs Increase humidity by placing the pot in a tray of moist peb-

Schefflera elegantissima

bles, but keep the pot above water level. Pinch regularly to achieve a bushy effect.

ARACEAE
Scindapsus pictus 'Argyraeus'
This plant, from Java to Borneo, is sold in its juvenile stage when it has striking, large, heart-shaped leaves of a satiny dark olive-green with irregular silver spots. Known as **satin pothos**, it will grow against the trunk of a tree in the wild. This can be replaced indoors with a piece of rough bark or a moss pole, or, the plant can be allowed to trail from a hanging basket.

Size Height 3 ft. (90 cm) or more.

Light Indirect sunlight.

Temperature Warm, minimum 65°F (18°C).

Moisture Keep moist from spring to fall. In winter, apply only enough water to prevent the soil drying out.

Feeding Apply standard liquid fertilizer every two weeks in spring and summer.

Propagation Take 4 in. (10 cm) tip cuttings in spring or early summer.

Special needs To maintain high humidity, place the pot on a tray of moist pebbles. Overwatering will cause root rot, drafts will damage the foliage, while too little light will cause the leaves to revert to green.

Schlumbergera truncata see *Cacti* p.127
Sedum see *Succulents* p.136

Selaginella kraussiana

Sinningia speciosa

SELAGINELLACEAE
Selaginella

The selaginella genus is a large one and includes several plants which are popular indoors for their pretty foliage. They are evergreen, mosslike plants, which spread by means of rhizomes and need constantly warm humidity to thrive, so are ideal for a bottle garden or terrarium. Some grow as low, mosslike, spreading mounds, others are more upright. The tips of the leaves bear spores, although selaginella is not classified as a fern. *S. kraussiana* originates from South Africa and is known as **spreading clubmoss** or **trailing spike moss**. It has masses of trailing, bright green foliage and spreads quite quickly, rooting as it goes. S.k. 'Aurea' has bright golden-green foliage and S.k. 'Variegata' has bright green foliage splashed with ivory white or pale yellow. *S. martensii*, from Mexico, is called **little club moss** or **spike moss**. It has upright, branching stems bearing tiny, bright green leaves. Stiff aerial roots grow down from the lower part of the stems to the soil, helping to support the weight of the upper part. *S. m.* 'Albolineata' has some leaves that are wholly or partially white and *S. m.* 'Watsoniana' has silver-tipped leaves.

Size Height 1 ft. (30 cm).
Light Partial shade.
Temperature Normal room.
Moisture Keep thoroughly moist at all times.
Feeding Give half-strength liquid fertilizer once a month all year round.
Propagation Take 2 in. (5 cm) tip cuttings in spring.
Special needs The foliage is particularly delicate and should never be allowed to dry out or it will turn brown. Touch it as little as possible and only mist with warm water; cold water will damage it.

GESNERIACEAE
Sinningia speciosa

This is the florist's **gloxinia** from Brazil, instantly recognizable by its enormous, furry leaves and large, bell-shaped flowers. Bought just as the buds begin to open, each plant will provide color for several weeks during the summer, with individual blooms lasting up to a week. Since its introduction during the nineteenth century, breeding has produced a rich range of flower colors, including white, pink, red, maroon, violet, and purple. Varieties include those with a white frill edging colored petals, speckles, or splashes of color on a white background, and blooms with a contrasting throat color.

Size Height 8 in. (20 cm).
Light Indirect sunlight or partial shade.
Temperature Normal room.
Moisture Keep moist at all times while in leaf.
Feeding Apply half-strength liquid tomato fertilizer every two weeks from when flowering stops to when the foliage dies down.
Propagation Take cuttings of the young leaves and stems or divide larger tubers in spring. Or sow seed, mixed with silver sand, and place in a

box in a position which receives bright, filtered light at 70°F (21°C) in late winter.
Special needs Avoid getting water on the leaves because they will scorch. The tuber can be stored dry over winter and brought back for a subsequent year by potting up in late winter, with hollow side up.

Solenostemon scutellarioides

URTICACEAE
Soleirolia soleirolii
Best known as **mind-your-own-business**, this species is from the western Mediterranean. It is a pretty, but deceptively quick-growing, evergreen perennial plant, which forms a low, creeping mat. It has delicate, intricately branching, almost translucent stems that root as they spread, and tiny, short-stalked, bright green leaves. Minute, solitary flowers are borne in the leaf axils. Positioned at the front of a mixed arrangement, it is an attractive way of hiding the container or softening the front edge. **Baby's tears**, **angel's tears**, and **Irish moss** are other popular names for this species. *S.s.* 'Aurea' has golden-green leaves and *S.s.* 'Variegata' has silver-variegated leaves.
Size Height 2 in. (5 cm), spread limited only by the container.
Light Indirect sunlight.
Temperature Cool.
Moisture Keep moist at all times.
Feeding Give half-strength liquid fertilizer every two weeks in spring and summer.
Propagation Divide rooted clumps.
Special needs Although this looks like an ideal plant for a bottle garden or terrarium, it is actually much too invasive and will swamp the other plants. Trim with scissors to keep it under control in a pot.

LABIATAE
Solenostemon scutellarioides (syn. Coleus blumei)
This is a subshrub originally from Malaysia and southeast Asia, known as **coleus** or **painted nettle**. It has semisucculent, 4-angled stems which are usually upright, but sometimes trail. The leaf colors include cream, yellow, orange, red, green, and brown in almost limitless shades and combinations, and the leaf shape varies from small and finely divided, to large and whole. It is a perennial, but often treated as annual and discarded as the foliage fades in fall. The key to successful cultivation is regular pinching to encourage bushing and never allowing the plant to produce its small, inconspicuous flowers.
Size Height up to 2 ft. (60 cm).
Light Direct sunlight, except noon in summer.
Temperature Normal room.
Moisture Keep thoroughly moist.
Feeding Use standard liquid fertilizer every two weeks in spring and summer.
Propagation Sow seed in spring, or take 3 in. (7 cm) tip cuttings in summer to ensure the survival of a particular favorite.
Special needs In high temperatures increase humidity by placing the pot on a tray of moist pebbles. Hard water splashes on the leaves will cause white marks.

PITTOSPORACEAE
Sollya heterophylla
This slender, evergreen, twining climber from Western Australia is also called **bluebell creeper** or **Australian bluebell**. It has rather weak stems bearing long-oval leaves, 1–2 in. (2.5–5 cm) long and mid- to deep green, paler beneath, on short stalks. The pretty, nodding, bell-like, blue flowers are produced in summer and fall, in clusters of 4–12. Each is slender-stalked, with five small

Sollya heterophylla

petals. Naturally preferring light woodland, it is hardy outdoors in mild areas; otherwise, it will do well in a cool, but well-lit conservatory.
Size Spread 5 ft. (1.5 m).
Light Indirect sunlight.
Temperature Cool.
Moisture Keep moist from spring to fall. In winter, water sparingly.
Feeding Use standard liquid fertilizer once a month from spring to fall.
Propagation Sow seed in spring, or take 4 in. (10 cm) tip cuttings in late spring or summer.
Special needs Avoid pinching shoots, because flowers are borne at the tips and the growing buds will be removed.

Sparrmannia africana

Spathiphyllum wallisii

TILIACEAE

Sparrmannia africana

A quick-growing, treelike shrub from South Africa, **African hemp** has large, evergreen, downy leaves of a pale apple-green and up to 10 in. (24 cm) long. The flowers are borne in long-stalked clusters, and can appear all year around if conditions are right. Each is white and 4-petaled, drooping down in bud, then straightening up as it opens, to reveal purple-tipped, golden yellow stamens. This is an ideal plant for a conservatory or cool porch where it has the room to grow and flourish. *S.a.* 'Flore Pleno' has double flowers and *S.a.* 'Variegata' has leaves marked with white.

Size Height 6–7 ft. (2–2.2 m).
Light Indirect sunlight.
Temperature Normal to cool room.

Moisture Keep thoroughly moist from spring to fall. In winter, apply only enough water to prevent the soil drying out.
Feeding Use standard liquid fertilizer every two weeks from spring to fall.
Propagation Take 6 in. (15 cm) tip cuttings in spring and root in soil mix or water.
Special needs Pinch shoot tips regularly to encourage bushing. It grows so quickly and roots so readily from cuttings that it is worth propagating every 2–3 years and then discarding the parent.

ARACEAE

Spathiphyllum wallisii

Originally from Panama and Costa Rica, the **peace lily** is a nearly stemless plant with glossy dark green leaves, up to 14 x 4 in. (36 x 10 cm), on stalks up to 8 in. (20 cm) long, which grow directly from the rhizome. The striking arum-like flowers are produced on stalks of up to 1 ft. (30 cm) long, and consist of a concave, oval spathe, which starts off white and gradually changes to green, surrounding a white, scented spadix.

Size Spread 3 ft. (90 cm).
Light Indirect sunlight.
Temperature Normal room.
Moisture Keep moist at all times.
Feeding Apply standard liquid fertilizer every two weeks from spring through to fall.
Propagation Divide in spring.
Special needs Avoid dry air at all times by placing the pot on a tray of moist pebbles. In warm conditions the plant will not have a definite rest period, so continue watering and fertilizing at a reduced level.

ASCLEPIADACEAE

Stephanotis floribunda

This climbing shrub from Madagascar is best known for its heavily-scented, waxy, white flowers (giving it its common names **Madagascar jasmine** and **wax flower**), but it also has wonderful leathery leaves of glossy, dark green. The $1\frac{1}{4}$ in. (3 cm) long flowers are produced in clusters of 10 or more. They are tubular, flaring out into five lobes. The plant needs supporting as

it grows, but will look equally attractive in a conservatory, trained against a wall, or indoors on a small trellis, wire wreath form, or over an archway, as long as it is positioned where its fragrance can be fully appreciated.
Size Spread 10 ft. (3 m) or more.
Light Indirect sunlight.
Temperature Normal to warm room.
Moisture Keep thoroughly moist from spring to fall. In winter, apply only enough water to prevent the soil drying out.
Feeding Use standard liquid fertilizer every two weeks from spring to summer.
Propagation Take tip cuttings.
Special needs Place in a tray of pebbles to increase humidity, and mist daily if the temperature rises. Pinch out growing tips regularly to encourage bushy growth.

GESNERIACEAE
Streptocarpus
This plant is also known as the **Cape primrose** and comes from South Africa. Many different hybrids have been bred, but the ones usually seen as indoor plants tend to be 'Constant Nymph' or 'John Innes' types. These have a rosette of coarse, primrose-like leaves arising directly from the base of the plant; from these, the flower stalks are produced, bearing single or multiple blooms in shades of purple, blue, mauve, red, pink, or white. The flowers may be followed by interesting, twisted seedpods, but these should be removed to promote further flowering. *S.* 'Constant Nymph' has pale blue-mauve flowers with darker lines in the throat and *S.* 'John Innes' hybrids have flowers ranging from pale pink to blue and purple.
Size Height 1 ft. (30 cm), spread 18 in. (45 cm).
Light Indirect sunlight.
Temperature Normal room.
Moisture Allow to dry slightly between waterings.
Feeding Give half-strength high potash liquid fertilizer every two weeks from spring to fall.
Propagation Take leaf cuttings, divide, or seed, in spring.
Special needs Keep away from drafts and cold air, and increase humidity in high temperatures, by placing on a tray of moist pebbles.

ARACEAE
Syngonium podophyllum
The arrowhead-shaped young leaves of the **arrowhead** or **goosefoot plant**, which originates from countries including Mexico to Brazil and Bolivia, are leathery, glossy, and brightly colored. As the plant ages, it grows long stems, which can either be trailed from a hanging basket or trained up a support. These stems bear the mature leaves, which are progressively 3- and then 5-lobed. The long stems should be cut off as they develop, as this will help to prolong the juvenile stage, with its particularly attractive foliage. *S.p.* 'Emerald Gem' has fleshy, shiny, dark green leaves, those of *S.p.* 'Silver Knight' are silver green, and those of *S.p.* 'Variegatum' are splashed pale green.
Size Height 6½–7 ft. (2–2.2 m).
Light Indirect sunlight.
Temperature Normal room.
Moisture Keep moist from spring to fall. In winter, apply only enough water to prevent the soil drying out.
Feeding Use standard liquid fertilizer every two weeks in spring and summer.
Propagation Take 4 in. (10 cm) tip cuttings in spring, or stem cuttings with aerial roots in spring or summer
Special needs This is an ideal subject for growing up a moss pole because it has aerial roots. Mist regularly, especially in high temperatures, to prevent the foliage from drying out.

Stephanotis floribunda

Streptocarpus

Syngonium podophyllum

the stalk into the soil, keeping the leaf in good contact with it.

Special needs If a tolmiea outgrows its alloted space, it can be planted outdoors and replaced indoors by a young plantlet.

COMMELINACEAE
Tradescantia
These are a tolerant, easy-to-grow group of plants. The characteristic flowers have 3 petals, 3 sepals, and 6 stamens, which although short-lived individually are produced continually over a period of many weeks.

T. fluminensis (syn. T. albiflora)
The stems of this plant from southeast Brazil will trail profusely from a shelf or hanging basket, each turning up at its lower end, hence the common name **wandering Jew**. The plant is also known as **spider lily** and **inch plant**. The leaves look translucent and arise directly from the succulent-looking stems, causing the stem to change direction slightly at each joint. Small, white or pale pink, 3-petaled flowers are produced in spring and summer in clusters on short stalks. Varieties include: T.f. 'Albovittata,' which has white-striped leaves; T.f. 'Aurea,' with yellow leaves; T.f. 'Laekenensis,' which has small leaves that are pale green, striped and banded white, and tinted purple; and T.f. 'Quicksilver,' a quick-grower with green and white striped leaves.
Size Stems to 18 in. (45 cm) long.
Light Some direct sunlight every day is important to maintain leaf color.
Temperature Normal room.
Moisture Keep thoroughly moist from spring to fall, drier during the winter.
Feeding Apply standard liquid fertilizer every two weeks from spring through to fall.
Propagation Take 4 in. (10 cm) tip cuttings from spring to fall. Root them in water or soil.
Special needs Pinch out tips regularly to encourage a bushy plant.

T. spathacea (syn. Rhoeo discolor)
The common names of this plant, **oyster plant**, **cradle lily**, and **Moses in the bulrushes**, arise from the unusual arrangement of the flower bracts, which are paired in the shape of a boat, with the small, white, 3-petaled flowers in the middle. These are set amid a loose rosette of lance-shaped, semisucculent leaves, which are dark green or dark blue-green above, purple beneath, atop a short, stout stem. T.s. 'Vittata' (syn. T.s. 'Variegata') has leaves striped cream above, deep purple beneath. T. spathacea originates in southern Mexico, Belize, and Guatemala.
Size Spread 18 in. (45 cm).
Light Indirect sunlight.
Temperature Normal room.
Moisture Keep moist from spring to fall, drier in winter.
Feeding Use standard liquid fertilizer every two weeks in spring and summer.
Propagation Remove offsets from the base of the plant after flowering.
Special needs It cannot tolerate drafts or dry air, so place it on a tray of moist pebbles.

Tulipa see *Bulbs* p.129
Vrisea splendens see *Bromeliads* p.122
Yucca filamentosa see *Palmlike Plants* p.138

ARACEAE
Zantedeschia
Many hybrids have been bred from the original six species of zantedeschia. These include those from Z. elliottiana (the golden arum), known as the Elliottiana Group, which have heart-shaped leaves often covered with white dots and golden-yellow spathes. Those from Z. rehmannii (the pink arum), known as the Rehmannii Group, have lance-shaped leaves, usually without markings, and white, pink, or purple spathes. **Z. aethiopica** is a rhizomatous plant from South Africa, also known as **arum** or **calla lily**, with long, glossy, deep green leaves, shaped like arrowheads. The flower head consists of a large, milk-white spathe which curls back to reveal a golden yellow spadix on a stalk up to 18 in. (45 cm) long. Unlike the many tropical hybrid zantedeschias, it is hardy outdoors in temperate regions, where flowering occurs during spring, after which there is a natural rest period. Indoor plants need to follow the same pattern, so after flowering, the plant should be placed in a cool spot, preferably outdoors, for the foliage to die down.
Size Height 3 ft. (90 cm).
Light Direct sunlight.
Temperature Cool to normal room.
Moisture As the plants come into leaf, and again as they die down after flowering, keep moist, but while they are in full flower, they need to be wet and can actually stand in water.
Feeding Give standard liquid fertilizer every two weeks, from when the plant is in full leaf until the end of the flowering season.
Propagation Divide in fall.
Special needs If the zantedeschia is planted outdoors after flowering, it will need a marshy or wet position.

Tradescantia spathacea 'Vittata'

Zantedeschia aethiopica

Glossary

Aerial roots Roots that emerge from the stem above soil level; they can often cling to trees and other supports.

Air-layering A means of propagation. A cut in an aerial stem is covered with spaghnum moss and sealed within a plastic bag to encourage rooting.

Annual A plant that completes its life-cycle, or grows from seed, flowers, produces seed and dies, within a single growing season.

Anther Pollen-producing part of the flower, often carried on a long filament.

Areoles A cushion-like raised or depressed area bearing spines, hairs or flowers in cacti.

Axil The angle between the stem and the leaf or leafstalk growing from it.

Biennial A plant that completes its life-cycle within two growing seasons.

Bract Modified leaf at the base of a flower or flower-head which can look like a leaf or a petal and can be brightly colored.

Bulbil Small, immature bulb formed at the base of mature bulbs or in the axil of a leaf, bract, or sometimes, flowerhead.

Calyx The outermost part of a flower, consisting of separate or joined sepals.

Capillary matting Porous material, which retains liquid. Capillary describes the action of a substance drawing water through the matting when the matting is in contact with water.

Carbohydrates Sugars and starches produced during photosynthesis, which feed the plant.

Corolla The petals, or primary decorative feature of a flower.

Cultivar (*abbrev* cv.) Usually a variety raised in cultivation, rather than occurring in the wild. Cultivar plant names tend to be in a modern language instead of Latin, enclosed within single quote marks.

Division Method of propagation which involves splitting a plant into two or more parts, each with its own roots and leaves.

Double Describes a flower with at least two full layers of petals.

Epiphyte A plant that naturally grows on the body of another plant, or sometimes on rocks, but which feeds independently.

Glochid A small, barbed bristle or hair arising from the areole of a cactus.

Heel Strip of bark and wood torn from the lower part of a main stem when a sideshoot is pulled off downwards.

Hybrid The natural or artificially produced offspring of genetically different parents belonging to the same family.

Layering Means of propagation, involving pegging a stem to the soil while still attached to the parent plant, so it will root separately.

Leaf node The point on a stem at which leaves and shoots arise.

Offsets Small plants that develop naturally at the bases of mature plants, especially bulbous plants.

Palmate Describes a leaf with three or more leaflets or lobes coming from a single point on a leafstalk; literally means "hand-shaped."

Perennial A plant that lives for three seasons and more, usually indefinitely.

Petiole Another term for leafstalk.

Photosynthesis The process by which plants convert carbon dioxide into starches and sugars.

Phototropism Occurs when a plant receives light from one direction only and grows towards it, resulting in lopsidedness.

Pinching out Removing the soft growing tips of a plant to encourage bushy growth of sideshoots.

Pinnae Leaflets of pinnate leaf or fern frond.

Plantlet Young, small plant that develops naturally on an older plant.

Pot-bound Describes a plant whose root system has outgrown its pot.

Pricking out Moving seedlings from the pots in which they were sown to plant them individually or farther apart in new containers.

Propagation The means by which plants increase or are increased.

Rest period A period of time during any 12-month season when a plant suspends active growth.

Rhizome Fleshy stem, usually horizontal and growing underground, which often acts as a storage system.

Semi-double Describes a flower with two or three times the number of petals of a single flower, usually in two or three layers.

Sepal A part of the calyx, which is sometimes colorful and petal-like but more often green and smaller than the petals.

Single A flower with only one layer of petals.

Spadix A special type of flower spike, usually embedded with tiny, stalk-less flowers, that often sits within a spathe.

Spathe Modified leaf or hood-like bract that surrounds the spadix.

Spore Reproductive unit of many non-flowering plants, such as ferns. Fern spores, which resemble dust, are often carried in spore cases on the undersides of the fronds.

Stamen The male, pollen-bearing part of a flower, usually comprising an anther carried on a filament.

Stigma The tip of the female flower organ, which receives pollen.

Stolon Horizontal or trailing stem that roots and produces new shoots at its tips.

Transpiration The loss of water via a plant's leaves.

Variegated Describes leaves which are streaked, spotted, or patterned with another color (usually cream or yellow).

Plant lists

Edible plants
x *Citrofortunella microcarpa*
Herbs including basil, mint, oregano, parsley and thyme

Easy plants for children to grow
Begonia x *hiemalis*
Bulbs, including crocus, hippeastrum, hyacinth, narcissus and tulip
Cacti, including
  Echinocactus, Mammilaria, Parodia and Rebutia
Chlorophytum
Herbs
Pelargonium
Saintpaulia
Sinningia
Thunbergia
Tradescantia

Plants for draughty places
Argyranthemum frutescens
Aspidistra elatior
Campanula isophylla
Cyclamen persicum
x *Fatshedera lizei*
Fatsia japonica
Gerbera jamesonii
Hedera sp.
Hydrangea macrophylla
Jasminum polyanthum
Narcissus
Nerium oleander
Pelargonium sp.
Primula sp.
Thunbergia alata
Tradescantia sp.

Plants for partially shady positions
Fittonia sp.
Howea fosteriana
Licuala grandis
Maranta leuconeura
Microlepia strigosa
Monstera deliciosa
Murraya paniculata
Nephrolepsis exaltata
  'Bostoniensis'
Philodendron sp.
Pteris cretica
Saintpaulia velutina

Architectural plants
Anthurium scherzerianum
Asparagus sp.
Caladium bicolor
Chyrsalidocarpus lutescens
Cocos nucifera
Cyperus papyrus
Dieffenbachia maculata
Fatsia japonica
Ficus sp.
Howea fosteriana
Licuala grandis
Nolina recurvata
Phoenix canariensis
Polyscias guilfoylei
Rhapsis excelsa
Schefflera sp.
Yucca filamentosa

Plants with colored flowers
Red
Achimenes sp.
Anthurium scherzerianum
Camellia japonica
Canna generalis
Capsicum annuum
Cyclamen persicum
Euphorbia pulcherrima
Gloriosa superba
  'Rothschildiana'
Guzmania lingulata
Hatiora gaertneri
Impatiens New Guinea
  hybrids
Kalanchoe blossfeldiana
Lotus berthelotii
Pelargonium sp.
Rebutia minuscula
Rosa chinensis 'Minima'
Vriesea splendens

Pink
Azalea
Begonia sp.
Billbergia nutans
Camellia japonica
Cyclamen persicum
Gerbera jamesonii
Hibiscus rosa-sinensis
Lantana camara 'Hybrida'
Mammillaria zeilmanniana
Mandevilla sanderi
Nerium oleander
Pelargonium sp.
Primula sp.
Ruellia makoyana
Saintpaulia velutina
Sinningia speciosa
Streptocarpus x *hybridus*
Tillandsia lindenii
Tradescantia sp.

Peach/orange
Begonia x *hiemalis*
Bougainvillea glabra
Gerbera jamesonii
Justicia brandegeana
Kalanchoe blossfeldiana
Lantana camara 'Hybrida'
Nerium oleander
Pelargonium sp.
Rosa 'Rouletii'
Schlumbergera x *buckleyi*
Thunbergia alata

Yellow
Allamanda cathartica
Aphelandra squarrosa
  'Louisae'
Calceolaria sp.
Canna generalis
Gerbera jamesonii
Hibiscus rosa-chinensis
Kalanchoe blossfeldiana
Lantana camara 'Hybrida'
Narcissus sp.
Opuntia microdasys
Parodia sp.
Primula sp.
Thunbergia alata

Blue/mauve
Browallia speciosa
Brunfelsia pauciflora
  'Macrantha'
Campanula isophylla
Exacum affine
Hydrangea macrophylla
Passiflora caerulea
Pelargonium sp.
Pericallis x *hybrida*
Plumbago auriculata
Primula sp.
Saintpaulia velutina
Sinningia speciosa
Sollya heterophylla
Streptocarpus x *hybridus*

White
Argyranthemum frutescens
Camellia japonica
Campanula isophylla
x *Citrofortunella microcarpa*
Clerodendrum thomsoniae
Cyclamen persicum
Euphorbia pulcherrima
Gardenia augusta
Hoya lanceolata spp. *bella*
Impatiens sp.
Lilium sp.
Orchids

Passiflora caerulea
Pelargonium sp.
Pentas lanceolata
Primula sp.
Spathiphyllum wallisii
Stephanotis floribunda
Streptocarpus x *hybrida*
Tolmiea menziesii
Tradescantia sp.

Foliage plants
Aglaonema crispum
Ananas bracteatus striatus
Asparagus sp.
Aspidistra elatior
Begonia rex
Caladium bicolor
Calathea makoyana
Chamaedorea elegans
Chlorophytum comosum
Chrysalidocarpus lutescens
Cissus sp.
Cocos nucifera
Codaeum variegatum var.
  pictum
Ctenanthe oppenheimiana
Cyperus papyrus
Dieffenbachia sp.
Epipremnum aureum
x *Fatshedera lizei*
Fatsia japonica
Ferns
Ficus sp.
Fittonia sp.
Grevillea robusta
Hedera sp.
Howea fosteriana
Hypoestes phyllostachya
Licuala grandis
Maranta leuconeura
Monstera deliciosa
Murraya paniculata
Musa acuminata
Nolina recurvata
Pelargonium crispum
Peperomia sp.
Philodendron sp.
Polyscias guilfoylei
Radermachera sp.
Saxifraga stolonifera
Schefflera sp.
Selaginella martensii
Senecio macroglossus
Soleirolia soleirolii
Syngonium podophyllum
Tolmeia menziesii
Tradescantia sp.
Yucca filamentosa
Zantedeschia aethiopica

Index

Acknowledgments

**The publishers and authors are also grateful to the following for
their help and support in the production of this book:**
Ann Barnes and Lynn Fauld Woods for the use of their homes for photography;
Hilary Bird for compiling the index; Dave Crook and Claudine Meissner for design
support; Lisa Dyer for editorial work; Alison Freegard for proofreading *Care and
Maintenance*; Peter Green at the Royal Botanic Gardens, Kew, Elvin McDonald
and Tony Lord for checking plant nomenclature; Amanda Lebentz, Ginny Surtees
and Catherine Ward for editing the book; Sampson Lloyd for photography in *Care
and Maintenance*; Leeann Mackenzie for styling the photography for *Containers*
and *Plants for the Place*; Debbie Mole for Art Directing the photography and
design; Mike Newton for photographing *Containers*, *Plants for the Place* and
Plant Displays; Lisa Pendreigh for editorial assistant work; Howard Rice for
photographing the plant portraits in the *Indoor Plant Directory*; George Taylor
for photographing some step by step sequences in *Care and Maintenance*;
Jo Weeks for copy-editing the *Indoor Plant Directory*;
and Kevin Williams for design.

Picture credits:
Garden Picture Library (Jenny Raworth's Conservatory), 1, 37.

**Jenny Raworth would also like thank the following for their help with
Containers, Plants for the Place and *Plant Displays*:**
Mike Newton, assisted by Richard Smith, for his photography;
Debbie Mole for her design; and Catherine Ward for her
support, enthusiasm and editorial guidance.

**Val Bradley would also like thank the following for their help with *Care and
Maintenance, Houseplant Doctor* and *Indoor Plant Directory*:**
Everyone at Collins & Brown who worked on the book, especially
Ginny Surtees for her invaluable help throughout; and Steve,
Chris and Nick Bradley for their support.